Communications in Computer and Information Science 1134

Commenced Publication in 2007
Founding and Former Series Editors:
Phoebe Chen, Alfredo Cuzzocrea, Xiaoyong Du, Orhun Kara, Ting Liu,
Krishna M. Sivalingam, Dominik Ślęzak, Takashi Washio, Xiaokang Yang,
and Junsong Yuan

More information about this series at http://www.springer.com/series/7899

Xiaoyan Zhu · Bing Qin · Xiaodan Zhu ·
Ming Liu · Longhua Qian (Eds.)

Knowledge Graph and Semantic Computing

Knowledge Computing and Language Understanding

4th China Conference, CCKS 2019
Hangzhou, China, August 24–27, 2019
Revised Selected Papers

 Springer

Editors
Xiaoyan Zhu
Department of Computer Science
and Technology
Tsinghua University
Beijing, China

Xiaodan Zhu
Queen's University
Kingston, Canada

Longhua Qian
Soochow University
Soochow, China

Bing Qin
Harbin Institute of Technology
Harbin, China

Ming Liu
Harbin Institute of Technology
Harbin, China

ISSN 1865-0929   ISSN 1865-0937 (electronic)
Communications in Computer and Information Science
ISBN 978-981-15-1955-0   ISBN 978-981-15-1956-7 (eBook)
https://doi.org/10.1007/978-981-15-1956-7

This Springer imprint is published by the registered company Springer Nature Singapore Pte Ltd.
The registered company address is: 152 Beach Road, #21-01/04 Gateway East, Singapore 189721, Singapore

Preface

This volume contains the papers from the China Conference on Knowledge Graph and Semantic Computing (CCKS 2019). CCKS 2019 is the result of two premier and relevant forums being merged: the Chinese Knowledge Graph Symposium (CKGS) and the Chinese Semantic Web and Web Science Conference (CSWS). CKGS was first held in Beijing in 2013, and then in Nanjing in 2014 and Yichang in 2015. CSWS was firstly held in Beijing in 2006, and has continually been the main forum for research on Semantic (Web) Technologies in China for nearly 10 years. The new conference, CCKS, brings together researchers from both forums and covers wider fields including Knowledge Graph, Semantic Web, Linked Data, NLP, Knowledge Representation, Graph Databases, etc. It aims to become the top forum on Knowledge Graph and Semantic Technologies for Chinese researchers and practitioners from academia, industry, and government. CCKS is organized by the Technical Committee on Language and Knowledge Computing of CIPS (Chinese Information Processing Society of China).

The coordinator of CCKS 2019 was Zhejiang University. Zhejiang University, referred to as the "University," formerly known as the College of Seeking, was founded in 1897 and is still one of the first Chinese founded modern institutions of higher learning. In 1928 it was renamed the National Zhejiang University. During the period of the Republic of China, Zhejiang University in Zhu Kezhen, under the leadership of the headmaster, grew into one of the top Chinese universities, and a famous British scholar, Joseph Needham, referred to the university as the "Cambridge of the east." Zhejiang University is China's first batch of 7 "211 Project" University, first batch of 9 "985 Project" University, a member of the Chinese University C9 Alliance, part of the World University League, a central university to the Pacific Union, and one of the most famous universities in China.

The theme for CCKS 2019 was "Knowledge Intelligence" which aimed to explore the key technologies and applications of language understanding, knowledge acquisition, and intelligent services in the context of big data. The conference included academic workshops, industrial forums, evaluation and competition, knowledge graph summit reviews, conference keynote reports, academic papers, etc. The conference invited well-known scholars, domestically and abroad, to give the lectures on the latest progress, development trends, and practical experience in the relevant fields. The forum also invited professional researchers in the industry to share their experience and promote industry-university-research cooperation. It had five sessions, including:

- Knowledge Graph Representation and Reasoning
- Information Extraction and Knowledge Graph Construction
- Link Data, Knowledge Integration, and Knowledge Graph Storage Management

- Natural Language Understanding, Semantic Computing, and Knowledge Graph Mining
- Knowledge Graph Application (Semantic Search, Q&A, Dialogue, Assistant Decision System, Recommendation, etc.)

The total number of papers received for CCKS 2019 exceeded 140. The acceptance rate was 37%, and 18 Engligh papers were accpeted to be published in this volume. All the accepted papers were peer reviewed by three qualified reviewers. The proceedings editors wish to thank the dedicated area chairs, and all the other reviewers for their contributions. We also thank Springer for their trust and for publishing the proceedings of CCKS 2019.

October 2019

Xiaoyan Zhu
Bing Qin
Xiaodan Zhu
Ming Liu
Longhua Qian

Organization

CCKS 2019 was organized by the Technical Committee on Language and Knowledge Computing of the Chinese Information Processing Society.

General Chair

Xiaoyan Zhu	Tsinghua University, China

Program Committee Chairs

Bin Qin	Harbin Institute of Technology, China
Xiaodan Zhu	Queen's University, Canada

Local Chair

Huajun Chen	Zhejiang University, China

Publicity Chairs

Bin Xu	Tsinghua University, China
Zhunchen Luo	Military Academy of Sciences, China

Publication Chairs

Ming Liu	Harbin Institute of Technology, China
Longhua Qian	Soochow University, China

Tutorial Chairs ATT

Wei Hu	Nanjing University, China
Ren Xiang	University of Southern California, USA

Evaluation Chairs

Xianpei Han	Institute of Software, Chinese Academy of Sciences, China
Zhichun Wang	Beijing Normal University, China

Top Conference Reviewing Chairs

GuiLin Qi	Southeast University, China
Zhiyuan Liu	Tsinghua University, China
Lei Zou	Peking University, China

Poster/Demo Chairs

Ru Li   Shanxi University, China
Haofen Wang   Leyan Technologies, China

Sponsorship Chair

Kang Liu   Institute of Automation, Chinese Academy of Sciences,
                               China

Industry Track Chairs

Shengping Liu   Beijing Unisound Information Technology, China
Yanghua Xiao   Fudan University, China

Area Chairs

Knowledge Graph Representation and Reasoning

Hai Wan   Sun Yat-sen University, China
Zhizheng Zhang   Southeast University, China

Information Extraction and Knowledge Graph Construction

Yubo Chen   Institute of Automation, Chinese Academy of Sciences,
                               China
Zhixu Li   Soochow University, China

Linked Data, Knowledge Integration, and Knowledge Graph Storage Management

Xin Wang   Tianjin University, China
Gang Wu   Northeastern University, China

Natural Language Understanding, Semantic Computing, and Knowledge Graph Mining

Chuan Shi   Beijing University of Posts and Telecommunications,
                               China
Zhichun Wang   Beijing Normal University, China

Semantic Search, Question Answering, Dialogue System, Assistant Decision System, and Recommendation

Feiliang Ren   Northeastern University, China
Wenliang Chen   Soochow University, China

Program Committee

Jeff Z. Pan	University of Aberdeen, UK
Yawei An	China General Technology, China
Yu Bai	Shenyang Aerospace University, China
Jie Bao	MEMECT, China
Xunliang Cai	Beijing Science and Technology Co., Ltd., China
Yi Cai	South China University of Technology, China
Daojian Zeng	Changsha University of Technology, China
Qingcai Chen	Harbin Institute of Technology Shenzhen, China
Wenliang Chen	Soochow University, China
Yidong Chen	Xiamen University, China
Yubo Chen	Institute of Automation, Chinese Academy of Sciences, China
Yunwen Chen	DataView Information Technology (Shanghai) Co., Ltd., China
Gong Cheng	Nanjing University, China
Xinyu Dai	Nanjing University, China
Xiao Ding	Harbin Institute of Technology, China
Jianfeng Du	Guangdong University of Foreign Languages and Trade, China
Yajun Du	Xihua University, China
Yongquan Fan	Xihua University, China
Chong Feng	Beijing Institute of Technology, China
Yansong Feng	Peking University, China
Feng Gao	Wuhan University of Science and Technology, China
Zhiqiang Gao	Southeast University, China
Jibing Gong	Yanshan University, China
Jinguang Gu	Wuhan University of Science and Technology, China
Jianyi Guo	Kunming University of Science and Technology, China
Saike He	Institute of Automation, Chinese Academy of Sciences, China
Shizhu He	Institute of Automation, Chinese Academy of Sciences, China
Tingting He	Central China Normal University, China
Guoping Hu	iFlytek, Co., Ltd., China
Linmei Hu	Peking University of Posts and Telecommunications, China
Wei Hu	Nanjing University, China
Minlie Huang	Tsinghua University, China
Xuanjing Huang	Fudan University, China
Zhisheng Huang	Free University of Amsterdam, The Netherlands
Donghong Ji	Wuhan University, China
Yantao Jia	Huawei, China
Xiaolong Jin	Institute of Computing Technology, Chinese Academy of Sciences, China

Binyang Li	University of International Relations, China
Daifeng Li	Sun Yat-sen University, China
Donghai Li	Beijing Yuandian Co., Ltd., China
Hang Li	ByteDance, China
Jinlong Li	Information Technology Department, China Merchants Bank, China
Jin Li	Yunnan University, China
Lishuang Li	Dalian University of Technology, China
Ru Li	Shanxi University, China
Yuanfang Li	Monash University, Australia
Changliang Li	Gold Peak Industries (Holdings) Ltd., China
Xiangwen Liao	Fuzhou University, China
Hongfei Lin	Dalian University of Technology, China
Bingquan Liu	Harbin Institute of Technology, China
Kewei Liu	China General Technology, China
Ming Liu	Harbin Institute of Technology, China
Shengping Liu	Beijing Unisound Information Technology Co., Ltd., China
Yao Liu	China Institute of Science and Technology Information, China
Yiqun Liu	Tsinghua University, China
Yongbin Liu	Nankai University, China
Zhiyuan Liu	Tsinghua University, China
Zuopeng Liu	Xiaomi Corporation, China
Zhunchen Luo	Military Academy of Sciences, China
Xianling Mao	Beijing Institute of Technology, China
Yao Meng	Fujitsu Research and Development Center Co., Ltd., China
Qingliang Miao	Lenovo Research Institute, China
Yue Pan	Microsoft, China
Longhua Qian	Soochow University, China
Tieyun Qian	Wuhan University, China
Likun Qiu	Alibaba Group, China
Xipeng Qiu	Fudan University, China
Weiguang Qu	Nanjing Normal University, China
Feiliang Ren	Northeastern University, China
Tong Ruan	East China University of Technology, China
Hao Shao	Gowild Co., Ltd., China
Libin Shen	Leyan Technologies, China
Zhifang Sui	Peking University, China
Jian Sun	Alibaba Group, China
Hongye Tan	Shanxi University, China
Buzhou Tang	Harbin Institute of Technology Shenzhen, China
Jie Tang	Tsinghua University, China
Jintao Tang	National University of Defense Technology, China

Yan Tang	Hohai University, China
Hai Wan	Sun Yat-sen University, China
Jing Wan	Beijing University of Chemical Technology, China
Bin Wang	Xiaomi Corporation, China
Hongjun Wang	TRS, China
Houfeng Wang	Peking University, China
Huizhen Wang	Northeastern University, China
Mingwen Wang	Jiangxi Normal University, China
Quan Wang	Baidu, China
Suge Wang	Shanxi University, China
Ting Wang	National University of Defense Technology, China
Wei Wang	深圳素问智能信息技术有限公司, China
Xiaoling Wang	East China Normal University, China
Xin Wang	Tianjin University, China
Xing Wang	Liaoning Technical University, China
Yongli Wang	Nanjing University of Technology, China
Zhichun Wang	Beijing Normal University, China
Gang Wu	Northeastern University, China
Gang Wu	北京知识图谱科技有限公司, China
Youzheng Wu	iQIYI, China
Tong Xiao	Northeastern University, China
Yanghua Xiao	Fudan University, China
Xin Xin	Beijing Institute of Technology, China
Fan Xu	Jiangxi Normal University, China
Tao Xu	Northwest University for Nationalities, China
Jingfang Xu	SOGO, China
Jun Yan	YIDU Cloud, China
Dong Yu	Beijing Language University, China
Zhengtao Yu	Kunming University of Science and Technology, China
Hongying Zan	Zhengzhou University, China
Weidong Zhan	Peking University, China
Hu Zhang	Shanxi University, China
Jiangtao Zhang	Chinese People's Liberation Army Hospital 305, China
Kuo Zhang	SOGO, China
Peng Zhang	Tianjin University, China
Qi Zhang	Fudan University, China
Richong Zhang	Beihang University, China
Wei Zhang	Alibaba Group, China
Xiaowang Zhang	Tianjin University, China
Yuzhi Zhang	Nankai University, China
Zhizheng Zhang	Southeast University, China
Shiqi Zhao	Baidu, China
Tiejun Zhao	Harbin Institute of Technology, China
Haitao Zheng	Tsinghua University Shenzhen, China
Junsheng Zhou	Nanjing Normal University, China

Contents

Adaptive Multilingual Representations for Cross-Lingual Entity Linking with Attention on Entity Descriptions

Chenhao Wang[1,2]([⊠]), Yubo Chen[2], Kang Liu[1,2], and Jun Zhao[1,2]

[1] University of Chinese Academy of Sciences, Beijing, China
[2] Institute of Automation, Chinese Academy of Sciences, Beijing, China
{chenhao.wang,yubo.chen,kliu,jzhao}@nlpr.ia.ac.cn

Abstract. Cross-lingual entity linking is the task of resolving ambiguous mentions in text to corresponding entities in knowledge base, where the query text and knowledge base are in different languages. Recent multilingual embedding based methods bring significant progress in this task. However, they still meet some potential problems: (1) They directly use multilingual embeddings obtained by cross-lingual mapping, which may bring noise and degrade the performance; (2) They also rely on the pre-trained fixed entity embeddings, which only carry limited information about entities. In this paper, we propose a cross-lingual entity linking framework with the help of more adaptive representations. For the first problem, we apply trainable adjusting matrices to fine-tune the semantic representations built from multilingual embeddings. For the second problem, we introduce attention mechanisms on entity descriptions to obtain dynamic entity representations, exploiting more clues about entity candidates according to the query mentions. Experiments on the TAC KBP 2015 Chinese-English cross-lingual entity linking dataset show that our model yields better performance than state-of-the-art models.

Keywords: Cross-lingual entity linking · Multilingual embedding · Attention mechanism

1 Introduction

Entity Linking (EL) is the task of resolving mentions in text to their corresponding entities in knowledge base (KB) (e.g., Wikipedia), which has been shown to be an important disambiguation component in information extraction, question answering and other systems. Recently, cross-lingual entity linking has begun to draw interest [6–8]. For languages that are limited in resources, cross-lingual EL is a valuable way to take advantage of abundant knowledge in other languages. We formalize it as follows: Given a mention m from a document d_A written in language A, the task is to find the corresponding entity e in reference KB that uses a different language B, or return NIL when there is no appropriate entity. For instance, as is shown in Fig. 1, 迈克尔·乔丹 (Michael Jordan) is an

© Springer Nature Singapore Pte Ltd. 2019
X. Zhu et al. (Eds.): CCKS 2019, CCIS 1134, pp. 1–12, 2019.
https://doi.org/10.1007/978-981-15-1956-7_1

ambiguous mention in Chinese text, and there are many entities named Michael Jordan in KB, so the cross-lingual EL system need to exploit English knowledge and decide which one is correct. In most cases, English Wikipedia is the reference KB because of its wide coverage and frequent updates.

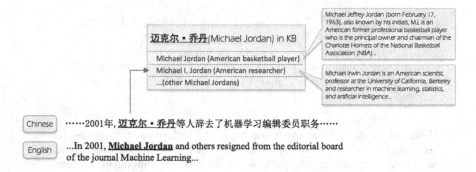

Fig. 1. An example of Chinese-English cross-lingual entity linking. 迈克尔·乔丹 **(Michael Jordan)** is an ambiguous mention in Chinese text, and there are many namesakes with respective English descriptions in KB. It is reasonable to ground the mention to American professor **Michael I. Jordan** rather than others, because there is a clue 机器学习 **(machine learning)** in the context.

EL systems usually utilize the clues in the context to decide the target entity. It is more challenging in cross-lingual setting where the context of the query mention and the descriptions of the candidates are in different languages. In recent years, multi-lingual embedding based methods [15, 16] have been introduced to cross-lingual EL task, which directly compare similarity across languages and yield better results than traditional methods. They first learn projections to map pre-trained embeddings in different languages into the same vector space, and then build representations based on such multilingual embeddings for comparing. As these methods utilize Wikipedia corpora to jointly learn and align embeddings in different languages, they can generalize to all languages in Wikipedia.

However, despite many advantages, there are several potential problems in existing multilingual embedding based methods. First, the projection matrices for mapping is learned from cross-lingual synonym dictionary. However, the mapping process can bring noise into cross-lingual EL. Directly applying the aligned embeddings into comparing may degrade the final performance. Thus it is worthwhile to build adaptive representations in cross-lingual EL task, emphasizing the useful part and restraining the noise.

Besides, existing methods rely on pre-trained entity embeddings. Such embeddings contain limited information about entities, and they are fixed when performing cross-lingual EL, so that they cannot adaptively exploit more useful clues in KB according to the query mention. Thus how to utilize more ready-to-use clues in KB when the query mention is given is still a problem.

To address the above problems, we propose Adaptive Multilingual Representations for Cross-lingual Entity Linking (ADXEL). In this framework, we introduce trainable adjusting matrices to fine-tune the word and entity representations before computing multiple contextual similarities, aiming to emphasize the useful part and restrain the noise. We also propose a novel module based on attention mechanism to exploit entity descriptions and build dynamic entity representations according to the query mention. Finally, a rank model is used to combine different features and output the final score for each candidate. The contributions of this paper are as follows:

- We propose Adaptive Multilingual Representations for Cross-lingual Entity Linking (ADXEL), an entity linking framework in cross-lingual setting.
- To improve semantic representations built from multilingual embeddings, we introduce trainable adjusting matrices to fine-tune representations.
- A novel module based on attention mechanism is used to exploit entity descriptions and build dynamic entity representations, so that more useful clues in knowledge base are taken into account.
- We conduct experiments on TAC KBP 2015 Chinese-English cross-lingual entity linking dataset, and the results show that our model yields better performance than previous state-of-the-art models. The code will be released on https://github.com/wch-wch/clel.

2 Related Work

In recent years, cross-lingual EL task is mainly driven by Text Analysis Conference (TAC) Knowledge Base Population (KBP) Entity Linking Tracks [6–8], where the target languages are Spanish and Chinese, and the mentions are linked to English Wikipedia or some KBs derived from it, such as Freebase. Generally, existing methods for cross-lingual EL can be divided in three classes: language link based methods, translation based methods, and cross-lingual clues based methods.

Most of traditional methods fall into the first two classes. They perform EL in the target language and afterwards find the corresponding entity in English Wikipedia by language links [14,17], or perform English EL with the help of translation or parallel corpora [10]. These methods rely on the completeness of KB in the target language or available translation resources, which make them difficult to generalize to lower resource languages. Some exceptions directly compare clues across languages by such as bilingual topic modeling [20], but they share the same problem.

Inspired by words embedding methods [11,12], jointly modeling the words and entities in the same continuous space has shown to benefits EL task [5,18,19]. As a further step, multi-lingual embedding based methods have been introduced to recent cross-lingual EL systems. Such methods simplify the assumption on resources, and directly compare clues across languages. WikiME [16] leverages canonical correlation analysis (CCA) [4] based model and inter-language links in Wikipedia to generate bilingual embeddings from pre-trained monolingual word-entity embeddings. Sil et al. [15] map word-entity embeddings in different languages into the vector space of English embeddings, so there is no need to maintain a pair of new embeddings for every two languages. These methods bring promotion in performance and better scalability on lower resource languages because they only use Wikipedia documents in different languages as corpora. However, they directly apply these multilingual embeddings in comparing clues, where the useless noise may limit the performance. Besides, they rely on pre-trained entity embeddings, which carry limited and fixed information about entities.

In this paper, we apply trainable matrices to emphasize the useful parts of the representations before comparing clues, and propose an additional architecture based on attention mechanisms to adaptively obtain dynamic entity representations from descriptions.

3   Methodology

In this section, we will first introduce multilingual embeddings and candidate generation process. Then we will describe each part in our proposed EL model in detail.

3.1   Multilingual Embeddings of Words and Entities

The first step is to jointly train embeddings of words and entities for each language. We build three corpora from Wikipedia documents. For the first one we take all documents and replace the anchor texts with target entity tokens. The second one is analogous but keep the surface forms of the anchor texts, so that all tokens are words. The third one only keep entity tokens in the first corpus to record the co-occurrence of entities. After that, we train Chinese and English monolingual embeddings on these corpora by Skip-Gram model [11,12].

The second step is to project different monolingual embeddings into the same vector space via a linear mapping. We take Chinese embeddings as source and English embeddings as target, and adopt MUSE [3] model to learn the mapping, which solves an Orthogonal Procrustes problem:

$$P_{zh \to en} = \arg\min_{\Omega} \|\Omega A_{zh} - A_{en}\|_F \quad \text{subject to} \quad \Omega^T \Omega = I \qquad (1)$$

where A_{zh} and A_{en} are matrices containing embeddings in the alignment dictionary, which is collected from Wikipedia inter-language links. The model minimizes the Frobenius norm so that the equivalent entity embeddings in different languages are drawn close. When the cross-lingual projection matrix $P_{zh \to en}$ is found, we apply it to all Chinese embeddings.

3.2   Candidate Generation

It is impractical to compare the query mention with every entity for there are great number of entities in knowledge base. Therefore, the candidate generation process is applied in EL tasks. Given a query mention m, the process is to find a small set $C_m = \{e_1, e_2, \cdots\}$, which consists of entity candidates that m may link to.

Like previous works [5,13,16], we build a mention-entity index from anchor texts and disambiguous pages in Wikipedia, then simply look up the index to find candidates for m. More specifically, we first build a basic cross-lingual index, where the key is Chinese mention and the value is its entity candidates in English Wikipedia. Then we also provide an additional augmented index by parting long names, and a pure English index. We first look up the basic index, and if the first step fails to find any, we then look up the augmented index and the English index. The candidates are sorted by a prior probability $P_{prior}(e_i|m)$, which is estimated from counts of $m \to e_i$ during building indexes. Finally the top K candidates are returned.

3.3   Local Context Modeling

The local context around the query mention provides important clues for disambiguation. We leverage gated recurrent unit (GRU) [2] to model the local context. GRU is a gated variant of recurrent neural network (RNN), which works as follow:

$$z_t = \sigma\left(W_z \cdot [h_{t-1}, x_t]\right) \tag{2}$$
$$r_t = \sigma\left(W_r \cdot [h_{t-1}, x_t]\right) \tag{3}$$
$$\tilde{h}_t = \tanh\left(W \cdot [r_t * h_{t-1}, x_t]\right) \tag{4}$$
$$h_t = (1 - z_t) * h_{t-1} + z_t * \tilde{h}_t \tag{5}$$

where x_t is the input vector at step t, h_{t-1} is the hidden state at last step, σ denotes the sigmoid function, and z_t, r_t are the update and reset gate.

In order to incorporate information from both sides of the query mention, we build two GRU networks. Given a embedding sequence of context words $S = \{x_0, \cdots, x_n\}$, where x_t is the embedding at step t and the query mention is from $t = p$ to $t = q$, we feed the forward GRU with $S_1' = \{x_0, \cdots, x_q\}$, and the backward GRU with $S_2' = \{x_n, \cdots, x_p\}$:

$$\overrightarrow{h_q} = \overrightarrow{GRU}(x_q, \overrightarrow{h_{q-1}}) \tag{6}$$
$$\overleftarrow{h_p} = \overleftarrow{GRU}(x_p, \overleftarrow{h_{p+1}}) \tag{7}$$
$$h_{local} = \overrightarrow{h_q} + \overleftarrow{h_p} \tag{8}$$

where h_{local} is the local context representation for the query mention.

3.4   Attention Mechanisms on Entity Abstracts

In Wikipedia, the first paragraph in a document usually tells the overview of the content, which we take as entity abstracts. To build an additional dynamic representation for every entity candidate considering the query mention, we exploit the entity abstracts during performing EL.

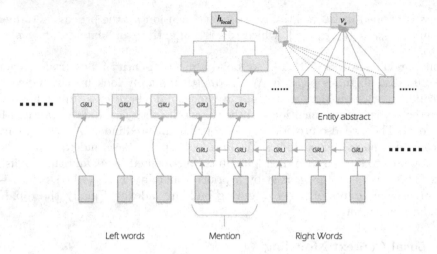

Fig. 2. The local context representation and dynamic entity representation

Attention mechanisms [1,9] can be described as mapping a query and a set of key-value pairs to an output. First a weight for every value is computed by a compatibility function of the query with corresponding key, and then the weighted sum of values are output.

$$E_i = f(Q, K_i) \tag{9}$$

$$a_i = softmax(E_i) = \frac{\exp(f(Q, K_i))}{\sum_j \exp(f(Q, K_j))} \tag{10}$$

$$Attention(Q, K, V) = \sum_i a_i V_i \tag{11}$$

where Q, K_i, V_i are the query, key and value, and $f(Q, K_i)$ is a compatibility function. We choose $f(Q, K_i) = Q^\top W_a K_i$, where W_a is trainable parameters.

We apply attention mechanisms on entity abstracts. Given a mention and a entity candidate e, the query is h_{local} from the previous section, and the keys and values are embeddings of words in the abstract. The output is the dynamic representation of the entity, written as v_e. The local context model and the attention mechanisms are shown in Fig. 2.

3.5 Candidate Ranking

In this step, we need to score every candidate, and find the most appropriate one as the result. We build several features based on representations obtained in previous steps, described as follows:

1. The basic local context feature S_1. S_1 is the cosine similarity of h_{local} and u_e, where u_e is the entity embedding.

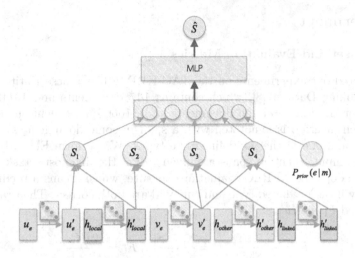

Fig. 3. The ranking model

2. The dynamic entity representation feature S_2. S_2 is the cosine similarity of h_{local} and v_e.
3. The other mentions feature S_3. Given a mention, we take the sum of word embeddings of other mentions in the same document as h_{other}. Then S_3 is the cosine similarity of h_{other} and u_e.
4. The linked entity feature S_4. We resolve mentions one-by-one in the same document, so the linked entities can be used. We take the sum of embeddings of the linked entities as h_{linked}. The cosine similarity of h_{linked} and u_e is S_4.
5. The prior probability $P_{prior}(e|m)$, estimated in candidate generation.

The representations are based on pre-trained multilingual embeddings. To fine-tune the representations, we did not directly use them to compute cosine similarities. Instead, we multiply h_{local}, h_{other}, h_{linked}, u_e and v_e by trainable diagonal matrices to obtain adaptive representations h'_{local}, h'_{other}, h'_{linked}, u'_e and v'_e. The diagonal matrices are initialized as identity matrices and updated during training.

The features are fed into a multilayer perceptron (MLP) neural network with a hidden layer to output the final score $\hat{S}$. The ranking model is as shown in Fig. 3. For every entity candidate $e_i \in C_m$, we compute its score $\hat{S}(e_i|m)$. Besides, to predict NIL when there is no appropriate target entity, we simply take e_{nil} as the last candidate in C_m and its score is trainable. Finally, we take the candidate with the highest score as prediction, and minimize the margin-based loss:

$$\hat{y} = arg\max_i \hat{S}(e_i|m) \tag{12}$$

$$loss(\hat{S}, y) = \frac{\sum_i max(0, \gamma - \hat{S}(e_y|m) + \hat{S}(e_i|m))}{|C_m|} \tag{13}$$

4   Experiment

4.1   Dataset and Evaluation Metrics

We conducted our experiments on the TAC KBP 2015 Chinese Entity Discovery and Linking Dataset [8], which contains 147 documents and 13112 query mentions for training, and 166 documents and 11066 query mentions for evaluating. Each mention is annotated with a span in some document, a Freebase ID or NIL, and one of the pre-defined five types. We perform EL with perfect mentions as input (mention spans are given, a.k.a. the diagnostic task in KBP 2015), and adopt the NERLC evaluation measure, which means a prediction is correct only if the predicted type and entity id are both correct. Then calculates the set-based F_1 metric:

$$P = \frac{|G \cap S|}{|S|} \quad R = \frac{|G \cap S|}{|G|} \quad F_1 = \frac{2PR}{P+R} \tag{14}$$

where G is gold and S is system prediction. We calculate the metrics by using the TAC KBP official evaluation tool[1].

4.2   Implementation

For embeddings, mention-entity indexes and abstracts, we download the Wikipedia dump and build corpora. We use the Word2Vec implementation in Gensim[2] to learn the word and entity embeddings with dimensionality 400 for Chinese and English, and then use MUSE[3] to learn the cross-lingual embedding mapping.

We train the model and conduct parameter selection on the training data. The size of candidate set $|C_m|$ is kept no more than 20. The words within a window $d_w = 20$ of the query mention are input as local context words. The size of hidden layer in scoring model is 200. The margin γ in the loss function is 0.1, and the learning rate is 0.0001.

For evaluation, the entity types should also be predicted. As previous works [15,16] did, we build a simple 5-class classifier, and take the mention context as well as the Freebase types of the predicted entity as input.

4.3   Compared with Previous Works

In Table 1, we compare our proposed model with previous state-of-the-arts methods on KBP 2015 Chinese-English Cross-lingual Entity Linking dataset. WikiME first introduced multilingual embeddings into cross-lingual EL, and outperformed the top TAC KBP 15 system. It used TF-IDF weighted context representations and a ranking SVM model. Sil et al. improved the performance

---

[1] https://github.com/wikilinks/neleval.
[2] http://radimrehurek.com/gensim/.
[3] http://github.com/facebookresearch/MUSE.

Table 1. Experimental results of our proposed model against other models.

Model	NERLC F_1
Top TAC'15 System [8]	83.1
WikiME [16]	83.6
Sil et al. [15]	84.4
ADXEL (This Work)	**86.4**

Table 2. Experimental results of simplified models.

Model	NERLC F_1
BASE	84.3
BASE+DIAG	85.3
BASE+ATT	85.6
BASE+DIAG+ATT	**86.4**

by applying long short-term memory (LSTM) and neural tensor networks (NTN) for modeling context, and then performing EL based on a sophisticated neural model architecture with features at multiple granularities.

The result shows that our model yields better performance than previous works. On the one hand, our context modeling is based on recurrent neural networks, which has been shown to work better than TF-IDF weighted representations for the task. On the other hand, we apply adjusting matrices to restrain the noise and emphasize useful parts in representations, and incorporate more information about candidates by dynamic entity representations. Similarly, Sil et al. also utilized the entity abstracts to build entity representations, however such representations are still independent from the query mention.

4.4 Effectiveness of Adjusting Matrices and Dynamic Entity Representations

In order to analyze the effectiveness of adjusting matrices and dynamic entity representations, we show the experimental results of several variant models:

- BASE: The model is used as strong baseline in our work, without adjusting matrices and dynamic entity representations. The local context representations solely compare with the pre-trained entity embeddings.
- BASE+ATT: Based on BASE model, we introduce attention based dynamic entity representations in this model.
- BASE+DIAG: Based on BASE model, we apply diagonal adjusting matrices.
- BASE+SQUARE: We replace the diagonal matrices in BASE+DIAG with general square matrices, and all parameters (not only diagonal) are trainable.
- BASE+SQUARE+ATT: In this model, we apply dynamic entity representations based on BASE+SQUARE model.
- BASE+ATT-EE: In this model, local context representations solely compare with the attention based entity representations, without the pre-trained entity embeddings.
- BASE+DIAG+ATT-EE: In this model, we apply diagonal adjusting matrices based on BASE+ATT-EE model.
- BASE+DIAG+ATT: The model is our proposed complete model.

From the results, we have several observations:

Table 3. Experimental results of comparing diagonal matrices with general matrices.

Model	NERLC F_1
BASE	84.3
BASE+SQUARE	84.6
BASE+DIAG	**85.3**
BASE+SQUARE+ATT	85.7
BASE+DIAG+ATT	**86.4**

Table 4. Experimental results of removing entity embeddings when computing the local context feature.

Model	NERLC F_1
BASE	84.3
BASE+ATT-EE	84.0
BASE+ATT	**85.6**
BASE+DIAG+ATT-EE	84.9
BASE+DIAG+ATT	**86.4**

- **Performance gains from proposed architectures.** In Table 2, the first three rows are simplified variants of the proposed model. The results show that both diagonal adjusting matrices and attention based dynamic entity representations are useful for improving the performance, but the effectiveness of the latter is more significant. With the effect of the two architectures, the model achieves 2.1% improvement in final performance.
- **Diagonal matrices is better than general matrices.** From Table 3, we observe that BASE+SQUARE only slightly outperforms BASE, but BASE+DIAG brings more significant improvement. It shows that diagonal adjusting matrices can work well with other architectures in the model. If they are replaced with general square matrices that have more trainable parameters, the model will be easier to overfit and degrade the performance.
- **Limitations of attention based entity representations.** From Table 4, we observe that BASE+ATT-EE has lower performance than BASE. It shows that though dynamic entity representations can incorporate more useful information and bring performance improvement in the complete model, they cannot completely replace the entity embeddings, and solely using them may degrade the performance. It is more appropriate to apply them together with the pre-trained entity embeddings.

4.5 Case Study and Error Analysis

We checked some examples produced by the model to verify the attention mechanism and error analysis. Some typical instances are listed as follows:

Sample 1: 我也很奇怪，快船老板**斯特林**不过电话里与情妇打情骂俏，在美国这么正常社会中也被搞下来了。(*I am also very surprised that* **Sterling**, *the boss of the Clippers, has been banned in such a normal society in the United States, just because of flirting with his mistress on the phone.*) In this sentence, **斯特林 (Sterling)** is the query mention, and our model successfully predicted the target entity **Donald T. Sterling**. We visualize the attention weights for the abstract, as in Fig. 4, which shows how the dynamic entity representation captures useful information in the abstract according to clues in mention context. We can find that *businessman* and *american* have higher weights. That may result from some clues in the context of query mention, such as 老板 (Boss) and 美国 (America).

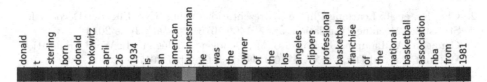

Fig. 4. Visualization of attention weights on different words in the abstract of entity **Donald T. Sterling**

Sample   2:   "你这一连套说**西班牙意大利**就算了，加上个**葡萄牙**，总感觉像岳不群把杀嵩山弟子，和魔教中人勾搭，偷辟邪剑谱一块说了一样。" (*It is barely ok that you have such arguments on* **Spain** *and* **Italy**; *when you add in* **Portugal**, *it seems like Yue Buqun puts killing Songshan disciples, hooking up with devils and stealing Evil Sword Spectrum together.*) Here, three country names are query mentions, and they actually refer to three national football teams, which our model failed to predict correctly. There is no explicit clues about football in the local context, but if we read other parts of the document, we can know it is about the World Cup. That shows our model is weak in global feature modeling, so more effective global methods may improve the performance.

5   Conclusion

We propose two new architectures for cross-lingual entity linking tasks based on multilingual embeddings. In order to restrain the noise and emphasize useful parts in multilingual representations, we apply diagonal adjusting matrices. Furthermore, to incorporate more useful information from entity descriptions, we introduce dynamic entity representations based on attention mechanisms. Experimental results show that our ranking model perform well on TAC KBP 2015 Chinese-English Cross-lingual Entity Linking dataset.

A direct future direction is to improve the global feature modeling and incorporate collective disambiguous methods. Besides, further research is needed to test and improve the transfer ability on different languages.

Acknowledgements. This work is supported by the National Natural Science Foundation of China (No. 61533018), the Natural Key R&D Program of China (No. 2017YFB1002101), the National Natural Science Foundation of China (No. 61806201, No. 61702512) and the independent research project of National Laboratory of Pattern Recognition. This work was also supported by Alibaba Group through Alibaba Innovative Research (AIR) Program and CCF-Tencent Open Research Fund.

References

1. Bahdanau, D., Cho, K., Bengio, Y.: Neural Machine Translation by Jointly Learning to Align and Translate. arXiv:1409.0473 [cs, stat], September 2014

2. Cho, K., et al.: Learning Phrase Representations using RNN Encoder-Decoder for Statistical Machine Translation. arXiv:1406.1078 [cs, stat], June 2014
3. Conneau, A., Lample, G., Ranzato, M., Denoyer, L., Jégou, H.: Word Translation Without Parallel Data. arXiv:1710.04087 [cs], October 2017
4. Faruqui, M., Dyer, C.: Improving vector space word representations using multilingual correlation. In: Proceedings of the 14th Conference of the European Chapter of the Association for Computational Linguistics, pp. 462–471. Association for Computational Linguistics, Gothenburg, Sweden (2014)
5. Ganea, O.E., Hofmann, T.: Deep Joint Entity Disambiguation with Local Neural Attention. arXiv:1704.04920 [cs], April 2017
6. Ji, H., Grishman, R., Dang, H.: Overview of the TAC 2011 knowledge base population track. In: Text Analysis Conference (TAC 2011), January 2011
7. Ji, H., Nothman, J., Hachey, B.: Overview of TAC-KBP2014 entity discovery and linking tasks. In: Text Analysis Conference (TAC 2014) (2014)
8. Ji, H., Nothman, J., Hachey, B., Florian, R.: Overview of TAC-KBP2015 tri-lingual entity discovery and linking. In: Text Analysis Conference (TAC 2015) (2015)
9. Luong, M.T., Pham, H., Manning, C.D.: Effective Approaches to Attention-based Neural Machine Translation. arXiv:1508.04025 [cs], August 2015
10. McNamee, P., Mayfield, J., Lawrie, D., Oard, D., Doermann, D.: Cross-language entity linking. In: Proceedings of 5th International Joint Conference on Natural Language Processing, pp. 255–263. Asian Federation of Natural Language Processing, Chiang Mai, Thailand, November 2011
11. Mikolov, T., Chen, K., Corrado, G., Dean, J.: Efficient Estimation of Word Representations in Vector Space. arXiv:1301.3781 [cs], January 2013
12. Mikolov, T., Sutskever, I., Chen, K., Corrado, G., Dean, J.: Distributed Representations of Words and Phrases and their Compositionality. arXiv:1310.4546 [cs, stat], October 2013
13. Shen, W., Wang, J., Han, J.: Entity linking with a knowledge base: issues, techniques, and solutions. IEEE Trans. Knowl. Data Eng. 27(2), 443–460 (2015)
14. Sil, A., Florian, R.: One for All: Towards Language Independent Named Entity Linking. arXiv:1712.01797 [cs], December 2017
15. Sil, A., Kundu, G., Florian, R., Hamza, W.: Neural cross-lingual entity linking. In: Thirty-Second AAAI Conference on Artificial Intelligence, April 2018
16. Tsai, C.T., Roth, D.: Cross-lingual wikification using multilingual embeddings. In: Proceedings of the 2016 Conference of the North American Chapter of the Association for Computational Linguistics: Human Language Technologies, pp. 589–598. Association for Computational Linguistics, San Diego (2016)
17. Wang, H., Zheng, J.G., Ma, X., Fox, P., Ji, H.: Language and domain independent entity linking with quantified collective validation. In: Proceedings of the 2015 Conference on Empirical Methods in Natural Language Processing, pp. 695–704. Association for Computational Linguistics, Lisbon, September 2015
18. Yamada, I., Shindo, H., Takeda, H., Takefuji, Y.: Joint learning of the embedding of words and entities for named entity disambiguation. In: Proceedings of The 20th SIGNLL Conference on Computational Natural Language Learning, pp. 250–259. Association for Computational Linguistics, Berlin (2016)
19. Yamada, I., Shindo, H., Takeda, H., Takefuji, Y.: Learning Distributed Representations of Texts and Entities from Knowledge Base. arXiv:1705.02494 [cs], May 2017
20. Zhang, T., Liu, K., Zhao, J.: Cross lingual entity linking with bilingual topic model. In: Twenty-Third International Joint Conference on Artificial Intelligence (2013)

Context-Dependent Representation
of Knowledge Graphs

Binling Nie$^{(\boxtimes)}$ and Shouqian Sun

Zhejiang University, Hangzhou, China
nbl1221@zju.edu.cn

Abstract. Recently, there is a growing interest of leveraging graph's structural information for knowledge representation. However, they fail to capture global connectivity patterns in knowledge graphs or depict unique structural properties of various graph context. In this paper, we propose a novel representation framework, Context-dependent Representation of Knowledge Graphs (CRKG), to utilize the diversity of graph's structural information for knowledge representation. We introduce triplet context to effectively capture semantic information from two types of graph structures around a triple. One is K-degree neighborhoods of a source entity in the target triple, which captures global connectivity patterns of entities. The other is multiple relation paths between the entity pair in the target triple, reflecting rich inference patterns between entities. Considering the unique characteristics of two kinds of triplet context, we design distinct embedding strategies to preserve their connectivity pattern diversities. Experimental results on three challenging datasets show that CRKG has significant improvements compared with baselines on link prediction task.

Keywords: Triplet context · Knowledge reasoning · Knowledge representation · Attention mechanism

1 Introduction

Knowledge graphs model factual information in the form of entities and relations to semantically represent the world's truth. In past few decades, a large number of knowledge graphs have been constructed, e.g., YAGO [27], DBpedia [2], NELL [10], WordNet [18], Freebase [3] and the Google Knowledge Graph [22]. This motivates researchers to study statistical models to predict new facts about the world given existing ones in the knowledge graph.

Existing knowledge graph embedding techniques can be categorized into two types: triple facts based methods and additional information enhanced methods. The prevailing methods based on triple facts alone [4,6,7,11,19] treat a given knowledge graph as a set of independent triples and derive the relationships between entities from interactions of their latent. Rich additional information is considered as supplementary for triple information that helps to learn representation of knowledge graphs. Particularly, structural information, which captures

© Springer Nature Singapore Pte Ltd. 2019
X. Zhu et al. (Eds.): CCKS 2019, CCIS 1134, pp. 13–24, 2019.
https://doi.org/10.1007/978-981-15-1956-7_2

the diversity of connectivity patterns in knowledge graph, has made significant contribution to this goal. Some researchers [12] incorporate different structural information into knowledge representation.

However, these approaches have not fully utilized the potential of the knowledge graph since they suffer from the following two limitations: (1) The state-of-art triple-based methods [11,19] capture limited graph structures of a triple, thus degrade their representation capability. (2) Structural information enhanced method [12] only takes the direct one-hop neighbor entities of the target entity into consideration and embed all types of graph context by averaging the embeddings of all entities and relations in a context as the representation of its context. The neighbor context only includes the direct one-hop neighbor entities of the target entity and can not capture global connectivity patterns (i.e., structural equivalences), which are observed in K-degree neighbors of the target entity. For example, in Fig. 1, the entity *RobinLi* and the entity *BillGates* share the same structural role of a hub entity. Such structural equivalences may reflect certain aspects of their semantics and help to model interactions with their neighborhoods precisely.

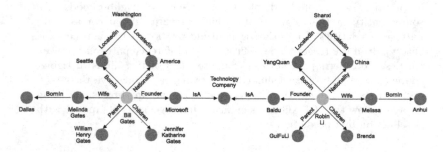

Fig. 1. An illustration of two entities' structural equivalence. The entity *RobinLi* and the entity *BillGates* share the same structural role of a hub entity.

To address the aforementioned issues, we propose a novel representation framework, Context-dependent Representation of Knowledge Graph (CRKG), to leverage the diversity of graph structures for knowledge representation. For a knowledge base, we not only treat it as a directed graph to capture various global connectivity patterns, but also view it as a set of separate triples. In addition, there are various relation paths between each entity pair in the target triple, which indicates complicated inference patterns between the entity pair. Thus, we take two types of graph structures around a triple into consideration, which are defined as triplet context. We divide triplet context of a target triple into neighborhood context and path context, and design distinct embedding strategies to preserve unique structural properties of two types of triplet context. Specifically, for a triple, neighborhood context is K-degree neighborhoods of a source entity in the target triple, which brings semantics of global connectivity patterns (i.e., structural equivalences) into the entity representation and helps model the entity more precisely. Path context consists of multiple relation paths between the entity pair in the target triple. We notice that different paths provide distinct evidence for semantics of the relation between the entity pair. For example, in Fig. 2, paths like *(RobinLi, BornIn, YangQuan, LocatedIn, ShanXi, LocatedIn, China)* and *(RobinLi, Founder, Baidu, LocatedIn, Beijing, LocatedIn, China)* are predictive of the triple fact *(RobinLi, Nationality, China)*, but the path *(RobinLi, Founder, Competitor, Google, FoundedBy, LaryPage, Visited, China)* isn't. To preserve the diversity of different structural information, we design distinct embedding strategies to effectively extract semantic presentations from two types of triplet context. Our experiments reveal that incorporating triplet context are competitive with state-of-the-art triple-based methods.

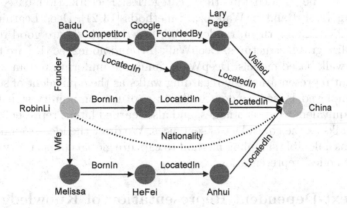

Fig. 2. Multiple paths between entities in a knowledge graph. Different relation paths have different representation power. The bottom three paths are predictive of the fact that the Nationality of Robin Li is China.

2   Related Works

2.1   Knowledge Graph Embedding

Recent years have witnessed rapid growth in knowledge graph embedding. We roughly categorize these methods into two groups: triple based embedding methods and additional information enhanced embedding methods.

Triple based embedding methods perform representation learning on the basis of triple facts. Many methods modeled latent features of entities to explain triples [4, 6, 7, 23]. Translation-based models [5, 16, 17, 20] aim to embed a knowledge graph into a continuous vector space for preserving certain information of the graph. Semantic Matching models [24, 31] compute each triple' score via similarity-based score function. Deep learning methods [11, 19] introduce convolutional neural network into knowledge base completion and performs best on this branch.

Additional information enhanced embedding methods incorporate a wide variety of information, e.g., entity types [14, 30], logic rules [26], textual descriptions [15, 28, 29], to further model entities and relations. The methods which leverage information about graph structures to learn entity and relation representation are most related to our study. GAKE [12] achieves state-of-the-art performance in this branch, which formulated a knowledge graph as a directed graph and leveraged the graph's structural information for representation learning. GAKE mainly considered graph structures related to entities. We extend it to take structure information around a triple into consideration, and define it as triplet context.

2.2 Network Embedding

There is a growing literature studying network embedding. Embedding approaches can be divided into three categories: Factorization based embedding methods [1,8], Random Walk based methods [13,21], Deep Learning based methods [9,25]. Among them, random walk based methods are good references for us to utilize graph structures. DeepWalk [21] and node2vec [13] are two typical random walk based models. DeepWalk simulated uniform random walks and learned latent representations by regarding walks as the equivalent of sentences. node2vec employed biased random walks to capture community structure and structural equivalence between nodes, and also learned latent representations by regarding walks as the equivalent of sentences. We draw the idea from node2vec, which designs a flexible sampling method to capture global connectivity patterns of nodes for nodes' representations.

3   Context-Dependent Representation of Knowledge Graphs

In this section, we present the details of Context-dependent Representation of Knowledge Graphs (CRKG).

3.1 Notations

We first describe the notations used in this paper. A knowledge graph consists of a set of triple facts. For any triple (h, r, t) in knowledge graph, two entities h, t pertain to the set of entities E, and the relation r belongs to the set of relations R. Let (h, p, t) be a path in knowledge graph, where $p = (h, r^1, r^2, ..., r^m, t)$, h/t are the start/end entities, and $r^1, r^2, ..., r^m$ are the relation edges. For a general entity pair (h, t), there is a path set containing multiple relation paths between them $P = \{p_1, p_2, ..., p_l\}$.

Triplet context contains neighborhood context and path context. To explore the diversity of graph structures, we learn two types of representation for each entity. We define h_n, t_n as neighborhood context representations of entities h and h_p, t_p as path context representations of entities h, and t. Similarly, r_n, r_p are neighborhood context representation and path context representation of the relation r. e_h, e_t are final representations of entities h and t. For multiple relation paths between entity pairs $p_1, p_2, ..., p_l$, we design various pooling techniques to obtain the relation path embeddings P.

3.2   Neighborhood Context Embedding

Neighborhood context is K-degree neighbor entities of a source entity in the target triple, which reflects global connectivity patterns of an entity and helps to model an entity more precisely. Different sampling strategies may generate different neighborhoods. Generally, there are two sampling strategies to generate neighborhood context.

- **Breadth-first Sampling (BFS)** The neighborhood context is restricted to entities which are immediate neighbors of the source, which is same as the neighbor context as GAKE. As in Fig. 3, for the target triple *(Bill Gates, Nationality, America)*, neighborhood context of the entity *Bill Gates* is *{ William Henry Gates, Jennifer Katharine Gates, Melinda Gates, Seattle, Microsoft}* when $K = 5$.
- **Depth-first Sampling (DFS)** The neighborhood context consists of entities sequentially sampled at increasing distances from the source node. In Fig. 3, DFS samples *{(Seattle, Washington, America, Uncle Sam), (Seattle, Washington, America, rose),(Melinda Gates, Dalas, Texas, America), (Microsoft, Sougou, WangXiaoChuan, America), (Microsoft, Seattle, Washington, America)}* when $K = 4$.

Appropriate neighborhood context is the key to learn richer representations. We encode the neighborhoods of entities following the idea of node2vec [13]. We apply a flexible neighborhood context sampling strategy which allows us to smoothly interpolate between BFS and DFS. By determining the right balance between BFS and DFS, we explore to capture diverse global connectivity patterns of the entity pairs. After obtain appropriate neighborhood context, we analogy neighborhood context of an entity as text context of a word and extend the Skip-gram architecture for representation learning.

Given an entity pair in a triple, we can maximize the log-likelihood of all entities given by their neighborhood contexts and obtain their neighborhood context representations as (h_n, t_n), which are then used to generate a neighborhood context representation of the relation in the triple by a subtraction operator $r_n = h_n - t_n$.

3.3   Path Context Embedding

Path context is multiple relation paths between the entity pair in the target triple, which indicates complicated inference patterns among relations in knowledge graphs. Different relation paths relevant to the target triple has different representation power. We design pooling techniques to handle this in path context embedding procedure.

We follow translation principles to learn path context representations. In this work, we simulate a random walk of maximum length $L = m$ to collect multiple paths of a triple, which provide distinct evidence for semantics of the relation. For a target triple, path context representation is to embed the vector P which contains semantic information of all paths relevant to the triple. We

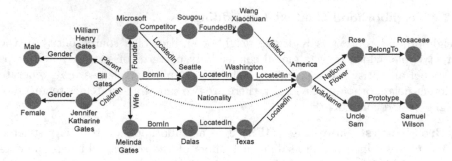

Fig. 3. An illustration of triplet context. For the triple *(Bill Gates, Nationality, America)*, triplet context contains neighborhood context and path context. Neighborhood of entity *Bill Gates* and entity *America* are *William Henry Gates, Jennifer Katharine Gates, Melinda Gates, Seattle, Microsoft* and *Wang Xiaochuan, Washington, Texas, Uncle Sam, Rose* respectively, when adopting BFS sampling and $K = 5$. Path context is *(Bill Gates, Founder, Microsoft, Competitor, Sougou, FoundedBy, WangXiaochuan, Visited, America), (Bill Gates, Founder, Microsoft, LocatedIn Seattle, LocatedIn Washington, LocatedIn, America), (Bill Gates, Wife, Melinda Gates, BornIn, Dalas, LocatedIn, Texas, LocatedIn, America)*.

design unique pooling techniques to learn representation power of different paths and embed the vector P. The highlight of pooling techniques is utilizing neighborhood context embeddings to decide representation power of different paths, which greatly reduce the computation complexity.

Max-pooling Mechanism. We only consider the max of path embeddings to represent semantics of the relation between the entity pair.

$$p = \operatorname{argmax} p_i \cdot r \tag{1}$$

where $p_i = r_n^1 + r_n^2 + ... + r_n^m$ and $r = r_n$.

After picking the appropriate path $p = (r^1, r^2, ..., r^m)$, we encode relation path embedding of the target triple.

$$P = r_p^1 + r_p^2 + ... + r_p^m \tag{2}$$

Attention Mechanism. We apply an attention-based multi-instance learning method to select top-k paths for the corresponding triple from all candidates. Formally,

$$att(p, r) = \frac{p \cdot r}{||p|| \cdot ||r||} \tag{3}$$

where $p = r_n^1 + r_n^2 + ... + r_n^m$ and $r = r_n$. Paths with higher att(p, r) could represent semantics of the corresponding relation more explicitly. Finally, we pick the top-k paths, and the weight of each path is as follows

$$w_i = \frac{att(p_i, r)}{\sum_{i=1,...,k} att(p_i, r)} \tag{4}$$

After selecting appropriate k paths, we model the target triple's relation path embedding.

$$P = \sum_{i=1,2,\ldots,k} w_i * p_i \tag{5}$$

where $p_i = r_p^1 + r_p^2 + \ldots + r_p^m$.

3.4 Optimization

To exploit various connectivity patterns for reasoning over entities and relations, we perform an addition operator to combine neighborhood context representations with path context embeddings.

$$e_h = h_n + h_p \tag{6}$$

$$e_t = t_n + t_p \tag{7}$$

$$r = r_p \tag{8}$$

Given a triple (h, r, t) and relation path representation P, the energy function is defined as follows:

$$E(h,r,t,P) = ||e_h + r - e_t||_2^2 + ||e_h + P - e_t||_2^2 \tag{9}$$

each component can be L_1 or L_2-norm, and the function is expected to be low when the triple holds and the representation of paths P is consistent with semantics of the relation r_p.

We utilize a margin-based score function as our training objective. The objective function is defined as follows:

$$L = \sum_{(h,r,t)\in T} \sum_{(h',r,t')\in T'} max(\gamma + E(h,r,t,P) - E(h',r,t',P),0) \tag{10}$$

where γ is a hyper parameter, T is the set of positive triples, T' is the set of invalid triples and P is the representation of the multiple-step path set related to the triple (h,r,t). And we set

$$||e_h||_2 \leq 1 \quad ||e_t||_2 \leq 1 \quad ||r||_2 \leq 1 \quad \forall h,r,t \tag{11}$$

For optimization, we employ a Stochastic Gradient Descent (SGD) algorithm to minimize the loss function.

4   Experiments and Analysis

We study and evaluate our approaches on the task: link prediction. We first present the dataset and implementation details. Then performance evaluation and analysis of the model are explained.

4.1   Datasets

In our experiments, we adopt three datasets: FB15k [5], FB15k-237 [11] and WN18RR [11]. FB15k is a classical benchmark dataset for knowledge graph embedding. However, FB15k contains many inverse relations, i.e., there are many triples such as $(h, hyponym, t)$ in test set while the training set contains its inverse $(t, hypernym, h)$. FB15k-237 is a subset of FB15k, where inverse relations are removed. Similarly, WN18RR is created to sanitize the reversible relation problem in WN18 [5]. We list both the statistics of FB15k, FB15k-237 and WN18RR in Table 1.

Table 1. Statistics of the experimental datasets

Dataset	#Rel	#Ent	#Triplet(Train/Valid/Test)		
FB15k	1341	14,541	483,142	59,071	57,803
FB15k-237	237	14,541	272,115	17,535	20,466
WN18RR	11	40,943	86,835	3,034	3,134

4.2   Implementation Details

Evaluation Metric. We use link prediction, which is widely used for knowledge graph embedding, to evaluate the performance of our model. The task is to predict the missing entity h or t in a triple (h, r, t) according to the embedding of another entity and relation. For each testing triple (h, r, t), we replace the head/tail entity by every entity in the knowledge graph, and give a ranking list of candidate entities in descending order of the scores calculated by score function $f(h, r, t)$. The score of the relation fact (h, r, t) is expected to be smaller than any other corrupted triples. We consider the proportion of correct entities in Top-10 ranked entities ($Hits@10$) as our evaluation metric. However, a corrupted triple may also exists in the knowledge graphs, which should also be considered as correct. The evaluation may rank these corrupted but correct triples high. To avoid such a misleading behavior, we may filter out these corrupted triples which have appeared in knowledge graph. Two evaluation settings are named as "raw" and "filter".

Experiment Details. We name the one as CRKG(-Max), which uses a max-pooling technique to learn path context representation. Meanwhile, the other is termed as CRKG(-Att), which adopts an attention mechanism to learn path context representation. As the dataset is same, we directly reference the results of several baselines from previous literatures. For parameters, we select the batch size B among 512, 1024, 2048, 4096, the learning rate α among 0.1, 0.01, 0.001, the dimension of relation embeddings d_e and the dimension of relation embeddings d_r among 100, 200, 300, 400. To get the optimum configuration, we have tried several settings on the validation dataset. For the optimal configuration of CKGR-Max, we set $d_e = d_r = 200, \alpha = 0.001, B = 4096$. For the datasets, we traverse all the training triples for 600 rounds. For the optimal configuration of CKGR-Att, we set $d_e = d_r = 400, \alpha = 0.001, B = 2048$. For the datasets, we traverse all the training triples for 800 rounds.

4.3 Performance Evaluation

Evaluation results of link prediction is shown in Table 2. From Table 2, we observe that: (1) CRKG(-Max) and CRKG outperform other baseline methods including GAKE significantly and consistently. It indicates that CRKG models are effective to capture connectivity patterns in knowledge graph by modeling graph context based on a triple. (2) PTransE, which merely model relation paths for knowledge graph embedding, does better than GAKE, thus showing taking transitional characteristics of relation paths can capture more rich inference patterns between entities than drawing an analogy between word context and relation paths. (3) Compared to GAKE, CRKG(-Max) increases by 18.97% and CRKG increases by 21.77%. It demonstrates that regarding the knowledge graph as a set of triples and a directed graph is preferable to extract more semantic information in varied viewpoints. It also proves our models preserve the diversity of different graph structures perfectly by performing distinct embedding methods on two types of graph context. (4) CRKG obtains better scores than CRKG(-Max), which illustrates the effect of two path context embedding strategies presented in Sect. 3.4. It is encouraging to see that considering information from multiple useful paths can provide more evidence for a prediction.

Table 2. Experimental results on link prediction

Data sets	FB15k			
	Mean rank		Hits@10	
Metric	Raw	Filter	Raw	Filter
TransE	243	125	34.9	47.1
TransH	211	84	42.5	58.5
TransR	226	78	43.8	65.5
PTransE	200	54	51.8	83.4
GAKE	228	119	44.5	64.8
CRKG(-Max)	209	59	51.81	83.8
CRKG	203	47	52.06	86.6

The relation in knowledge graphs can be divided into four classes: 1-to-1, 1-to-N, N-to-1, and N-to-N relations [5]. From Table 3, we observe that: (1) Our models achieve improvements under four classes of relations when predicting head and tail entities. This indicates our models take advantage of various graph context and significantly improve the performance of embedding in relation-level. (2) Compared to TransR, the improvements on predicting N side, such as "N-To-1" of predicting head entities, "1-To-N" of predicting tail entities, and "N-To-N" on both sides, are especially significant. Predicting on N side is a drawback of translation-based methods. It shows our models model more precise representations of entity pairs and their complex correlations by utilizing different types of graph context. The impact may also be great than relation-specific projection.

Table 3. Experimental results on FB15K by mapping properties of relations.(%)

Tasks	Prediction head (*Hits*@10)				Prediction tail (*Hits*@10)			
Relation category	1-To-1	1-To-N	N-To-1	N-To-N	1-To-1	1-To-N	N-To-1	N-To-N
TransE	43.7	65.7	18.2	47.2	43.7	19.7	66.7	50.0
TransH	66.7	81.7	30.2	57.4	63.7	30.1	83.2	60.8
TransR	76.9	77.9	38.1	66.9	76.2	38.4	76.2	69.1
CRKG(-MAX)	83.8	94.0	**61.0**	**84.0**	83.8	**68.3**	93.2	**86.8**
CRKG	90.9	95.9	**69.1**	**86.2**	89.7	**74.0**	94.4	**89.0**

4.4 Model Analysis

In this section, we compare the CRKG with its two variants, CRKG(-N) and CRKG(-P), to demonstrate the effectiveness of different kinds of triplet context. The two variants are summarized in the following:

- CRKG(-N): We only take neighborhood context into count. The path context representations of entities and relations are set to zero vectors except that the entity pair's direct relation embedding is randomly initialized and optimized.
- CRKG(-P): Similar with CRKG(-N), we only incorporate path context into triple's representation learning. The neighborhood context representations of entities and relations are set to zero vectors.

The performance of CRKG and its variants on datasets are given in Table 4. From the table, we can have the following observations: (1) Both CKRG(-N) and CKRG(-P) beat all single triple representation learning methods, which reveals that modeling two kinds of triplet context for representation learning of knowledge graph can capture semantic representation more effectively. (2) CRKG gives better performance than CKRG(-N) and CKRG(-P), which implies combining two kinds of triplet context together can boost the performance of knowledge representation learning, and they really cooperate to learn effective features of entities and relations.

5   Conclusion

In this paper, we propose Context-dependent Representation of Knowledge Graphs (CRKG) to leverage the diversity of graph structures for knowledge

Table 4. Experimental results on WN18RR and FB15k-237

Data sets	WN18RR		FB15k-237	
Metrics	Mean Rank	*Hits*@10	Mean Rank	*Hits*@10
TransE	3384	50.1	347	46.5
ConvE	5277	48	246	49.1
ConvKB	2254	52.5	257	51.7
CRKG(-N)	1247	52.4	187	52.8
CRKG(-P)	1256	52.7	183	53.2
CRKG	962	56.2	171	55.4

representation. We take different graph structures around a triple into account, termed as triplet context. Triplet context consists of neighborhood context and path context. To fully preserve the uniqueness and diversity of connectivity patterns in two kinds of triplet context, we design distinct embedding strategies for knowledge representation. Experiment results on three datasets show that CRKG outperforms all the baseline methods, indicating utilizing semantic information from different graph structures could model entities and relations more precisely, especially for complex relations.

References

1. Ahmed, A., Shervashidze, N., Narayanamurthy, S., Josifovski, V., Smola, A.J.: Distributed large-scale natural graph factorization. In: WWW, pp. 37–48 (2013)
2. Auer, S., Bizer, C., Kobilarov, G., Lehmann, J., Cyganiak, R., Ives, Z.: DBpedia: a nucleus for a web of open data. In: Aberer, K., et al. (eds.) ASWC/ISWC -2007. LNCS, vol. 4825, pp. 722–735. Springer, Heidelberg (2007). https://doi.org/10.1007/978-3-540-76298-0_52
3. Bollacker, K.D., Evans, C., Paritosh, P., Sturge, T., Taylor, J.: Freebase: a collaboratively created graph database for structuring human knowledge. In: SIGMOD, pp. 1247–1250 (2008)
4. Bordes, A., Glorot, X., Weston, J., Bengio, Y.: Joint learning of words and meaning representations for open-text semantic parsing. In: AISTATS, pp. 127–135 (2012)
5. Bordes, A., Usunier, N., Garciaduran, A., Weston, J., Yakhnenko, O.: Translating embeddings for modeling multi-relational data. In: NIPS, pp. 2787–2795 (2013)
6. Bordes, A., Weston, J., Collobert, R., Bengio, Y.: Learning structured embeddings of knowledge bases. In: AAAI, pp. 301–306 (2011)
7. Bordes, A., et al.: A semantic matching energy function for learning with multi-relational data. Mach. Learn. **94**(2), 233–259 (2014)
8. Cao, S., Lu, W., Xu, Q.: Grarep: learning graph representations with global structural information. In: CIKM, pp. 891–900 (2015)
9. Cao, S., Lu, W., Xu, Q.: Deep neural networks for learning graph representations. In: AAAI, pp. 1145–1152 (2016)
10. Carlson, A., Betteridge, J., Kisiel, B., Settles, B., Hruschka, E.R., Mitchell, T.M.: Toward an architecture for never-ending language learning. In: AAAI, pp. 1306–1313 (2010)

11. Dettmers, T., Minervini, P., Stenetorp, P., Riedel, S.: Convolutional 2D knowledge graph embeddings. In: AAAI (2018)
12. Feng, J., Huang, M., Yang, Y., Zhu, X.: GAKE: graph aware knowledge embedding. In: COLING, pp. 641–651 (2016)
13. Grover, A., Leskovec, J.: node2vec: Scalable feature learning for networks. In: SIGKDD, pp. 855–864 (2016)
14. Guo, S., Wang, Q., Wang, B., Wang, L., Guo, L.: Semantically smooth knowledge graph embedding. In: ACL, pp. 84–94 (2015)
15. Han, X., Liu, Z., Sun, M.: Neural knowledge acquisition via mutual attention between knowledge graph and text. In: AAAI (2018)
16. Lin, Y., Liu, Z., Luan, H., Sun, M., Rao, S., Liu, S.: Modeling relation paths for representation learning of knowledge bases. In: EMNLP, pp. 705–714 (2015)
17. Lin, Y., Liu, Z., Sun, M., Liu, Y., Zhu, X.: Learning entity and relation embeddings for knowledge graph completion. In: AAAI, pp. 2181–2187 (2015)
18. Miller, G.A.: Wordnet: a lexical database for English. Commun. ACM **38**(11), 39–41 (1995)
19. Nguyen, D.Q., Nguyen, T.D., Nguyen, D.Q., Phung, D.Q.: A novel embedding model for knowledge base completion based on convolutional neural network. In: NAACL, pp. 327–333 (2018)
20. Nickel, M., Tresp, V., Kriegel, H.: Knowledge graph embedding by translating on hyperplanes. In: WWW, pp. 271–280 (2012)
21. Perozzi, B., Alrfou, R., Skiena, S.: Deepwalk: online learning of social representations. In: SIGKDD, pp. 701–710 (2014)
22. Singhal, A.: Introducing the knowledge graph: things, not strings. https://www.blog.google/products/search/introducing-knowledge-graph-things-not/. Accessed 28 Aug 2018
23. Socher, R., Chen, D., Manning, C.D., Ng, A.Y.: Reasoning with neural tensor networks for knowledge base completion. In: NIPS, pp. 926–934 (2013)
24. Trouillon, T., Welbl, J., Riedel, S., Gaussier, E., Bouchard, G.: Complex embeddings for simple link prediction. In: ICML, pp. 2071–2080 (2016)
25. Wang, D., Cui, P., Zhu, W.: Structural deep network embedding. In: SIGKDD, pp. 1225–1234 (2016)
26. Wang, Q., Wang, B., Guo, L.: Knowledge base completion using embeddings and rules. In: ICAI, pp. 1859–1865 (2015)
27. Wang, Z., Zhang, J., Feng, J., Chen, Z.: Factorizing YAGO: scalable machine learning for linked data. In: AAAI, pp. 1112–1119 (2014)
28. Wang, Z., Zhang, J., Feng, J., Chen, Z.: Knowledge graph and text jointly embedding. In: EMNLP, pp. 1591–1601 (2014)
29. Xie, R., Liu, Z., Jia, J., Luan, H., Sun, M.: Representation learning of knowledge graphs with entity descriptions. In: AAAI, pp. 2659–2665 (2016)
30. Xie, R., Liu, Z., Sun, M.: Representation learning of knowledge graphs with hierarchical types. In: AAAI, pp. 2965–2971 (2016)
31. Yang, B., Yih, W., He, X., Gao, J., Deng, L.: Embedding entities and relations for learning and inference in knowledge bases. In: ICLR (2015)

Construction and Application of Teaching System Based on Crowdsourcing Knowledge Graph

Jinta Weng[1] ⓘ, Ying Gao[1(✉)], Jing Qiu[1], Guozhu Ding[2], and Huanqin Zheng[1]

[1] School of Computer Science and Cyber Engineering, Guangzhou University, Guangzhou, China
552122632@qq.com, falcongao@sina.com.cn
[2] School of Education, Guangzhou University, Guangzhou, China

Abstract. [Objective] Through the combination of crowdsourcing knowledge graph and teaching system, research methods to generate knowledge graph and its applications. [Method]Using two crowdsourcing approaches, crowdsourcing task distribution and reverse captcha generation, to construct knowledge graph in the field of teaching system. [Results] Generating a complete hierarchical knowledge graph of the teaching domain by nodes of school, student, teacher, course, knowledge point and exercise type. [Limitations] The knowledge graph constructed in a crowdsourcing manner requires many users to participate collaboratively with fully consideration of teachers' guidance and users' mobilization issues. [Conclusion] Based on the three subgraphs of knowledge graph, prominent teacher, student learning situation and suitable learning route could be visualized. [Application] Personalized exercises recommendation model is used to formulate the personalized exercise by algorithm based on the knowledge graph. Collaborative creation model is developed to realize the crowdsourcing construction mechanism. [Evaluation] Though unfamiliarity with the learning mode of knowledge graph and learners' less attention to the knowledge structure, system based on Crowdsourcing Knowledge Graph can still get high acceptance around students and teachers.

Keywords: Educational knowledge graph · Learning analysis · Information extraction · Semantic network · Crowdsourcing

1 Introduction

Proposed by Google in 2012, Knowledge graph is a new dynamically correlated knowledge representation, which represent entity and entity' relationship through nodes and links. With the help of knowledge graph, the association and visualization of knowledge will be friendly presented.

Generally, human's cognition of teaching knowledge is always based on our culture and history, and this knowledge is always closely related to its corresponding author, object, history, emotion and other entities. We use the Chinese educational knowledge in the Mu Du's poem, "the southern dynasty four hundred and eighty temple, how

X. Zhu et al. (Eds.): CCKS 2019, CCIS 1134, pp. 25–37, 2019.
https://doi.org/10.1007/978-981-15-1956-7_3

many buildings in the misty rain" as an example, and then chooses manual way to get the following entities:

(1) The author is Mu Du.
(2) there are temples and rain.
(3) The dynasty was tang dynasty.
(4) The emotion of ancient poetry is the beauty of Jiang Nan.

By (1), (2), (3), (4) in series four short sentences, it is not difficult to draw, because the author Mu Du live in the ancient millennium, the poem use "temples" "rain" such nice hazy type of entity to represent "the beauty of Jiang Nan".

With Chinese "Education informatization 2.0 Action Plan" pointing out [2]: it is necessary to change the concept of education resource and turn it into continuous and connective view of 'Big Source'. The view of Big Resource means that we should reveal the mobility and interconnection between knowledge and data, and treat educational objects in an interdisciplinary, dynamic and connectable way.

Knowledge Graph subsequently become the popular way to represent educational knowledge. Hu tracked the relevant data in the learning process of learners and drew the learning path diagram through knowledge graph [3]. Zhu classified English exercises and generated knowledge graph of English exercises for intelligent topic selection [4]. Kang and Wang generated a large biological knowledge base, and constructed an intelligent system for answering questions [5]. However, relationships among different disciplines, courses, knowledge and resources is often neglected in current KG educational systems, resulting in low interoperability and knowledge reusability of educational data. Secondly, crowdsourcing-construction method can also realize in a large degree by massive students and teachers' efforts. Therefore, this paper will introduce and design two crowdsourcing methods to develop a way to general educational knowledge graph.

2   Motivation of Crowdsourcing

2.1   General Construction of KG

Construction of Knowledge graph is information extraction matter. It can be dividing into NER (Named entity recognition) step and RE (Relation extraction) step. Entity annotation, also known as Named Entity Recognition. Relationship extraction, through a certain method, such as TransE [6], to generate the relationship between the different entities. Both extracting methods are consist of automatic construction method and manual annotation method.

(1) Automated Construction
     Automated construction method can be divided into two types: Feature Matching and Classification. Feature Matching means full consideration to self-feature, contextual feature and self-restriction of the type of the specified word. Classification method mainly includes HMM proposed by Sahara et al. [7], decision tree model proposed by Sahara [8], SVM model proposed by Sahara and Matsumoto [9] and distance-based model TransE. Classification also contains propose

appropriate neural network model for deep learning, such as CNN, RNN, and CRF+LSTM method. Thought out the probably existing problem of polysemy in the process of automated construction, word2vec, TF-IDF model, BM25 model, proximity model and semantic feature model facilitate Entity disambiguation and relation disambiguation.

It can be seen that in the field of automatic annotation, whether it is entity annotation or knowledge representation learning, the selected model not only relies heavily on the existing data type and data amount, but also has low accuracy for atlas data with rapid knowledge update and change.

(2) Manually Annotated

Manual annotation method means that developers can arrange a certain number of non-user groups to develop and implement the data graph according to certain input specifications. For example, Tian et al. used manual annotation to optimize video retrieval [12].This method is often used to build query manuals and professional dictionaries. Because data entry personnel are generally intelligent, the knowledge graph generated can reflect specialization and standardization, but it cannot reflect the diversity and complexity of individual knowledge of human brain.

Although these two methods can solve the problem of knowledge system construction to a certain extent, there are also problems of large expensive manual assistance and high demand for data.

2.2 Crowdsourcing Within Students' Effort

Crowdsourcing results have been certificated better than each of individual annotations in swarm intelligence task like group collaboration [13]. Surowiecki found crowdsourcing translation is far better than a single machine translation in low error rate [14].

With the combination of crowdsourcing way and automatic construction, this paper purpose students' group crowdsourcing [15] and backward verification code to use crowdsourcing. As shown in Fig. 1, different supervised algorithm to realize Named entity recognition, and then use TransE, CNN+LSTM method or other RE algorithm within desirable entities to generate relations which will subsequently save in the triple database. In the part of crowdsourcing, we adopt two methods to generate more triples.

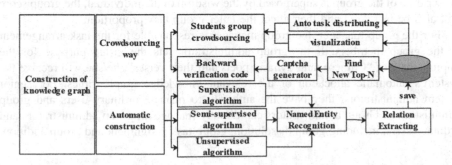

Fig. 1. Our construction approach of KG

First, we design an auto task distributing method to dispense constant type of triples in the corresponding group and develop a visualization tool that enable user directly edit or delete triples. Especially, we use the backward verification code by captcha generator from the Top-N triple.

2.3   Crowdsource Task Distribution

As Fig. 2 shown, at the beginning of the crowdsourcing task module, users will be authenticated and divided into three types: common users, group users and system administrators. For common users, the system will judge whether the user has joined the group. User will accept the task distributed by the group administrator and complete corresponding task after join the group.

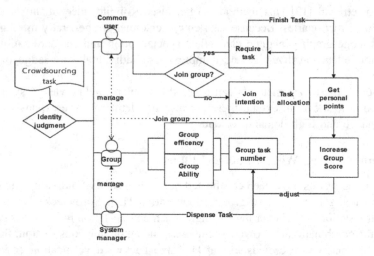

Fig. 2. Our construction approach of KG

The types of tasks can be one of triple verification, perfection of concept and attribute, relationship expansion. Every time common users complete a task, they will automatically trigger the system's reward mechanism and obtain a certain score. Since the wisdom of the group is superposed by the wisdom of the individual, the group score will also be increased and then affect the latter group task proportion.

For the group manager, the group manager is responsible for the task arrangement of the group members. If the group administrator sets the group purpose for the improvement of "Chinese tang dynasty poets and their verses", he/she will receive the system's automatic allocation of the relevant knowledge graph triples. For senior system administrators, they have the authority to manage ordinary users and group administrators. Group administrators can directly manage all group administrators and ordinary users, including group dissolution, group task assignment and group addition.

2.4   Reverse Captcha Generation

Reverse captcha generation is mainly reflected in the generation of captchas in the system login page, so captchas generated by captchas generator will extract triples existing in the database and then pack into Full-in-blank type or confirmatory question.

As Fig. 3 depicted, owing to knowledge grape is make up of entities and links. Question can be divided into entity concept catechism; entity attributes question or relations judgment problem like type 1 to 3.

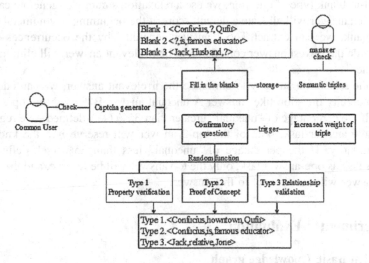

Fig. 3. Reverse captcha generation

By calling on the existing network verification code generated interface two type of generated authentication code like Fig. 4 in the login page, the user has to input verification code instead of traditional numeric verification or image-recognition verification. At last, it will make the weight of generated triples rise in the Confirmatory question or storage new semantic triple in the Fill in the blanks process. All the high score and low score of Top-N triples can be chosen to check again by manager or

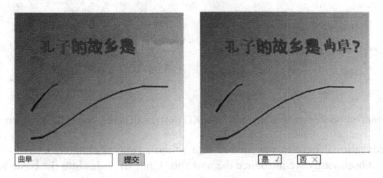

Fig. 4. Two type of knowledge Reverse Captcha triple

recirculate in the new round finally. Since the system will review the user's task by generated captchas, if the views are consistent, the credibility will be proved to be high and the score will be increased.

2.5 Different Answer Within Crowdsourcing

During the above two crowdsource task distribution, group task allocation and reverse captcha generation task, may result ambiguity question or irrelevant answer.

For fill-in-blank type of question, we use a relaxation strategy to generate candidate answer. Each answer will allocate a default score at the beginning. By numerable input into the blank, we can extract Top-2 answer generated by the occurrences of each answer, while the lowest answer considered to be irrelevant answer will eliminate after a new cycle.

After the relaxation strategy to eliminate the irrelevant answer, we can add a new type of ambiguity question like "answer A unequal answer B?" used the top-2 answer A and B. If the percentage of "unequal" greater than 35% (self-defined), we regard this task as multi-answer task, both of the top-2 answer will reserve into the knowledge graph. Similarity, If the percentage of "unequal" less than 35% (self-defined), we regard this task as one-answer task, only the top answer will be reserve, and the second-highest answer will auto-reflect to this answer.

3 Experimental Evaluation

3.1 Design Basic Knowledge graph

To construct a knowledge graph in educational field, we take subject of educational technology (ET) as an example. The basic entity of a subject is course nodes. As the Fig. 5 depicted, the knowledge graph only exists two kind of nodes, subject node and course node. Relation between then call "course-subject" relation.

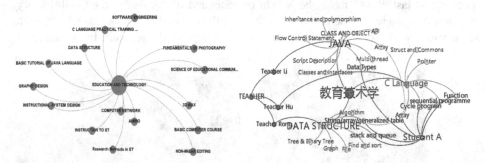

Fig. 5. From introduce course nodes into basic KG (left) to all nodes (right) (Color figure online)

As Educational entities can divide into school, course, chapter, knowledge and resource, subsequently we introduce the new four kinds of nodes into the basic KG and use different colors to represent the same class to build a distinct knowledge graph, like Fig. 5 (right).

3.2   Results Visualization

Based on the node and relationship model built above, we use the visualization plug-in of Echart3.0 to present the construction results in a visual form. As shown in Fig. 6, the knowledge graph of education domain is composed of schools, courses, knowledge elements, resources and creators.

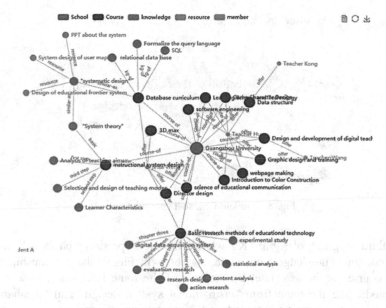

Fig. 6. Visualization of the Educational field

3.3   Different Subgraph of KG

By analyzing "teacher" nodes and their offered "course" node, not only we can judge detached teacher and cooperative teacher, but we can also find the teacher ability by the connective nodes. Furthermore, each course nodes can fall into the same category,

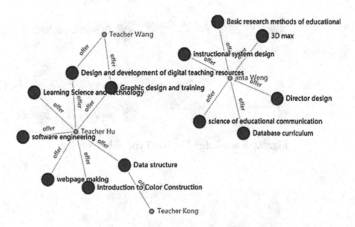

Fig. 7. Teacher-Course-Type subgraph

which make analyses the ability type of teacher possible. We extract the Teacher and their offered course from the KG to formula a subgraph In Fig. 7.

To master and compare the learning situation of different students to locate the poor student and excellent student, we extract the teacher nodes and their offered course from the KG to automatically formula a subgraph as Fig. 8 shown.

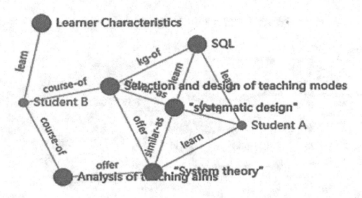

Fig. 8. Student-Course-Type subgraph

The third subgraph of Kg are Knowledge-Course-Type subgraph, which make of course node and knowledge-point node. As show in Fig. 9, the relationship within different course can be associate. By the help of the route from one course node to another node, like the route from "instructional system design" and "database curriculum", we can generate a suitable learning route to student.

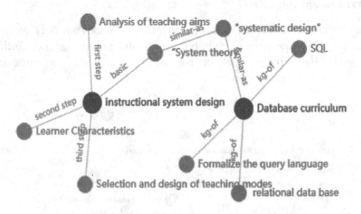

Fig. 9. Knowledge-Course-Type subgraph

4 Application

4.1 Personalized Exercises Recommendation

Personalized exercises recommendation is an important application of knowledge graph to recommend the most suitable resources for learners. For this application, following factors are generally considered:

(1) Incremental recommendation: Based on the recent learning topics, it recommends exercises of characteristic knowledge points under specific courses, exercises of related knowledge points under specific courses, exercises of characteristic knowledge points under related courses, and exercises of related knowledge points under related courses. For incremental recommendation, learners' learning situation and curriculum structure developed by teachers will be involved. The nodes involved include students, courses and knowledge. The learning situation of student A is divided into "learned courses" and "unlearned courses", as shown in Fig. 10.

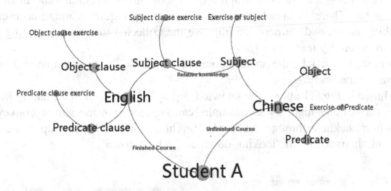

Fig. 10. Incremental recommended form of storage

(2) Past recommendation: Recommend high error rate of exercises node to learners in the past learning.

For the past recommendation, it will involve entity of students, sub-knowledge and exercises. We put forward an algorithm to recommend the suitable problem set in Eqs. (1) and (2). The learner's learning situation LS is reflected by the rate R of finished resources node and the error rate E of exercises node. Rate of resources node graph are the proportion of sum of finished entity within the all resource of same current topic.

In the case that exercises are same error rate, learners who have learned more related resources have lower learning ability than those who have not learned or have learned less about the same number of resources, that is, the former needs to spend more time to complete consolidation exercises. Based on the above conditions, the evaluation algorithm is developed:

$$LS = \frac{1}{R} * E*100\%$$ (1)

$$R = \frac{\sum_1^{course\ num}(exercise + video + note + other\ resource)}{Number\ of\ all\ resouces}$$ (2)

By setting a certain threshold value P, when the value is greater than the standard threshold value, the default is that the answer is good; when the answer is lower than the threshold value, the answer is considered to be poor. When 20% is set as the comparison threshold in specified topic, the P value above 20% is considered to be more recommended for exercises under this topic, while less than 20% is not recommended. For the determination of contrast threshold, teachers need to make dynamic adjustment according to the average level of students.

4.2   Collaborative Creation

Knowledge graph with a good extensible graph structure and human-readable visualization, we develop a knowledge graph tool to allow users add nodes and links to the graph together. Therefore, teachers can carry out group inquiry learning according to the teaching needs, and learners can improve the collected materials according to the topics carried out by teachers.

In this study, we take the ancient poem "Jing Ye Si" as an example and make a preliminary experiment.

As shown in Fig. 11 above, the knowledge graph drawn by user A, taking Bai Li's thoughts on A quiet night as an example, can be seen that the author conveys the author's homesickness through the words "bright moon" in "looking up at the bright moon" and "hometown" in "looking down at the hometown".

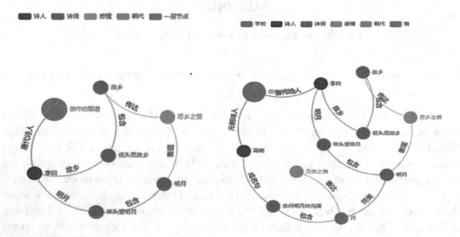

Fig. 11. Knowledge graph drawn by user A and user B, left knowledge graph is drawn by User A while right one drawn by User A.

Basing on A's knowledge graph, student B join and improve the classical knowledge graph. According to the moon in poet "the moon according to ditch" of the author Ming Gao in the yuan dynasty, Ming Gao thought out the moon to convey inner helpless mood. Although the entity moon in this poet within Bai Li poem refers to the same one, it expresses different meaning by the different crowdsourcing user.

To sum up, the cognitive levels of user A and user B are different. Most users can know the "homesick" moon in "Thinking at Quiet Night", but they cannot know the "Helplessness" conveyed by the moon in "Pipa Xing". Therefore, this collaborative creation method can highlight the individual differentiation level under the cognitive level.

5 Evaluation and Summary

To certificate the practicality and reliability, we propose two applications and evaluate our knowledge teaching system by 20-point questionnaire. We invite 20 users which make up of 5 teachers and 15 students to ask the question shown in Table 1, the average score of questionnaires can fluctuate up and down within 4 points in all dimensions. According to the Richter scale, a score of 4 indicates that respondents have a high sense of system identity. The total average score of the dimensions explored in this study is 3.94, which is approximately equal to 5(highest) * 0.8(80%), indicating that the surveyor's satisfaction with the system is close to 80%.

Table 1. Statistical results

Problem list	Mean
I think this system can help me find the key knowledge points of this subject	4.00
I think this system can improve my cognitive structure	3.75
I think this system can conveniently display my learning context (learning portrait)	3.80
I think this system can facilitate me to master the learning situation of other learners	3.70
In my opinion, this system can be used as a tool for classroom knowledge network creation and knowledge resource storage	4.15
I think this system can facilitate teachers' classroom teaching	3.85
I can use different classification rules to reason on the knowledge graph	4.20
In my opinion, this knowledge graph can meet the needs of related data search I quickly mastered the use of knowledge graph	4.15
I can accept the operating interface display of this system	3.75
I am more interested in the learning method with the help of knowledge graph than the traditional learning method	3.95
I think the learning method with the help of knowledge graph is better than the traditional learning method	3.95
20 Total	3.94

Therefore, we believe that our teaching system based on knowledge graph can solve the shortcomings of traditional adaptive learning system, and teachers and students generally agree with the teaching system based on knowledge graph. However, the above table can also point out the shortcomings of the system: (1) systematic proficiency in question 9 indicates that learners are relatively unfamiliar with the learning mode of knowledge graph; (2) according to question 3, learners do not pay too much attention to the knowledge structure. (3) The teaching practicality of the sixth question highlights the lack of certain teaching practice in this system. Knowledge graph constructed in a crowd-sourced manner requires many users to participate collaboratively, and needs to fully consider the teacher guidance and User mobilization issues.

Acknowledgment. This work was supported by Guangzhou teaching achievement cultivation project ([2017]93), Guangdong Province Higher Education Teaching Reform Project ([2018] 180).

References

1. Hou, H.: Mapping knowledge domain—a new field of information management and knowledge management **27**(01), 30–37+96 (2009)
2. Wang, Z.: Education informationization 2.0: core essence and implementation suggestions. https://doi.org/10.13541/j.cnki.chinade.20180725.001. Accessed 21 Apr 2019
3. Hu, W.: Learning path graph generation graph based on knowledge map. Beijing University of Posts & Telecommunications (2017)
4. Zhu, Z.: Topic selection system and application of junior middle school English based on knowledge graph. Minzhu University in China (2016)
5. Kang, Z., Wang, D.: Question answer system of biology based on knowledge graph. Comput. Eng. Softw. **39**(02), 7–11 (2018)
6. Nadeau, D., Sekine, S.: A survey of named entity recognition and classification. Lingvisticae Investigationes **30**(1), 3–26 (2007)
7. Sekine, S.: NYU: description of the Japanese NE system used for MET-2. In: Message Understanding Conference (1998)
8. Borthwick, A., Sterling, J., Agichtein, E., et al.: NYU: description of the MENE named entity system as used in MUC-7. In: Message Understanding Conference (1998)
9. Asahara, M., Matsumoto, Y.: Japanese named entity extraction with redundant morphological analysis. In: Conference of the North American Chapter of the Association for Computational Linguistics on Human Language Technology. Association for Computational Linguistics (2003)
10. Mccallum, A., Li, W.: Early results for named entity recognition with conditional random fields, feature induction and web-enhanced lexicons. In: Conference on Natural Language Learning at HLT-NAACL. Association for Computational Linguistics (2003)
11. Bordes, A., Usunier, N., Garciaduran, A., et al.: Translating embeddings for modeling multi-relational data. In: International Conference on Neural Information Processing Systems. Curran Associates Inc. (2013)
12. Ya, R.: Design and Implementation of Manual Annotation Video Retrieval System. Beijing Jiaotong University (2015)
13. Ke, Y., Yu, S., Sui, Z., et al.: Research on corpus annotation method based on collective intelligence. J. Chinese Inf. Process. **31**(4), 108–113 (2017)

14. Surowiecki, J.: The wisdom of crowds: why the many are smarter than the few and how collective wisdom shapes business, economies, societies, and nations. Pers. Psychol. **59**(4), 982–985 (2010)
15. Kohli, S., Arora, S.: Domain specific search engine based on semantic web. In: Pant, M., Deep, K., Nagar, A., Bansal, J. (eds.) Soft Computing for Problem Solving. AISC, vol. 259, pp. 217–224. Springer, Heidelberg (2014). https://doi.org/10.1007/978-81-322-1768-8_20

Cross-Lingual Entity Linking
in Wikipedia Infoboxes

Juheng Yang and Zhichun Wang[✉]

Beijing Normal University, Beijing, People's Republic of China
yangjuheng@163.com, zcwang@bnu.edu.cn

Abstract. Infoboxes in Wikipedia are valuable resources for extracting structured information of entities, several large-scale knowledge graphs are built by processing infobox data, including DBpedia, YAGO, etc. Entity links annotated by hyper-links in infoboxes are the keys for extracting entity relations. However, many entity links in infoboxes are missing because the mentioned entities do not exist in the current language versions of Wikipedia. This paper presents an approach for automatically linking mentions in infoboxes to their corresponding entities in another language, when the target entities are not in current language. Our approach first builds a cross-lingual mention-entity vocabulary from the cross-lingual links in Wikipedia, which is then used to generate cross-lingual candidate entities for mentions. After that, our approach performs entity disambiguation by using a cross-lingual knowledge graph embedding model. Experiments show that our approach can discover cross-lingual entity links with high accuracy.

Keywords: Cross-lingual · Entity linking · Wikipedia · Infobox

1 Introduction

Wikipedia infoboxes contain rich structured information of entities, describing various relations and attributes of entities in the form of tables. Several large-scale knowledge graphs such as DBpedia [1] and YAGO [9] have been built by extracting structured information from Wikipedia infoboxes. In Wikipedia infoboxes, entity relations are specified by infobox attributes and hyper-links to other wiki pages in the attribute values. For example in the infobox of *United States*, the attribute 'President' has a value containing a link to the wiki page of *Donald Trump*; hence a triple *(United States, President, Donald Trump)* can be extracted from the infobox. Most entity links in Wikipedia infoboxes are monolingual links; if a mentioned entity does not exist in the current language version of Wikipedia, there will be no entity link in the infobox. For example, Fig. 1 shows part of the infobox of *TCL Corporation* in English Wikipedia, which is a famous Chinese corporation. For the attributes of *Industry* and *Subsidiaries* in the infobox, there are links to wiki pages of *Consumer Electronics* and *TCL Multimedia*, respectively. But for the attribute *Founder*, the attribute value only

© Springer Nature Singapore Pte Ltd. 2019
X. Zhu et al. (Eds.): CCKS 2019, CCIS 1134, pp. 38–49, 2019.
https://doi.org/10.1007/978-981-15-1956-7_4

contains the name of the funder, *Li Dongsheng*; there is no link to the wiki page of *Li Dongsheng* because it does not exist in English Wikipedia.

Although there are many links missing in the infoboxes because of the absence of the target entities, we find that some entities can be found in another language version of Wikipedia. Considering the example shown in Fig. 1, there is not an entity of *Li Dongsheng* in English Wikipedia, but this entity does exist in Chinese Wikipedia. We have done statistical analysis on the data of English Wikipedia; we randomly selected 100 infoboxes of famous Chinese persons or organizations from English Wikipedia, and manually analyzed these infoboxes. It is found that all of these infoboxes have missing entity links caused by the absence of corresponding entities in English Wikipedia. We then further discovered that 78 missing entity links can be established from these infoboxes to entities in Chinese Wikipedia. If such cross-lingual entity links can be automatically detected and added to infoboxes, relations between entities will be largely enriched in Wikipedia.

Based on the above observations, we propose an approach for cross-lingual entity linking in Wikipedia infoboxes (CELF). The goal of our approach is to discover cross-lingual entity links in infoboxes when monolingual links cannot be established. CELF works in three steps, mention identification, candidate entity selection and entity disambiguation. The first step is to identify mentions in infoboxes; then in the step of candidate entity selection, a cross-lingual mention-to-entity vocabulary is built, based on which candidate entities in another language are selected for each mention. In the step of entity disambiguation, the target entity of each mention is determined. To bridge the language gap, CELF trains a cross-lingual knowledge graph embedding model, and performs entity disambiguation based on the learned entity embeddings. We conduct experiments on three datasets of different language pairs of Wikipedia. The results show that our approach achieves over 90% *Hits@1* in all the three datasets, and outperforms baseline approach by over 20%.

The rest of this paper is organized as follows, Sect. 2 discusses related work; Sect. 3 describes the proposed approach in detail; Sect. 4 shows the experiment results; Sect. 5 concludes our work.

2   Related Work

2.1   Entity Linking

Entity linking is the task of determining the identity of entities mentioned in texts and linking them to their corresponding entities in a given knowledge base. The problem of entity linking has been studied for years, and many entity linking approaches have been proposed. Shen et al. [8] and Wu et al. [14] gave exhaustive reviews of previous work in entity linking. In this section, we mainly discuss some most related work to our approach.

Xu et al. published an early work of discovering missing entity links in infoboxes [15]. Their approach can automatically discover missing entity links in Wikipedia's infoboxes. The proposed approach first identifies entity mentions in

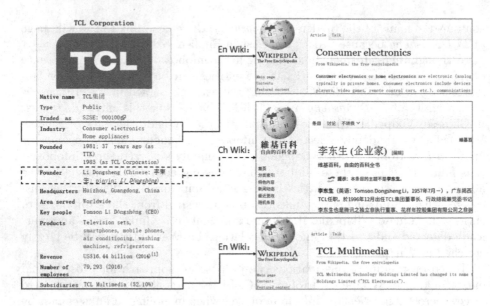

Fig. 1. TCL's English version of infobox

the infoboxes; and then it computes several features to estimate the possibilities that a given attribute value might link to a candidate entity. A logistic regression model is used to learn the weights of different features, and predict the target entity for each mention.

In the work of [7] and [13], knowledge bases are built from Wikipedia, Baidu Baike and Hudong Baike. In the process of extracting entity relations from infoboxes, missing entity links are completed by matching the mentions with entity names. Name matching works for small portion of missing entity links, but it will fail to correctly find the link if a mention is ambiguous.

The above work solves the problem of entity linking in infoboxes, but they only focus on monolingual entity links. The problem of cross-lingual entity linking is more challenging because of the language gap.

2.2 Knowledge Graph Embedding

In our work, cross-lingual knowledge graph embedding model is used to perform entity disambiguation. Here we briefly review the work on knowledge graph embedding.

Knowledge graph embedding models embed entities and relations in a knowledge graph into a low-dimensional vector space while preserving the original knowledge. The embeddings are usually learned by minimizing a global loss function of all the entities and relations in a KG, which can be further used for relation prediction, information extraction, and some other tasks. TransE is a representative knowledge graph embedding approach [2], which projects both entities and relations into the same vector space; if a triple (h, r, t) holds, TransE wants that $h + r \approx t$. The embeddings are learned by minimizing a margin-based ranking criterion over the training set. TransE model is simple but powerful, and it gets promising results on link prediction and triple classification problems. To further improve TransE, several enhanced models based on it have been proposed, including TransR [5], TransH [12] and TransD [4] etc. By introducing new representations of relational translation, later approaches achieve better performance at the cost of increasing model complexity. There are many other KG embedding approaches, recent surveys [6,11] give detailed introduction and comparison.

MTransE [3] and JAPE [10] are two models for learning embeddings for cross-lingual knowledge graphs. MTransE encodes entities and relations of each KG in a separated embedding space by using TransE; it also provides transitions for each embedding vector to its cross-lingual counterparts in other spaces. The loss function of MTransE is the weighted sum of two component models' loss (i.e., knowledge model and alignment model). JAPE is also based on TransE model, which learns vector representations of entities in the overlay graph of two knowledge graphs. JE and MTransE are two similar models for dealing with heterogeneous knowledge graphs, which can be easily adapted to cross-lingual knowledge graphs.

Our approach uses a similar embedding model as MTransE and JAPE, but the learned embeddings are used to perform entity disambiguation, instead of discovering entity alignments. Therefore, our knowledge graph embedding model focuses on linking prediction.

3   The Proposed Approach

This section presents our approach CELF in details. Given a set of Wikipedia infoboxes in one language L, the goal of our approach is to identify entity mentions in these infoboxes and to link them to entities in another language L' in Wikipedia. Our approach CELF works in three main steps: mention identification, candidate entity selection and entity disambiguation.

3.1   Mention Identification

Mention identification is to find entity mentions in an infobox. In this work, mentions are only discovered in the attribute values with no hyper-links in the infoboxes. In order to find the mentions potentially having the target entities in another language, our approach uses the clues in the infoboxes. In Wikipedia's infoboxes of one language, e.g. English, there are usually native mentions coming after their English mentions in brackets if the target entities are missing in the current language version of Wikipedia. Taking the infobox in Fig. 1 as an example, the value of the attribute *Founder* is "Li Dongsheng (Chinese:)". Here "Chinese: 李東生" shows the Chinese name of the founder, telling that *Li Dongsheng* is an entity mention and its corresponding Chinese form is 李東生. Base on this observation, our approach process all the attribute values in the

Table 1. An example of mention-entity vocabulary ($L = English$, $L' = Chinese$). ([EN:...] are translations of the entities in L' to facilitate reading.)

$Mention_L$	$Mention_{L'}$	Candidate entities in L'
Queer as Folk	同志亦凡人	同志亦凡人 _(英國電視劇) [EN: *Queer_as_Folk_(UK_TV_series)*] 同志亦凡人 _(2000 年電視劇) [EN: *Queer_as_Folk_(U.S._TV_series)*]
The Republicans	共和黨	共和黨 _(法國)[EN: *The_Republicans_(France)*] 共和黨 _(美國)[EN: *The_Republicans_(United States)*] 共和黨 _(德國)[EN: *The_Republicans_(Germany)*] 共和黨 _(愛爾蘭)[EN: *Fianna_Fail*]
Labour Party	工党	工党 _(英國)[EN: *Labour_Party_(UK)*] 工党 _(挪威)[EN: *Labour_Party_(Norway)*] 工党 _(爱尔兰)[EN: *Labour_Party_(Ireland)*]
...	...	...

given infoboxes, and find whether there are brackets with language annotations. Attribute values matching the pattern [$mention_L$ (language: $mention_{L'}$)] are recorded; and $mention_L$ will be identified as an entity mention in language L, its corresponding mention in language L' is $mention_{L'}$.

3.2   Candidate Entity Selection

After identifying mentions in language L, our approach selects candidate entities in language L' for each mention. To select candidate entities, we first build a cross-lingual mention-entity vocabulary. The structure of vocabulary is shown in Table 1. Each record in the vocabulary can be represented as ($m_L, m_{L'}, c_{L'}$), which contains a mention m_L in language L, its corresponding mention $m_{L'}$ in language L', and a set of candidate entities $C_{L'}$ in language L'. Mentions in two languages are directly obtained in the step of mention identification. To get the candidate entities for each mention, we select entities in L' having $m_{L'}$ as their surface forms, and take them as the candidate entities.

The following components of Wikipedia in language L' are used as the sources for getting entities and their surface forms:

– **Page titles:** Each entity page in Wikipedia describes a single entity and contains the information focusing on this entity. Generally, the title of each page is the most common name for the entity described in this page, e.g., the page title 'Microsoft' for that giant software company headquartered in Redmond. Therefore page titles are taken as the surface forms of the corresponding entities. When the name of an entity is ambiguous, there will be a qualifier in brackets in the page title. For example, the name of "Transformers" is ambiguous; so the movie of *Transformers* has the title of "Transformers (film series)", and the comics of *Transformers* is named as "Transformers (comics)". For those page titles having brackets, we take the parts before the brackets as the surface forms of the entities.

- **Redirect pages:** A redirect page in Wikipedia has no content except a link to another page. The page title of a redirect page can be taken as a surface form of the entity it links to. For example, the page of *UK* redirects to the page of *United Kingdom*, so "UK" is taken as the surface form of entity *United Kingdom*.

- **Disambiguation pages:** When multiple entities in Wikipedia have the same name, a disambiguation page is created to separate them. A disambiguation page contains a list of references to distinct entities which might be referred by the title of the disambiguation page. Here we take the titles of disambiguation pages as the surface forms of entities listed on them.

3.3 Entity Disambiguation

Once entity mentions and their candidate entities are obtained, our approach uses a cross-lingual knowledge graph embedding model to disambiguate entities. In the following, we will fist introduce how the cross-lingual embedding model is defined and trained; and then the method of using embeddings for entity disambiguation is presented.

Cross-Lingual Embedding Model. Our approach uses a cross-lingual embedding model works similarly as MTransE and JAPE. The model embeds entities in two different languages into a unified low-dimensional vector space. Based on the learned embeddings, relations between entities can be conveniently scored, which helps accurately disambiguate entities. Before learning entity embeddings, two knowledge graph $G_L = (E_L, R_L, T_L)$ and $G_{L'} = (E_{L'}, R_{L'}, T_{L'})$ are firstly obtained by extracting triples from the infoboxes in L and L', respectively. Here $E_{L/L'}, R_{L/L'}$ are sets of entities and relations, respectively; $T_{L/L'} \subset E_{L/L'} \times R_{L/L'} \times E_{L/L'}$ is the set of triples. In our approach, infobox triples in DBpedia of language L and L' are directly used as G_L and $G_{L'}$, because they are all extracted from Wikipedia's infoboxes. Cross-lingual links in Wikipedia are also used in our embedding model, which is denoted as $X = \{(e_{i_1}, e_{i_2}) | e_{i_1} \in E_L, e_{i_2} \in E_{L'}\}_{i=1}^{m}$.

In our cross-lingual embedding model, two knowledge graphs G_L and $G_{L'}$ are integrated into one combined knowledge graph G. Then TransE model is employed on learning embeddings of elements in G. Entities and relations are all represented as vectors in $\mathbb{R}^k$. If a triple (e, r, e') exists in G, the model wants $e + r \approx e'$; e, r and e' are vectors of e, r and e' respectively.

In the training process of TransE, we want entity pairs in X (i.e. entities connected by cross-lingual links) share the same vector representations. Because entities connected by cross-lingual links corresponds to the same thing, their vectors need to be the same. To pose this constraint on the TransE model, we revise the loss function of TransE as:

$$Loss = \sum_{(h,r,t)\in G} \|h + r - t\| + \lambda \sum_{(e,e')\in X} \|e - e'\| \qquad (1)$$

where λ is a weight parameter. The loss function is optimized by stochastic gradient descent (SGD) with mini-batch strategy. The loss function has a penalty part of cross-lingual links. During the learning process, vectors of two entities at both ends of a interlanguage link will get closer and closer. By optimizing the loss function of this cross-lingual embedding model, entities in two languages are mapped into one unified vector space. Base on the learned embeddings, probabilities of relations between entities from different languages can be estimated.

Entity Disambiguation Based on Embeddings. After training cross-lingual embedding model, we get vector representations of all the entities and relations in G_L and $G_{L'}$. These embeddings are used for entity disambiguation. In the infobox of entity h, supposing a mention m_L is identified in the value of attribute r, the set of selected candidate entities is $C_{L'}$; the goal of entity disambiguation is to find the correct entity $e_{L'}^{\star}$ for the mention. In our approach, the disambiguation is performed by computing scores for candidate entities based on the embeddings. For each candidate entity $e_{L'}$ in $C_{L'}$, our approach computes its score as:

$$score = \|h + r - e_{L'}\| \qquad (2)$$

The smaller this score is, the more likely the entity is the target entity. Therefore, our approach computes scores for every entity in $C_{L'}$, and it then ranks the candidate entities by the ascending order of their scores. The entity in the top 1 place is output as the target entities of mention m_L.

4   Experiment

4.1   Datasets

We use datasets from DBpedia. DBpedia has abundant structural knowledge extracted from Wikipedia's pages. According to three different language versions of database in DBpedia, Chinese, Japanese and French, we build up our experiment datasets. For each language, its datasets include test set, answer set and training set. Test set contains some broken triples in English, whose tail entities are manually removed, of which the effect is the same as the truly uncompleted triples. Intuitively, we are based on the interlanguage links to find the removed tail entities' corresponding entities in language L', which constitute the answer set. Training set contains the triples involved in all the entities and relations, and some interlanguage links where the interlanguage links to the removed tail entities are kicked out.

The statistics of all the datasets are listed in Table 2.

Table 2. Statistics of the datasets

Datasets		Entities	Triples	Mentions	Candidate entities	Answer entities
zh_en	en	148,068	317,550	3,002	6,468	3,002
	zh	109,602	239,680			
ja_en	en	140,021	302,067	2,787	5,023	2,787
	ja	99,629	234,005			
fr_en	en	149,927	329,003	2,942	5,528	2,942
	fr	110,803	243,742			

4.2 Evaluation Metrics

We use $Hits@1$ to assess the performance of our method. $Hits@1$ measures the proportion of correctly aligned entities ranked in the top 1. For instance, there are five candidate entities for one cross-lingual mention, and we separately calculate the score between each candidate entity and the sum of h and r. The highest score among those five scores represents the appearance of the target entity. A higher $Hits@1$ indicates a better performance.

4.3 Baseline

Because there has not been any presented work for the cross-lingual entity linking in infobox yet, we propose a baseline for comparison. The first two steps of Baseline are the same as CELF, from [15], in the disambiguating step, we choose an approach evaluating the likelihood between mention and candidate entities through three semantic features: *Link Probability*, *Local Entity Occurrence* and *Foreign Entity Occurrence*

- **Link Probability**

  Link Probability feature approximates the probability that a mention m links to an entity e:

  $$f_1(m, e) = \frac{count(m, e)}{count(m)} \tag{3}$$

  where $count(m, e)$ denotes the number of links from m to e, and the $count(m)$ denotes the number of times that m appears in Wikipedia.

- **Local Entity Occurrence**

If there has already been a link to a certain entity in the text of article, there will likely be a link to this entity in the infobox. Here, we define an Local Entity Occurrence feature to capture this information:

$$f_2(e, m) = \begin{cases} 1 & e \in E_L(m) \\ 0 & otherwise \end{cases} \tag{4}$$

where $E_L(m)$ is the set of the cross-lingual entities. These entities are linked to those entities, which are in the text of the article containing mention m, by the interlanguage links. Entity e is one of mention m's cross-lingual candidate entities.

- **Foreign Entity Occurrence**

The same as the Local Entity Occurrence, Foreign Entity Occurrence also evaluate whether the entity appears, not in the article of English Wiki, but in one infobox of language L' version of Wiki. Conspicuously, the premise is that there must be an interlanguage link for the article containing mention m, if not, we let the score equal zero:

$$f_3(e, m) = \begin{cases} 1 & e \in E_{L'}(m) \\ 0 & otherwise \end{cases} \tag{5}$$

where $E_{L'}(m)$ is the set of entities. According to the interlanguage link for the entity representing the article containing mention m, we find the its cross-lingual entity in language L', and all the entities in $E_{L'}(m)$ are all from the text of that cross-lingual entity's article. Entity e is one of mention m's cross-lingual candidate entities.

We compute the weighted sum of features between mentions and entities by the following score function:

$$S(m, e) = \mathbf{w} \cdot \mathbf{f}(\mathbf{m}, \mathbf{e}) \tag{6}$$

where $\mathbf{w} = (\omega_1, \omega_2, \omega_3)$ and $\mathbf{f}(\mathbf{m}, \mathbf{e}) = (f_1(m, e), f_2(m, e), f_3(m, e))^T$. Here, we use the already existing entity links $<m_i, e_i>$ in infoboxes as training data, and train a logistic regression model to get the weights of different features. For mention m, we separately calculate the candidate entities' score, and then screen the target entity which have the highest score.

4.4 Experiment Setup

For our proposed method, when training our model, we set the learning rate λ to 0.01, the dimensionality of embedding vectors among $\{50, 75, 100, 125, 150\}$, and the ratio hyper-parameter λ_1 ranging from 0 to 1. Through changing values of dimensionality and hyper-parameter, we find that when the dimensionality equals 75 and ratio hyper-parameter equals 1, the performances are all better than ever. So, we set the dimensionality to 75 and hyper-parameter to 1 firmly when training our model. As for the baseline, we train a logistic regression model and then get the weights of different features and the expression of $S(m, e)$.

4.5 Results

For our proposed method and the baseline, we separately find the experimental cross-lingual target entities. Then we calculate all the $Hits@1$ in every methods for each language pair. The outcomes are shown below in Fig. 2:

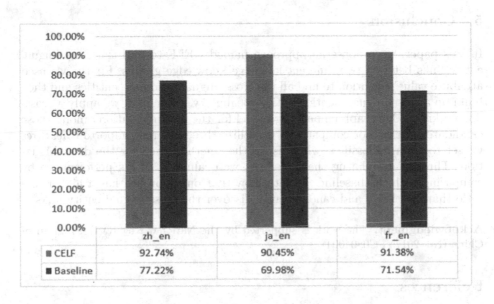

	zh_en	ja_en	fr_en
■ CELF	92.74%	90.45%	91.38%
■ Baseline	77.22%	69.98%	71.54%

Fig. 2. The $Hits@1$ of CELF and baseline

From the results, we find that for each candidate language, our method's $Hits@1$ is always conspicuously much higher than that based on the proposed baseline. We have to say that our proposed baseline is a little bit brutal, but our method CELF's experimental outcomes are better, and there are many other disambiguation methods waiting for being applied in cross-lingual entity linking in infobox.

4.6 NIL Clustering

In our task, we should consider that, if there is no correct cross-lingual candidate entity of a mention existing in Wiki, what the criterion of nothingness is and what we should do. Because of the utilization of cosine similarity to evaluate whether the cross-lingual candidate entity is the object or not, intuitively we set the criterion according to the cosine value. After normal training step, for each mention, we remove its cross-lingual target entity according to the answer set from the training data, and retrain the model, and then, again find the largest cosine value of each mention. Among all the found cosine values (the number of which equals the number of mentions), we choose the largest value as the criterion of NIL clustering in chosen language, which means that if the cosine value of a mention's target entity is lower than the criterion, we regard the object belonging to that mention as nothingness and assign a new ID to it. After training, we get three criteria: zh_en's criterion is 0.30, ja_en's criterion is 0.27, and fr_en's criterion is 0.30.

5 Conclusion

In this paper, we propose an approach named CELF to find the cross-lingual entity links between two different language knowledge graphs. Firstly, we used attribute value's mention to find all the cross-lingual candidate entities and then build up a cross-lingual mention-entity vocabulary. After that, we apply a cross-lingual knowledge graph embedding model for the disambiguation among those candidate entities. For comparison, we utilize three different important features we set to train a classifier, which is another method used for the disambiguation. Through calculating the hits ratio, we evaluate CELF's performance by comparing with the baseline. Results show that our approach has a higher hits ratio than baseline's and can efficiently discover the cross-lingual entity links.

Acknowledgment. The work is supported by the National Key R&D Program of China (No. 2017YFC0804004).

References

1. Bizer, C.: DBpedia-a crystallization point for the web of data. J. Web Semant. **7**(3), 154–165 (2009)
2. Bordes, A., Usunier, N., Garcia-Duran, A., Weston, J., Yakhnenko, O.: Translating embeddings for modeling multi-relational data. In: Proceedings of Advances in Neural Information Processing Systems (NIPS 2013), pp. 2787–2795 (2013)
3. Chen, M., Tian, Y., Yang, M., Zaniolo, C.: Multilingual knowledge graph embeddings for cross-lingual knowledge alignment. In: Proceedings of the Twenty-Sixth International Joint Conference on Artificial Intelligence (AAAI 2017), pp. 1511–1517 (2017)
4. Ji, G., He, S., Xu, L., Liu, K., Zhao, J.: Knowledge graph embedding via dynamic mapping matrix. In: Proceedings of the 53rd Annual Meeting of the Association for Computational Linguistics and the 7th International Joint Conference on Natural Language Processing, vol. 1, pp. 687–696 (2015)
5. Lin, Y., Liu, Z., Sun, M., Liu, Y., Zhu, X.: Learning entity and relation embeddings for knowledge graph completion. In: Proceedings of the Twenty-Ninth AAAI Conference on Artificial Intelligence (AAAI 2015), vol. 15, pp. 2181–2187 (2015)

6. Nickel, M., Murphy, K., Tresp, V., Gabrilovich, E.: A review of relational machine learning for knowledge graphs. Proc. IEEE **104**(1), 11–33 (2016)
7. Niu, X., Sun, X., Wang, H., Rong, S., Qi, G., Yu, Y.: Zhishi.me - weaving Chinese linking open data. In: Aroyo, L., et al. (eds.) ISWC 2011. LNCS, vol. 7032, pp. 205–220. Springer, Heidelberg (2011). https://doi.org/10.1007/978-3-642-25093-4_14
8. Shen, W., Wang, J., Han, J.: Entity linking with a knowledge base: issues, techniques, and solutions. IEEE Trans. Knowl. Data Eng. **27**(2), 443–460 (2015)
9. Suchanek, F.M., Kasneci, G., Weikum, G.: Yago: a core of semantic knowledge. In: Proceedings of the 16th International Conference on World Wide Web, WWW 2007, pp. 697–706. ACM, New York (2007)
10. Sun, Z., Hu, W., Li, C.: Cross-lingual entity alignment via joint attribute-preserving embedding. In: d'Amato, C., et al. (eds.) ISWC 2017. LNCS, vol. 10587, pp. 628–644. Springer, Cham (2017). https://doi.org/10.1007/978-3-319-68288-4_37
11. Wang, Q., Mao, Z., Wang, B., Guo, L.: Knowledge graph embedding: a survey of approaches and applications. IEEE Trans. Knowl. Data Eng. **29**(12), 2724–2743 (2017)
12. Wang, Z., Zhang, J., Feng, J., Chen, Z.: Knowledge graph embedding by translating on hyperplanes. In: Proceedings of the Twenty-Eighth AAAI Conference on Artificial Intelligence (AAAI 2014), vol. 14, pp. 1112–1119 (2014)
13. Wang, Z.C., Wang, Z.G., Li, J.Z., Pan, J.Z.: Knowledge extraction from Chinese wiki encyclopedias. J. Zhejiang Univ. Sci. C **13**(4), 268–280 (2012)
14. Wu, G., He, Y., Hu, X.: Entity linking: an issue to extract corresponding entity with knowledge base. IEEE Access **6**, 6220–6231 (2018)
15. Xu, M., et al.: Discovering missing semantic relations between entities in Wikipedia. In: Alani, H., et al. (eds.) ISWC 2013. LNCS, vol. 8218, pp. 673–686. Springer, Heidelberg (2013). https://doi.org/10.1007/978-3-642-41335-3_42

Incorporating Domain and Range of Relations for Knowledge Graph Completion

Juan Li, Wen Zhang, and Huajun Chen[✉]

Zhejiang University, Hangzhou, China
{lijuan18,wenzhang2015,huajunsir}@zju.edu.cn

Abstract. Knowledge graphs store facts as triples, with each containing two entities and one relation. Information of entities and relations are important for knowledge graph related tasks like link prediction. Knowledge graph embedding methods embed entities and relations into a continuous vector space and accomplish link prediction via calculation with embeddings. However, some embedding methods only focus on information of triples and ignore individual information about relations. For example, relations inherently have domain and range which will contribute much towards learning, even though sometimes they are not explicitly given in knowledge graphs. In this paper, we propose a framework TransX$_C$ (X can be replaced with E, H, R or D) to help preserve individual information of relations, which can be applied to multiple traditional translation-based embedding methods (i.e. TransE, TransH, TransR and TransD). In TransX$_C$, we use two logistic regression classifiers to model domain and range of relations respectively, and then we train the embedding model and classifiers jointly in order to include information of triples as well as domain and range of relations. The performance of TransX$_C$ are evaluated on link prediction task. Experimental results show that our method outperforms the corresponding translation-based model, indicating the effectiveness of considering domain and range of relations into link prediction.

Keywords: Knowledge graph completion · Domain and range of relations · Knowledge graph embedding

1 Introduction

Knowledge graphs (KGs), like Freebase [1] and WordNet [15], are useful for a variety of natural language processing tasks such as relation extraction [20] and question answering [26]. They are organized in form of triples *(head entity, relation, tail entity)* (denoted as (h, r, t)). For example, *(Beijing, capitalOf, China)* indicates that Beijing is the capital of China. However, knowledge graphs are still suffering from incompleteness, for instance, 71% of people have no birth information and 75% have no nationality information in Freebase [6]. Therefore,

© Springer Nature Singapore Pte Ltd. 2019
X. Zhu et al. (Eds.): CCKS 2019, CCIS 1134, pp. 50–61, 2019.
https://doi.org/10.1007/978-981-15-1956-7_5

knowledge graph completion is a meaningful task for the development of KGs, which aims at predicting new triples based on existing triples.

In recent years, knowledge graph embedding has been proposed to learn vector representations for entities and relations in continuous vector spaces, which can be used for knowledge graph completion. One kind of simple and effective embedding methods are translation-based models, which regard relations as translations from head entities to tail entities, including TransE [2] and its extensions, such as TransH [27], TransR [13] and TransD [8]. These translation-based models utilize information of triples, while ignoring domain and range of relations. Domain and range are restrictions on class memberships of two individuals interconnected by a certain property in OWL2. In KGs, entities correspond to individuals in OWL2 and relations between entities correspond to properties. Even though domain and range of relations might not be explicitly mentioned in a knowledge graph, they are inherently exist.

In order to illustrate that domain and range of relations are important for link prediction task, we give real examples from FB15k [2] in Table 1. Domain of "genre titles" should be in the class *GENRE*, but TransE ranks "United Kingdom" on the top, which belongs to *COUNTRY* and apparently does not satisfy domain of relation "genre titles". Similarly, the range of relation "actor of film" ought to be class *FILM*, however, the first candidate tail entity is "Wall Street", belonging to the class *LOCATION*, which does not satisfy range of "actor of film". Thus, domain and range of relations are useful for filtering false positive candidates in link prediction.

Table 1. Link prediction results for the missing entity (head or tail entity) given one entity and relation of a triple from TransE. Entities rank in top 2 or top 3 are shown for each example. Terms in bold are relations.

Positive triples	Candidate head entities	Candidate tail entities
(Mockumentary, **genre titles**, This Is Spinal Tap)	United Kingdom*(COUNTRY)*	The Opposite of Sex
	Parody*(GENRE)*	Spiceworld
	Slapstick*(GENRE)*	–
(Tommy Lee Jones, **actor of film**, Space Cowboys)	Morgan Freeman	Wall Street*(LOCATION)*
	Dennis Franz	Cowboys & Aliens*(FILM)*
	Samuel L. Jackson	–
(Beauty and the Beast, **film has actor**, David Ogden Stiers)	Mary Poppins*(FILM)*	Ashley Tisdale
	Hercules*(PERSON)*	Madeline Kahn
	The Little Mermaid*(FILM)*	Howard Ashman

In this paper, we propose a new framework TransX$_C$, which incorporates domain and range of relations into translation-based models (i.e. TransE, TransH, TransD and TransR). In TransX$_C$, the translation-based model utilizes information of observed triples, and two logistic regression classifiers are introduced to discuss whether domain and range constraints of relations are satisfied. One of the two classifiers takes relation and head entity as input to justify whether the head entity satisfy domain of the relation, and the other classifier is to justify whether the tail entity meets range of the relation. The translation-based model and logistic regression classifiers are trained jointly.

We evaluate TransX$_C$ on link prediction task with four benchmark datasets (WN18 [2], FB15k [2], WN18RR [5] and FB15k-237 [22]). Experiment results show that our methods achieve significant improvements compared with corresponding original translation-based models.

To summarize, our contributions are as follows:

- We combine relation's domain and range with knowledge representation learning for link prediction, making the prediction conducted not only based on triples, but also properties of relations to achieve better results;
- Our framework TransX$_C$ introduces two logistic regression classifiers to encode domain and range of relations, which can be applied to multiple knowledge graph embedding methods.

2   Related Work

2.1   Knowledge Graph Embedding

Knowledge graph embedding models can be trained solely on the basis of observed triples, or through integrating extra information beyond triples to enhance models. Since our framework is used on translation-based models which are learning from triples, models that utilize information from observed triples are introduced here.

Translation-Based Models. For a triple (h, r, t), when it is true, TransE [2] assumes $\mathbf{h} + \mathbf{r} \approx \mathbf{t}$, where $\mathbf{h}$, $\mathbf{r}$ and $\mathbf{t}$ are embedding vectors of h, r and t respectively. TransH [27] introduces hyperplanes related to specific relations, enabling entities to have different representations in different relations. In TransR [13], entities and relations are represented in different spaces and entities are projected into a relation-specific space for the calculation of scores for triples. TransD [8] uses different mapping matrices for head entities and tail entities to further improve TransR. TranSparse [9] simplifies TransR by enforcing sparseness of the projection matrix. TransM [7] associates each triple with a weight depending on the specific relation, and lower weights on complex relations allow the tail entity $\mathbf{t}$ to lie further away from $\mathbf{h} + \mathbf{r}$. TransA [28] introduces a symmetric nonnegative matrix for each relation and uses an adaptive Mahalanobis distance to define the score function.

Other Models. RESCAL [19] is a collective matrix factorization model. DistMult [29] represents each relation as a diagonal matrix. However, DistMult can not model asymmetric relations, ComplEx [23] extends it into complex number field where entities and relations are represented as complex vectors. HolE [18] uses circular correlations to combine entity embeddings. ANALOGY [14] optimizes the latent representations with respect to the analogical properties of the embedded entities and relations. ConvE [5] and ConvKB [16] are based on convolutional neural networks. CapsE [17] employs capsule network [21] to model relationship triples. KBGAN [3] concentrates on generating better negative facts to improve a range of existing knowledge graph embedding models.

2.2   Domain and Range of Relations

RDF-Schema provides `rdfs:domain` and `rdfs:range` concepts to declare the class of entities for relations. Domain restricts the class of head entities and range restrictions indicate what class tail entities should belong to in KGs.

Domain and range of relations have been used as type constraints of entities to improve embedding methods. [12] adds prior knowledge about relations to the factorization through directly introducing domain and range constraints into least-squares cost function of RESCAL [19]. Typed-RESCAL [4] excludes triples of incompatible domain and range constraints from the loss. [11] integrates domain and range constraints based on observed triples into TransE, RESCAL and the multiway neural network approach, enforcing subject entities are corrupted through the subset of entities that belong to the domain, while the corrupted object entities are sampled from the subset of entities that belong to the range of the given relation. Although choosing entities from domain and range of relations can reduce calculation, these methods may filter out positive entities.

3   Our Method

In this section, we first discuss how to define domain and range of relations in KGs. Then, we describe translation-based models used as baselines without our framework. Finally, we introduce details of this proposed framework TransX$_C$.

3.1   Domain and Range of Relations

The concept of domain and range are derived from OWL2. For example, for the relation "hasWife", axioms corresponding to domain and range constraints are `ObjectPropertyDomain(:hasWife :Man)` and `ObjectProperty Range(:hasWife :Woman)`, which means class of the subject entity should be *MAN* and the object entity should be *WOMAN*. Thus, for one relation, domain constrains the class of the subject entity and range decides what class the object entity should belong to.

Domain and range of relations exist inherently, but they might be missing in many knowledge graphs. Using domain and range constraints from OWL2, we should consider that head entities ought to belong to domain of relations, and tail entities belong to relations' range in KGs. And domain and range can be used to help filter false positive entities in link prediction.

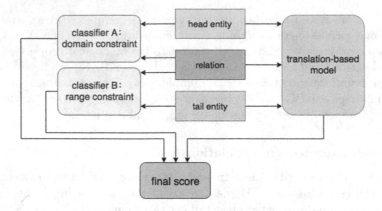

Fig. 1. Basic idea of TransX$_C$.

3.2   Translation-Based Models

In general, a knowledge graph embedding model can be formulated as a score function $f(h, r, t)$, where h and t are the head and the tail entity respectively, and r denotes the relation between h and t. Scores calculated from score function are the basis for ranking, which contribute to evaluation metrics of link prediction. For translation-based models, the score function is defined as:

$$S = f(h, r, t) = \|\mathbf{h}_\perp + \mathbf{r} - \mathbf{t}_\perp\|_{L_1/L_2} \tag{1}$$

where $\mathbf{h}_\perp$ and $\mathbf{t}_\perp$ indicate projection vectors of the head entity and the tail entity. We choose TransE, TransH, TransD and TransR as our basic models, and their respective score functions are listed in Table 2.

Table 2. A summary for translation-based methods used in our framework. All boldface lower case letters represent vectors in $\mathbb{R}^d$, and boldface upper case letters represent matrices in $\mathbb{R}^{(d \times d)}$. $\mathbf{I}$ denotes identity matrix. n_e and n_r are the number of entities and relations respectively. d denotes the embedding dimension.

Model	Score function $S(h, r, t)$	#Number of parameters
TransE	$\|\mathbf{h} + \mathbf{r} - \mathbf{t}\|_{L_1/L_2}$	$(n_e + n_r)d$
TransH	$\|(\mathbf{h} - \mathbf{w}_r^\top \mathbf{h}\mathbf{w}_r) + \mathbf{r} - (\mathbf{t} - \mathbf{w}_r^\top \mathbf{t}\mathbf{w}_r)\|_{L_1/L_2}$	$(n_e + 2n_r)d$
TransR	$\|\mathbf{M}_r \mathbf{h} + \mathbf{r} - \mathbf{M}_r \mathbf{t}\|_{L_1/L_2}$	$(n_e + n_r)d + n_r d^2$
TransD	$(\mathbf{r}_p \mathbf{h}_p^\top + \mathbf{I})\mathbf{h} + \mathbf{r} - (\mathbf{r}_p \mathbf{t}_p^\top + \mathbf{I})\mathbf{t}\|_{L_1/L_2}$	$2(n_e + n_r)d$

In TransH, for a triple (h, r, t), r is modeled as a vector $\mathbf{r}$ on a hyperplane, where $\mathbf{w}_r$ is the normal vector of the hyperplane which means $\|\mathbf{w}_r\| = 1$. $\mathbf{h}$ and $\mathbf{t}$ are projected onto a hyperplane according to $\mathbf{w}_r$ and will be connected by the translation vector $\mathbf{r}$. In TransR, each relation has a projection matrix $\mathbf{M}_r$, which is related with a specific relation r to project entities from entity space to relation space. The relation-specific projection makes head entity and tail entity that hold the relation close to each other, and entity pairs that do not hold the relation far away. TransD learns two vectors for each entity and relation, $\mathbf{h}_p$, $\mathbf{r}_p$ and $\mathbf{t}_p$ are vectors to make projection vectors for head entities and tail entities.

3.3 The TransX$_C$ Model

As translation-based models solely consider triple information of KGs during training, ignoring individual information of relations. Our framework, illustrated in Fig. 1, will be jointly trained with consideration of information from not only triples, but also domain and range of relations.

In TransX$_C$, for each triple (h, r, t), the head entity and tail entity are represented as vectors $\mathbf{h}, \mathbf{t} \in \mathbb{R}^k$ and relation vector is set as $\mathbf{r} \in \mathbb{R}^d$, where k and d are the dimension of entity vectors and relation vectors. Considering domain and range of a relation, we introduce two different logistic regression classifiers, one is used for dealing with domain constraint of relations, and the other is for range constraint. Input of domain classifier is $\mathbf{x}_{rh} = [\mathbf{r}, \mathbf{h}] \in \mathbb{R}^{(k+d)}$ and range classifier's input is $\mathbf{x}_{rt} = [\mathbf{r}, \mathbf{t}] \in \mathbb{R}^{(k+d)}$. $[\mathbf{x}, \mathbf{y}]$ represents concatenation of $\mathbf{x}$ and $\mathbf{y}$. The output of the classifiers are defined as follows:

$$P_{rh} = \sigma(\mathbf{w}_{rh} \cdot \mathbf{x}_{rh} + b_{rh}) \tag{2}$$

$$P_{rt} = \sigma(\mathbf{w}_{rt} \cdot \mathbf{x}_{rt} + b_{rt}) \tag{3}$$

where $\mathbf{w}_{rh}$, $\mathbf{w}_{rt} \in \mathbb{R}^{(k+d)}$ are different weights for domain and range classifiers, and b_{rh}, $b_{rt} \in \mathbb{R}^1$ are corresponding bias terms. $\mathbf{x} \cdot \mathbf{y}$ is the dot product of the vector $\mathbf{x}$ and $\mathbf{y}$. $\sigma = 1/(1 + e^{-x})$ is a sigmoid function. $P_{rh} \in (0, 1)$ denotes the probability that head entity h satisfy domain constraint of relation r and $P_{rt} \in (0, 1)$ represents the probability that tail entity t satisfy range constraint.

In order to incorporate information from triples and domain and range of relations into learning at the same time, we train embeddings of entities and relations as well as domain and range classifiers jointly. The score function S_f of TransX$_C$ is finally defined as:

$$S_f(h, r, t) = S + \alpha((1 - P_{rh}) + (1 - P_{rt})) \tag{4}$$

where α is a hyperparameter reflecting the weight of domain and range constraints during link prediction. As an embedding model aims to define a score function to assign each triple a score, and golden triples should receive lower scores than corrupted triples. Thus if (h, r, t) is a golden triple, domain and range constraints are satisfied, score S from translation-based models will be close to 0 and score S_f also ought to be close to 0. Since probabilities P_{rh} and P_{rt} should close to 1 for (h, r, t), we use $(1 - P_{rh})$ and $(1 - P_{rt})$ instead of P_{rh} and P_{rt} in score function to make the two parts close to 0, which will be consistent with embedding scores. Then the final score S_f of a golden triple will close to 0. For corrupted triples, probabilities from $(1 - P_{rh})$ and $(1 - P_{rt})$ will close to 1, and S_f will be larger than score of golden triples.

We define the following margin-based ranking loss as training objective:

$$L = \sum_{(h,r,t)\in\triangle} \sum_{(h',r',t')\in\triangle'} max(0, S_f(h,r,t) + \gamma - S_f(h',r',t')) \qquad (5)$$

where $\triangle$ is the set of positive triples and $\triangle'$ denotes the set of negative triples. Positive triples $(h,r,t) \in \triangle$ come from the existing knowledge graph, and (r, h) is a positive example of domain classifier and the positive example of range classifier is (r, t). While the negative triples $(h',r',t') \in \triangle'$ are generated by replacing head entity or tail entity of the triple (h,r,t). Instead of randomly replacing entities, we also insure concatenation of the replaced entity and the relation is a negative sample for domain (or range) classifier via checking whether it is a head (or tail) entity of relation r in the whole knowledge graph. γ is a margin, and $max(0,x)$ is the maximum value between 0 and x. The learning objective of TransX$_C$ is to minimize L.

4 Experiments

To evaluate our proposed framework, we test performance of TransX$_C$ on link prediction task with four translation-based models, including TransE, TransH, TransR and TransD.

4.1 Datasets and Experiment Settings

Datasets. Experiments are conducted on four benchmark datasets: WN18 [2], FB15k [2], WN18RR [5] and FB15k-237 [22]. The statistics of these datasets are summarized in Table 3. WN18 is a subset of WordNet [15] where entities are synsets corresponding to distinct word senses and relations are lexical relations of synsets. FB15k is a subset of Freebase [1], a large-scale knowledge graph containing a large number of relational facts. FB15k-237 is a subset of FB15k where inverse triples are removed and WN18RR is a subset of WN18 where inverse relations are deleted.

Table 3. Statistics of four experiment datasets

Dataset	#Relations	#Entities	#Train	#Valid	#Test
WN18	18	40943	141442	5000	5000
FB15k	1345	14951	483142	50000	59071
WN18RR	11	40943	86835	3034	3134
FB15k-237	237	14541	272115	17535	20466

Evaluation Metrics. Link prediction is to predict h given $(?, r, t)$ or predict t given $(h, r, ?)$. For each test triple, one entity will be removed and replaced with all entities in the knowledge graph. Scores of these corrupted triples are calculated via score function and be ranked in ascending order. After getting the rank of correct entities, we compute the mean reciprocal rank (MRR) of these rankings, which is regarded as a more robust measure than mean rank, since a single bad ranking can influence mean rank largely. Another metric hit@k $(k = 1, 3, 10)$ is the proportion of correct entities in top-k ranked entities. A good link prediction result should achieve higher MRR and higher hit@k. This is called "raw" setting. We also adopt "filter" setting to filter out the corrupted triples that exist in training, validation, or test datasets before ranking.

Implementation Details. Since TransX$_C$ incorporates domain and range of relations into translation-based models, we compare our models with translation-based models, our baselines include TransE, TransH, TransR and TransD. For each dataset, we train every model for 1000 epochs, each was divided into 100 mini-batches. We select margin γ among $\{1, 2, 4, 5\}$, and both the dimension of entity vectors k and the dimension of relation vectors d are among $\{50, 100, 200\}$. Learning rate λ is set to be 0.01 or 0.001. We tried hyperparameter $\alpha = 0.01, 0.1, 1$ and L_1 or L_2 distance for TransE$_C$, TransH$_C$, TransD$_C$ and TransR$_C$. The same parameters for these models on the four datasets are as follows: learning rate $\lambda = 0.001$, $\alpha = 0.01$ and L_1 distance is taken as dissimilarity.

The optimal configurations for TransE$_C$ are $\gamma = 5$, $k = d = 200$ on WN18; $\gamma = 4$, $k = d = 200$ on FB15k, WN18RR and FB15k-237. For TransH$_C$, the optimal settings are $\gamma = 5$, $k = d = 200$ on WN18, WN18RR and FB15k-237; $\gamma = 4$, $k = d = 200$ on FB15k. And the optimal configurations for TransR$_C$ are: $\gamma = 5$, $k = d = 200$ on FB15k and FB15k-237; $\gamma = 5$, $k = d = 50$ on WN18; $\gamma = 4$, $k = d = 50$ on WN18RR. Optimal settings for TransD$_C$ are $\gamma = 5$, $k = d = 100$ on WN18; $\gamma = 4$, $k = d = 200$ on FB15k; $\gamma = 5$, $k = d = 50$ on WN18RR; and $\gamma = 5$, $k = d = 200$ on FB15k-237.

4.2   Results

Results of our experiments as well as baselines are shown in Tables 4 and 5. Incorporating domain and range of relations into training process of translation-based models brings pronounced improvements to baselines, indicating that our framework is effective.

Experimental results on WN18 and FB15k are illustrated in Table 4. As shown in Table 4, we observe that: (1) TransE$_C$ and TransH$_C$ beat their corresponding baseline implementations, besides, TransR$_C$ and TransD$_C$ have slight improvements, which demonstrates incorporating domain and range of relations would benefit embedding. (2) Our framework on FB15k produces better improvement than on WN18, because the more relations contained in KGs, the more information will be preserved via consideration of domain and range constraints,

Table 4. Results on WN18 and FB15k for link prediction. Results of TransE and TransR are from SimplE [10]. Hit@10 of TransH and TransD are from their original paper. Others are from [25]. The best results of TransX and its corresponding TransX$_C$ are in bold.

Method	WN18					FB15k				
	MRR		Hit@			MRR		Hit@		
	Filter	Raw	1	3	10	Filter	Raw	1	3	10
TransE [2]	0.454	0.335	0.089	**0.823**	**0.934**	0.380	0.221	0.231	0.472	0.641
TransE$_C$	**0.645**	**0.443**	**0.457**	0.818	0.909	**0.556**	**0.260**	**0.417**	**0.650**	**0.798**
TransH [27]	0.361	0.268	0.048	0.624	0.823	0.283	0.183	0.173	0.332	0.644
TransH$_C$	**0.601**	**0.417**	**0.359**	**0.836**	**0.903**	**0.556**	**0.260**	**0.418**	**0.649**	**0.796**
TransR [13]	0.605	0.427	0.335	**0.876**	**0.940**	0.346	**0.198**	0.218	0.404	0.582
TransR$_C$	**0.646**	**0.469**	**0.482**	0.786	0.896	**0.374**	0.191	**0.234**	**0.458**	**0.621**
TransD[8]	–	–	–	–	0.922	–	–	–	–	**0.773**
TransD$_C$	0.490	0.345	0.106	0.880	**0.949**	0.518	0.261	0.374	0.616	0.767

Table 5. Results on WN18RR and FB15k-237 for link prediction. Results of TransD and TransE with † are from [24]. Results with ‡ are from [30]. The best results of TransX and its corresponding TransX$_C$ are in bold.

Method	WN18RR				FB15k-237			
	MRR	Hit@1	Hit@3	Hit@10	MRR	Hit@1	Hit@3	Hit@10
TransE [2]	0.178[‡]	–	–	0.432[†]	0.242[†]	0.166[†]	0.276[†]	0.424[†]
TransE$_C$	**0.191**	0.036	0.323	**0.438**	**0.294**	**0.203**	**0.328**	**0.472**
TransH [27]	0.186[‡]	–	–	0.451[‡]	0.233[‡]	–	–	0.401[‡]
TransH$_C$	**0.207**	0.043	0.350	**0.462**	**0.298**	0.208	0.330	**0.479**
TransR [13]	–	–	–	–	–	–	–	–
TransR$_C$	0.176	0.010	0.326	0.409	0.217	0.135	0.238	0.389
TransD [8]	0.190[‡]	–	–	0.428[†]	0.280[†]	–	–	0.453[†]
TransD$_C$	**0.196**	0.022	0.335	**0.469**	**0.297**	0.204	0.329	**0.483**

WN18 has 18 relations but FB15k has 1345 relations. (3) On FB15k, TransE$_C$ improves hit@1, hit@3 and hit@10 by 18.6%, 17.8% and 15.7%. For TransH$_C$, hit@1, hit@3 and hit@10 jump by 24.5%, 31.7% and 15.2% respectively.

Table 5 shows link prediction results on WN18RR and FB15k-237, confirming that domain and range of relations help to improve the performance of baselines. Results of baselines are taken from previous literature. From this table, we conclude that: (1) Comparing with baselines, MRR and hit@10 of TransE$_C$, TransH$_C$ and TransD$_C$ have small improvements on WN18RR. (2) On FB15k-237, TransE$_C$, TransH$_C$ and TransD$_C$ improve hit@10 by 4.8%, 7.8% and 3% than corresponding baselines respectively. (3) Hit@1 of TransX$_C$ produce better performance on FB15k-237 than on WN18RR, we owe to the FB15k-237 have more relations and WordNet is a lexical database.

Table 6. Examples of predicted entities on FB15k using TransX and TransX$_C$. The first two examples are results of TransE and TransE$_C$, the last two examples correspond to results of TransH and TransH$_C$. Each example contains the positive triple, where terms in bold indicate the entity to be replaced, and its predicted entities which rank in top 2 or top 3 are listed in this table.

(Tommy Lee Jones, actor of film, **Space Cowboys**)	
Predictions of TransE	**Predictions of TransE$_C$**
Wall Street*(LOCATION)*	Extremely Loud and Incredibly Close*(FILM)*
Cowboys & Aliens*(FILM)*	Space Cowboys*(FILM)*
Space Cowboys*(FILM)*	−
(**The Dark Knight Rises**, film release region, Uruguay)	
Predictions of TransE	**Predictions of TransE$_C$**
Hugo*(PERSON)*	Life of Pi*(FILM)*
Life of Pi*(FILM)*	The Dark Knight Rises*(FILM)*
Men in Black 3*(FILM)*	−
(Testicular cancer, parent disease, **Cancer**)	
Predictions of TransH	**Predictions of TransH$_C$**
Genetic disorder*(DISEASE)*	Genetic disorder*(DISEASE)*
Testicular cancer*(DISEASE)*	Testicular cancer*(DISEASE)*
Public limited company*(COMPANY)*	Cancer*(DISEASE)*
(Law&Order: Special Victims Unit, award work of winner, **Ann Margret**)	
Predictions of TransH	**Predictions of TransH$_C$**
NBC*(COMPANY)*	Ellen Burstyn*(PERSON)*
John Corbett*(PERSON)*	Brenda Blethyn*(PERSON)*
Brenda Blethyn*(PERSON)*	Amanda Plummer*(PERSON)*

4.3   Case Study

To demonstrate our framework does consider domain and range of relations, we list some prediction results of TransE, TransE$_C$, TransH and TransH$_C$ on FB15k in Table 6.

Comparing candidate entities from TransX$_C$ with predicted candidates from basic TransX, entities dissatisfy domain or range of relations are filtered out by our models. In the first example, range should be in the class *FILM*, and in TransE$_C$, the top two candidates are in the class *FILM*, but the top one entity predicted by TransE belongs to an entirely different class *LOCATION*. In the second example, prediction results of domain from TransE rank an entity in the class *PERSON* as the first one, which does not satisfy domain constraint, while TransE$_C$ filters out this entity. The third and fourth example are to predict tail entity. In the third example, the top three results from TransH$_C$ are all in the class *DISEASE*, however, an entity in the class *COMPANY* ranks third in TransH. The fourth example constrains the tail entity to be in the class *PERSON*, TransH makes an entity in the class *COMPANY* as the best prediction result, which can be filtered out by TransH$_C$ with incorporating domain and range of relations.

Since TransX$_C$ can filter out candidate entities that do not satisfy domain or range constraints, incorporating individual information of relations are efficient to link prediction task.

5 Conclusion and Future Work

We propose a framework TransX$_C$ based on translation-based models to improve these original models, and this framework trains a translation-based model and logistic regression classifiers jointly to preserve information of triples and domain and range of relations. To illustrate the efficiency of our framework, we test it with four translation-based models on four datasets and evaluate joint models on link prediction task. Results show that TransX$_C$ achieve significant improvements compared with corresponding basic models.

For future works, we will try to seek better classifiers to encode domain and range of relations. We also plan to explore more ways to incorporate domain and range constraints or other implicit information from observed triples in KGs.

Acknowledgements. This work is funded by NSFC 61473260/61673338, and Supported by Alibaba-Zhejiang University Joint Institute of Frontier Technologies.

References

1. Bollacker, K.D., Evans, C., Paritosh, P., Sturge, T., Taylor, J.: Freebase: a collaboratively created graph database for structuring human knowledge. In: SIGMOD Conference, pp. 1247–1250. ACM (2008)
2. Bordes, A., Usunier, N., García-Durán, A., Weston, J., Yakhnenko, O.: Translating embeddings for modeling multi-relational data. In: NIPS, pp. 2787–2795 (2013)
3. Cai, L., Wang, W.Y.: KBGAN: adversarial learning for knowledge graph embeddings. In: NAACL-HLT, pp. 1470–1480. Association for Computational Linguistics (2018)
4. Chang, K., Yih, W., Yang, B., Meek, C.: Typed tensor decomposition of knowledge bases for relation extraction. In: EMNLP, pp. 1568–1579. ACL (2014)
5. Dettmers, T., Minervini, P., Stenetorp, P., Riedel, S.: Convolutional 2D knowledge graph embeddings. In: AAAI, pp. 1811–1818. AAAI Press (2018)
6. Dong, X., et al.: Knowledge vault: a web-scale approach to probabilistic knowledge fusion. In: KDD, pp. 601–610. ACM (2014)
7. Fan, M., Zhou, Q., Chang, E., Zheng, T.F.: Transition-based knowledge graph embedding with relational mapping properties. In: PACLIC, pp. 328–337. The PACLIC 28 Organizing Committee and PACLIC Steering Committee/ACL/Department of Linguistics, Faculty of Arts, Chulalongkorn University (2014)
8. Ji, G., He, S., Xu, L., Liu, K., Zhao, J.: Knowledge graph embedding via dynamic mapping matrix. In: ACL (1), pp. 687–696. The Association for Computer Linguistics (2015)
9. Ji, G., Liu, K., He, S., Zhao, J.: Knowledge graph completion with adaptive sparse transfer matrix. In: AAAI, pp. 985–991. AAAI Press (2016)

10. Kazemi, S.M., Poole, D.: Simple embedding for link prediction in knowledge graphs. In: NeurIPS, pp. 4289–4300 (2018)
11. Krompaß, D., Baier, S., Tresp, V.: Type-constrained representation learning in knowledge graphs. In: Arenas, M., et al. (eds.) ISWC 2015. LNCS, vol. 9366, pp. 640–655. Springer, Cham (2015). https://doi.org/10.1007/978-3-319-25007-6_37
12. Krompass, D., Nickel, M., Tresp, V.: Large-scale factorization of type-constrained multi-relational data. In: DSAA, pp. 18–24. IEEE (2014)
13. Lin, Y., Liu, Z., Sun, M., Liu, Y., Zhu, X.: Learning entity and relation embeddings for knowledge graph completion. In: AAAI, pp. 2181–2187. AAAI Press (2015)
14. Liu, H., Wu, Y., Yang, Y.: Analogical inference for multi-relational embeddings. In: ICML. Proceedings of Machine Learning Research, vol. 70, pp. 2168–2178. PMLR (2017)
15. Miller, G.A.: WordNet: a lexical database for English. Commun. ACM **38**(11), 39–41 (1995)
16. Nguyen, D.Q., Nguyen, T.D., Nguyen, D.Q., Phung, D.Q.: A novel embedding model for knowledge base completion based on convolutional neural network. In: NAACL-HLT (2), pp. 327–333. Association for Computational Linguistics (2018)
17. Nguyen, D.Q., Vu, T., Nguyen, T.D., Nguyen, D.Q., Phung, D.Q.: A capsule network-based embedding model for knowledge graph completion and search personalization. CoRR abs/1808.04122 (2018)
18. Nickel, M., Rosasco, L., Poggio, T.A.: Holographic embeddings of knowledge graphs. In: AAAI, pp. 1955–1961. AAAI Press (2016)
19. Nickel, M., Tresp, V., Kriegel, H.: A three-way model for collective learning on multi-relational data. In: ICML, pp. 809–816. Omnipress (2011)
20. Rocktäschel, T., Singh, S., Riedel, S.: Injecting logical background knowledge into embeddings for relation extraction. In: HLT-NAACL, pp. 1119–1129. The Association for Computational Linguistics (2015)
21. Sabour, S., Frosst, N., Hinton, G.E.: Dynamic routing between capsules. In: NIPS, pp. 3859–3869 (2017)
22. Toutanova, K., Chen, D.: Observed versus latent features for knowledge base and text inference. In: Proceedings of the 3rd Workshop on Continuous Vector Space Models and their Compositionality, pp. 57–66 (2015)
23. Trouillon, T., Welbl, J., Riedel, S., Gaussier, É., Bouchard, G.: Complex embeddings for simple link prediction. In: ICML. JMLR Workshop and Conference Proceedings, vol. 48, pp. 2071–2080. JMLR.org (2016)
24. Wang, K., Liu, Y., Xu, X., Lin, D.: Knowledge graph embedding with entity neighbors and deep memory network. CoRR abs/1808.03752 (2018)
25. Wang, P., Dou, D., Wu, F., de Silva, N., Jin, L.: Logic rules powered knowledge graph embedding. CoRR abs/1903.03772 (2019)
26. Wang, Q., Mao, Z., Wang, B., Guo, L.: Knowledge graph embedding: a survey of approaches and applications. IEEE Trans. Knowl. Data Eng. **29**(12), 2724–2743 (2017)
27. Wang, Z., Zhang, J., Feng, J., Chen, Z.: Knowledge graph embedding by translating on hyperplanes. In: AAAI, pp. 1112–1119. AAAI Press (2014)
28. Xiao, H., Huang, M., Hao, Y., Zhu, X.: TransA: an adaptive approach for knowledge graph embedding. CoRR abs/1509.05490 (2015)
29. Yang, B., Yih, W., He, X., Gao, J., Deng, L.: Embedding entities and relations for learning and inference in knowledge bases. In: ICLR (2015)
30. Zhang, Y., Yao, Q., Dai, W., Chen, L.: AutoKGE: searching scoring functions for knowledge graph embedding. CoRR abs/1904.11682 (2019)

REKA: Relation Extraction with Knowledge-Aware Attention

Peiyi Wang[1], Hongtao Liu[1]([⊠]), Fangzhao Wu[2], Jinduo Song[1], Hongyan Xu[1], and Wenjun Wang[1]

[1] College of Intelligence and Computing, Tianjin University, Tianjin, China
{wangpeiyi9979,htliu,songjinduo,hongyanxu,wjwang}@tju.edu.cn
[2] Microsoft Research Asia, Beijing, China
wufangzhao@gmail.com

Abstract. Relation extraction (RE) is an important task and has wide applications. Distant supervision is widely used in RE methods which can automatically construct labeled data to reduce the manual annotation effort. This method usually results in many instances with incorrect labels. In addition, most of existing relation extraction methods merely rely on the textual content of sentences to extract relation. In fact, many knowledge graphs are off-the-shelf and they can provide useful information of entities and relations, which has the potential to alleviate the noisy data problem and improve the performance of relation extraction. In this paper, we propose a knowledge-aware attention model to incorporate the knowledge graph information into relation extraction. In our approach, we first learn the representations of entities and relations from knowledge graph using graph embedding methods. Then we propose a knowledge-aware word attention model to select the informative words in sentences for relation extraction. In addition, we also propose a knowledge-aware sentence attention model to select useful sentences for RE to alleviate the problem of noisy data brought by distant supervision. We conduct experiments on a widely used dataset and the results show that our approach can effectively improve the performance of neural relation extraction.

Keywords: Relation extraction · Knowledge graph · Attention

1 Introduction

Relation extraction (RE) aims to extract relational fact between a pair of entities from texts [19]. For example, given a sentence "Microsoft was founded by Bill Gates", relation extraction methods can predict that there is a `Founder` relation between the entity `Bill_Gates` and the entity `Microsoft`. Relation extraction is an important task in natural language processing and data mining fields [10, 19], and has wide applications such as automatic knowledge base construction [13], question answering [1], and so on.

© Springer Nature Singapore Pte Ltd. 2019
X. Zhu et al. (Eds.): CCKS 2019, CCIS 1134, pp. 62–73, 2019.
https://doi.org/10.1007/978-981-15-1956-7_6

Existing methods for relation extraction are usually based on supervised learning techniques [8,19]. These methods require a large amount of labeled data for model training, while it is time-consuming to annotate. In order to handle this problem, distant supervision is widely used to automatically generate labelled data for training relation extraction models [11]. In distant supervision, a large text corpus is aligned with knowledge bases (KBs) under the assumption that if two entities have a relation in KBs, then all sentences mentioning these two entities would be annotated with this relation [11]. The sentences containing the same entity pair are usually regarded as a bag. However, distant supervision usually results in a large number of samples with incorrect labels. For example, since the relation **Founder** exists between "Bill Gates" and "Microsoft" in knowledge graph, the sentence "Bill Gates left Microsoft in 2014" would be wrongly labeled as **Founder** relation. Several methods have been proposed to alleviate the noise data problem of distant supervision for relation extraction [12,13,15,18]. For example, Zeng et al. [18] applied convolutional neural networks (CNN) to encode sentences and utilized multi-instance learning (MIL) to select the correct instance. Lin et al. [10] introduced attention mechanism to assign different weights to different sentences in each bag. However, these methods usually only rely on the textual content of sentences to extract the relations between entities, and the useful information of entities and relations in knowledge graph is not considered.

Our work is motivated by following observations. First, many high-quality knowledge graphs (KBs) such as Freebase [3] and DBpedia [2] have been built and are off-the-shelf. These knowledge graphs contain a huge number of entities and their relations. Second, the entities and relations in knowledge graphs can provide useful information for relation extraction. Specifically, the knowledge of relations in KBs can provide important information for inferring whether a sentence is relevant to a relation and can help alleviate the problem of incorrect labels in distant supervision. For example, for two sentences "Microsoft was founded by Bill Gates" and "Bill Gates left Microsoft in 2014", the structure information of **Founder** relation in KBs can help judge that the first sentence is more related to **Founder** than the second one. In addition, the knowledge of entities can help identify important words in sentences. For example, in sentence "Mel Karmazin, the chief executive of Sirius, made many phone calls", the word "chief" is more informative than "phone" for relation extraction. Thus, exploiting the useful information in knowledge graphs has the potential to alleviate the problem of noisy data and improve the performance of relation extraction.

In this paper we propose a neural Relation Extraction approach with hierarchical Knowledge-aware Attentions (REKA). In our approach we first learn the representations of entities and relations from knowledge graphs using graph embedding methods such as TransE [4]. Considering that there are some entities not included by KBs, we propose a context-aware model to reconstruct the embeddings of those entities based on the text information. We propose a knowledge-aware word attention network by using the entity embeddings from knowledge graphs as entity-specific attention vectors to help our approach attend to informative words which are relevant to entity mentions. In addition, we propose a knowledge-aware sentence attention network to help our approach select informative sentences for relation extraction by using the relation embeddings from knowledge graphs as attention vectors.

The contributions in this paper include:

(1) We integrate the rich information about entities and relations in knowledge bases into relation extraction via knowledge graph embedding and hierarchical attention.
(2) We propose a knowledge-aware word attention based on entity embedding for focusing on more informative words in one sentence.
(3) We propose a knowledge-aware sentence attention based on relation embedding to alleviate the problem of noisy data.
(4) We evaluate our method on a widely used dataset and the experimental results show that our approach achieves significant improvement over the existing methods.

2 Related Work

Existing works in supervised relation extraction mainly relied on a large amount of annotated data to train models [5,8,19]. These methods are of supervised paradigm and require quite a lot labelled training sentences. To address the labelled problem, Mintz et al. [11] proposed a distant supervision approach to automatically generate labelled data via aligning plain text with existing knowledge bases, which could result in wrong labelling problems. To alleviate this issue, some works applied multi-instance learning in distant supervised relation extraction [6,12,15]. They relaxed the original strong assumption in distant supervision and adopted a multi-instance methods via feature-based approaches.

With the development of deep learning, various works based on neural network have been proposed. Zeng et al. [18] utilized convolutional neural networks to represent sentences and designed a at-least-one strategy to alleviate the wrong labelling issue. Zhou et al. [20] proposed a word-level attention model based on Bidirectional Long short Term memory (BiLSTM) to capture the most important semantic information in a sentence. Lin et al. [10] introduced sentence-level attention over instances that can learn different weights for sentences. These attention based works have achieved significant progress. However, the query vectors in previous attention models are randomly initialized, which is insufficient and difficult to tune with the noise data in distant supervision. Our hierarchical knowledge attention model utilizes the embeddings of entities and relations as query vectors, which could improve the performance of the relation extraction task.

In this paper, we integrate the prior structure information of knowledge bases into relation extraction models via Knowledge Graph Embedding (KGE). We will introduce KGE briefly next. KGE aims to transform entities and relations into low-dimensional vectors, which would preserve the structure information of KG. Recently, many methods about KGE have been proposed. TransE (Bordes et al. [4]) is one of the most widely used model, which aims to hold $\mathbf{h} + \mathbf{r} \approx \mathbf{t}$ in knowledge graph, where $\mathbf{h}, \mathbf{r}, \mathbf{t}$ are the embedding vectors of head entity h, relation r, tail entity t respectively. Afterwards, various methods based on TransE were proposed, such as TransA [16], TransR [9] and etc. In this paper, we adopt TransE as our knowledge base embedding method to get the prior knowledge representations of entities and relations.

3   Our Approach

In this section, we will present our model REKA in details. First, we will describe the relation extraction problem in distant supervision. Afterwards, our approach will be introduced, including knowledge embedding module, knowledge-aware word attention module, sentence encoder and knowledge-aware sentence attention module; the two attention parts are both based on entity and relation semantic representation. The overview of our approach is shown in Fig. 1.

3.1   Problem Definition

In distant supervision, given head entity h and tail entity t, we denote the bag including n sentences mentioning the two entities as $B = \{s_1, s_2, \cdots, s_n\}$, where $s_i = \{w_1, \cdots, h, \cdots, t, \cdots, w_N\}$ is the i-th sentence in the bag B, the goal of relation extraction is to predict which semantic relation $r_j, 1 \leq j \leq N_r$ exists between h and t, where N_r is the number of relations. In other words, relation extraction models aim to estimate the probability $p(r_j|B)$ and determine the most likely relation.

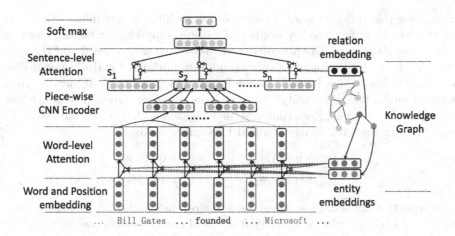

Fig. 1. The framework of our *REKA* approach.

3.2 Knowledge Embedding Module

In this section, we learn the representation of entities and relations from knowledge graphs. Given a triplet (h, r, t) composed of two entities h and t as well as their relation r, we choose TransE [4] to learn embedding vectors of entities and the relation. TransE is under such an assumption that $\mathbf{h} + \mathbf{r} \approx \mathbf{t}$ holds, where $\mathbf{h}, \mathbf{t}$ and $\mathbf{r}$ are the representations of h, t and r. The loss function can be formulated as: $\mathcal{L} = \max(\gamma + ||\mathbf{h} + \mathbf{r} - \mathbf{t}|| - ||\mathbf{h}' + \mathbf{r} - \mathbf{t}'||, 0)$, where h' and t' are negative entities generated in negative sampling and the triple (h', r, t') doesn't hold in KBs.

In the test phase, there may be entities out-of-KB. To address this issue, we construct the embeddings of those entities using the text information in sentences. Given a sentence $s = \{w_1, w_2, \cdots, e, \cdots, w_N\}$, where e is an out-of-KB entity, we first utilize a convolution neural network and max-pooling layer to encode the sentence s denoted as $\mathbf{c}$, which is regarded as the semantic vector of s. Then we construct the embedding of this entity $\mathbf{e^t}$ via concatenating with the word embedding $\mathbf{e^w}$ and a Multi-layer Perceptron (MLP) is followed:

$$\mathbf{e}^t = f(\mathbf{W}[\mathbf{c}, \mathbf{e^w}] + b), \tag{1}$$

where f is non-linear function and $\mathbf{W}$ is the parameter matrix in MLP, b is the bias item. In training phase, this module is trained via:

$$\mathcal{L}_{KB} = ||\mathbf{e} - \mathbf{e^t}||_2^2, \tag{2}$$

where $\mathbf{e}$ is the entity embedding learned by TransE in KB.

3.3 Knowledge-Aware Word Attention

Considering that different words in a sentence are differentially informative, it is important to identify those key words and will be helpful for extracting features of sentences. Zhou et al. [20] proposed a word-level attention based on BiLSTM. However, the query vector in [20] was randomly initialized and did not utilize the rich side knowledge fully. As a result, we design a knowledge-aware word attention model based on entity semantic representation. Given a sentence $s = \{w_1, h, \cdots, t, \cdots, w_N\}$, we compute the weight of each word by bilinear form attention with the embeddings of $\mathbf{h}$ and $\mathbf{t}$ as query vectors:

$$\alpha_i^h = \frac{\exp(\mathbf{h} \cdot \mathbf{w_i})}{\sum_{j=1}^N \exp(\mathbf{h} \cdot \mathbf{w_j})}, \quad \alpha_i^t = \frac{\exp(\mathbf{t} \cdot \mathbf{w_i})}{\sum_{j=1}^N \exp(\mathbf{t} \cdot \mathbf{w_j})},$$

where $\mathbf{w_i}$ is the embedding vector of the i-th word in s and α_i^h, α_i^t are the importance weight of w_i under head entity h and tail entity t respectively. We adopt average of α_i^h and α_i^t as the final weight and denote $\hat{\mathbf{w}}_i$ as the representation of w_i:

$$\alpha_i = \frac{\alpha_i^h + \alpha_i^t}{2}, \quad \hat{\mathbf{w}}_i = \alpha_i \mathbf{w_i}.$$

3.4   Sentence Encoder Module

In this part, we will introduce the sentence encoder in order to represent sentences into feature vectors. Since our knowledge-aware attention mechanism is flexible and can be applied in various sentence encoder models, we adopt a widely used and basic method PCNN [18] to represent sentences in our approach.

Word Embedding. Given a sentence $s = \{w_1, h, \cdots, t, \cdots, w_N\}$, besides the word embedding $\hat{w}_i$ obtained above, we utilize the position feature as well, which is defined as the relative distances from the current word to the two entities h and t. For example, in the sentence "Bill_Gates founded Microsoft years ago.", the relative distance from founded to Bill_Gates is -1, and to Microsoft is 1. The distances of word w_i are encoded as position embedding vectors, denoted as $\mathbf{pf}_i^h, \mathbf{pf}_i^t$ for head entity h and tail entity t respectively. Afterwards, we concatenate them together and get the final embedding of the word: $\mathbf{w_i} = [\hat{\mathbf{w}}_i, \mathbf{pf}_i^h, \mathbf{pf}_i^t] \in \mathcal{R}^{d_w + 2 \times d_p}$, where d_p is the dimension of position embedding.

Convolution. Each sentence s_i can be denoted as a matrix of word embeddings: $S = [\mathbf{w_1}, \mathbf{w_2}, \cdots, \mathbf{w_N}]$. Here, we will utilize a convolution neural network to encode S. Given there are K convolutional kernels denoted as $\{k_1, k_2, \cdots, k_K\}$ and the window size of kernels l, the convolutional operation between the i-th kernel and the j-th window of input sequence is defined as:

$$c_{i,j} = \mathbf{k_i} \odot \mathbf{w}_{j:j+l-1},$$

where $1 \leq i \leq K, 1 \leq j \leq N - l + 1$, $\odot$ is the inner-product between vectors. Then we can get the output of convolution denoted as a matrix $\mathbf{C} = [\mathbf{c_1}, \mathbf{c_2}, \cdots, \mathbf{c_K}]$.

Piece Wise Max Pooling. Here we adopt piece wise max pooling [18] instead of the single max pooling which would be too coarse to capture fine-grained features for relation extraction. Each sentence is divided into three segments by the head entity and tail entity and we conduct max pooling in each segment: $p_{i,j} = \max(c_{ij})\ 1 \leq i \leq N, j = 1, 2, 3$, then we can get a 3-dimension vector output for each kernel (i.e., $\mathbf{p_i} = [p_{i1}, p_{i2}, p_{i3}]$ for kernel k_i) rather than 1-dimension in tradition max-pooling. Then the final output is denoted as $\mathbf{S_i} = \tanh([\mathbf{p_1}, \mathbf{p_2}, \cdots, \mathbf{p_K}]) \in \mathcal{R}^{3K}$ (i.e., the representation of sentence s_i).

3.5   Knowledge-Aware Sentence Attention

Given the representation of sentences, next we will compute the representation of a bag $B = \{s_1, s_2, \cdots, s_n\}$. We adopt selective attention in sentence-level following [7, 10] to de-emphasize the noise sentences and emphasize the positive sentences, denoted as:

$$\mathbf{B} = \sum_i \alpha_i \mathbf{S_i}, \quad \alpha_i = \frac{\exp(\mathbf{S_i A r})}{\sum_j \exp(\mathbf{S_j A r})},$$

where α_i is the weight of sentence s_i in the bag B, and $\mathbf{r}$ is the attention query vector associated with a relation, $\mathbf{A}$ is the harmony matrix in attention. Instead of randomly initializing r, we adopt the relation embedding learned in TransE as the attention query vector, which provides rich structure knowledge about the connection between entity pair and relation.

$\mathbf{B} \in \mathcal{R}^{3K}$ is the final representation of the bag B, which integrates the text information and structure knowledge in KBs. Afterwards, we compute the score of all relations associated with the bag:

$$\mathbf{o} = \mathbf{MB} + \mathbf{b},$$

where $\mathbf{b}$ is the bias item. $\mathbf{M} \in \mathcal{R}^{N_r \times 3K}$ and $\mathbf{M}_i$ is the weight of i-th relation to compute the score $\mathbf{o}_i$. Afterwards, the conditional probability that the bag B can express the relation $r_i, 1 \le i \le N_r$ is defined with a soft-max layer as:

$$p(r_i|B, \theta) = \frac{\exp(\mathbf{o}_i)}{\sum_{j=1}^{N_r}(\mathbf{o}_j)}, \tag{3}$$

where θ is the set of parameters of our model.

3.6 Objective Function and Optimization

Firstly, we have defined a loss $\mathcal{L}_{KB}$ in Sect. 3.2. Next, we define the cross entropy loss function by maximizing the likelihood in the training data:

$$\mathcal{L}_{text} = -\sum \log p(r_i|B_i, \theta).$$

Besides, we believe that the relation embeddings learned in TransE should be close to the relation vectors in $\mathbf{M}$; as a result, to utilize the knowledge of KBs more fully, we design a regularization item as another loss:

$$\mathcal{L}_{reg} = ||\mathbf{Wr_i} - \mathbf{M_i}||_2^2, \tag{4}$$

where $\mathbf{r_i}$ is the relation embedding learned in knowledge graph embedding TransE and $\mathbf{W}$ is a harmony matrix.

The final loss function is defined:

$$\mathcal{L} = \lambda_1 \mathcal{L}_{KB} + \mathcal{L}_{text} + \lambda_2 \mathcal{L}_{reg},$$

where λ_1, λ_2 are two balance weight for different loss items.

In the training phase, we adopt Adadelta [17] to optimize the objective $\mathcal{L}$. In addition, we use Dropout [14] technology to prevent overfitting.

4   Experiments

We conduct extensive experiments to evaluate the performance of our approach. In this section, we first introduce the dataset and experimental settings and then report and analyze the results in details.

4.1 Experimental Settings

Dataset. We evaluation our method on a widely used dataset NYT+Freebase, developed by [12]. This dataset was generated in distant supervision via aligning a three-year New York Times corpus from 2005 to 2007 with Freebase. All sentences are annotated with two entities and their relation fact. Following previous works [10,18], we use the 2005–2006 sentences as training data and the sentences in year 2007 as testing data. Besides, we only use the triplets in training dataset to learn the prior embeddings of entities and relations via TransE. The dataset contains 53 relation labels including a special one "NA" denoting that there are no relations between the two entities. There are 522,611 sentences, 281,270 entity pairs and 18,252 positive instances (i.e., not "NA") in the training data and 172,448 sentences, 96,678 entity pairs and 1,950 positive instances in the testing data.

Evaluation Metrics. Since there may be wrong labels in distant supervision, we could not compute the commonly-used metrics (e.g., Accuracy, F1-Score) directly. Following the previous works [7,10,18], we evaluate our approach via held-out evaluation, which is an approximate measure that compares the predicted relations with those in Freebase. We present our results with Precsion-Recall Curves and Precision@N (Top N in precision) in our experiments.

Parameter Settings. We explore different combinations of hyper parameters in our model via cross-validation to tune them. The best configurations are: word embedding dimension $d_w = 50$, position embedding dimension $d_p = 5$, number of kernels $K = 230$, the window size of kernels $l = 3$, loss weight $\lambda_1 = 1, \lambda_2 = 0.005$, the dropout rate 0.5.

4.2 Performance Comparison

To evaluate the effect of our model, in this part we will present experimental results of the held-out metrics (i.e., the Precision-Recall curves and Precision@N). The baselines include:

(1) **Mintz** [11]: a feature-based method which extracted human-designed features from sentences.
(2) **MultiR** [6]: a multi-instance learning model which can handle overlapping relations via graphical model.
(3) **MIMLRE** [15]: a multi-instance and multi-label method for distant supervision.
(4) **PCNN** [18]: a relation extraction model based on multi-instance learning and piecewise convolutional neural network.
(5) **BGRU+ATT** [20]: a word-level attention model based on BGRU, and its extended model **BGRU+2ATT** with both word-level and sentence-level attention.
(6) **PCNN+ATT** [10]: adopts a selective attention to reduce the weight of noise data based on PCNN.

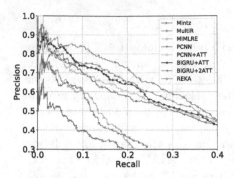 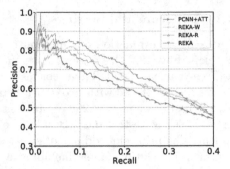

Fig. 2. Precision-Recall curves of REKA and baselines

Fig. 3. Precision-Recall curves of REKA, REKA-R and REKA-W.

Table 1. Precision under Top K of predicted results.

P@N (%)	100	200	300	400	500	600	700	800	Avg
Mintz	52.3	50.2	45.1	41.3	39.7	37.1	35.7	34.6	42.0
MultiR	70.3	65.2	61.8	54.4	48.1	43.6	41.4	40.0	53.1
MIML	70.9	62.7	61.2	56.7	50.7	46.6	43.0	41.8	54.2
PCNN	72.3	69.7	64.1	62.4	59.9	57.6	55.1	54.3	61.9
PCNN+ATT	76.2	73.1	67.4	66.0	63.8	60.8	59.1	57.0	65.4
BGRU+ATT	82.0	76.5	71.3	70.2	66.3	62.3	60.2	57.8	68.3
BGRU+2ATT	81.0	76.0	72.7	71.3	68.2	65.3	62.5	60.0	69.3
REKA	**84.8**	**84.0**	**79.0**	**75.8**	**71.6**	**66.8**	**64.4**	**61.3**	**73.5**

The Precision-Recall curves are shown in Fig. 2 and the Precision@N results are listed in Table 1. We find that PCNN+ATT outperforms PCNN and BGRU+2ATT outperforms BGRU+ATT. Both results demonstrate that attention based methods can improve the performance in relation extraction. This is because the attention can reduce the weight of noise data. Moreover, our knowledge-aware attention model REKA achieves the best results both in PR curves and the top precision@N metrics by integrating useful information in KBs. The reason is that the relational facts information in KBs can help alleviate the wrong labeled problem and focus on useful words and sentences. These results indicate that incorporating knowledge can effectively improve the performance for relation extraction.

4.3 Effect of Knowledge-Aware Attention

To demonstrate the incremental effectiveness of different modules in our model, in this section we further explore the effect of entity and relation knowledge respectively. We remove the entity knowledge and adopt randomly-initialized attention vectors in word-level attention denoted as REKA-W (i.e., there is only relation knowledge-aware attention). Besides, we remove the relation knowledge module and adopt randomly-initialized query vector in sentence-level attention denoted as REKA-R (i.e., there are only entity knowledge-aware attention). PCNN+ATT [10] is the method without any knowledge attention.

Table 2. Precision under Top K of predicted results.

P@N (%)	100	200	300	400	500	600	700	800	Avg
PCNN+ATT	82.0	71.0	69.3	66.0	63.8	60.8	59.1	57.0	66.1
REKA-R	81.2	78.1	74.7	69.5	65	63.5	61.1	58.8	69.0
REKA-W	78.6	80.5	74.5	71.0	67.8	63.5	62.1	59.3	69.7
REKA	**84.8**	**84.0**	**79.0**	**75.8**	**71.6**	**66.8**	**64.4**	**61.3**	**73.5**

The results are shown in Fig. 3 and Table 2. We can find that REKA-W and REKA-R both outperform PCNN+ATT, which indicates that the effectiveness of our knowledge-aware attention under word-level and sentence-level. This is because the different words in a sentence are of different importance and our word-level knowledge attention can effectively select those more useful words towards to entity pair. Besides, the combination of word-level and sentence-level attention (i.e., REKA) achieves the best performance. This shows the two-level knowledge-aware attentions are complementary for relation extraction and can make full use of the useful knowledge in KBs.

4.4 Flexibility of Knowledge Attention

In this part we apply our knowledge attention in two other sentence encoders (CNN and BGRU) to evaluate the flexibility of our approach. We report the areas under Precision Recall Curves in Figs. 4 and 5. We can see that either entity attention (+W) or relation attention (+R) outperform the pure CNN or BGRU and the combination (+W+R) of the two knowledge attention achieves the best performance, which indicates that our prior knowledge attention is flexible and can improve the performance significantly in different encoders.

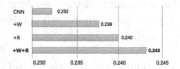   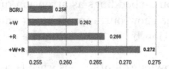

Fig. 4. Areas under PR curves for CNN   **Fig. 5.** Areas under PR curves for BGRU

4.5   Case Study

In this section, we show a case study for qualitative analysis to further explain the effect of our knowledge-aware attention intuitively. As shown in Table 3, we select a entity pair (*rice_university, houston*) with the relation */location/contains/*, there are three sentences (the first two are noise data and the third one is positive instance) in the bag. We present the weights of the sentences in PCNN+ATT and our model REKA. We can see that in PCNN+ATT, the first negative sentence is assigned with a much higher weight of 0.36 while the weight in our model is only 0.02. This indicates that incorporating knowledge in KBs can effectively alleviate the wrongly labeled problem, and can focus on those more informative sentences in entity-pair bags.

Table 3. The attentions of sentences for entity pair (**rice_university, houston**) and relation /location/contains/.

Sentence	PCNN+ATT	REKA
(1) ...city of **houston**, higher education finance corporation,... revenue bonds for **rice_university** Negative	0.36	0.02
(2) ken kennedy, a **rice_university** computer scientist ... died wednesday in **houston** Negative	0.001	0.001
(3) an energy expert at the james a. baker iii institute for public policy at **rice_university** in **houston** Postive	0.639	0.979

5   Conclusion

In this paper, we propose a neural approach for relation extraction which can leverages the useful information of entities and relations in knowledge graphs. In our approach we first learn the embeddings of entities and relations from knowledge graphs using graph embedding methods. Then we propose a knowledge-aware word attention network to select important words for relation extraction by using the entity embeddings as attention query vectors. In addition, we propose a knowledge-aware sentence attention network to select informative sentences and alleviate the problem of incorrectly labeled instances by using the relation embeddings as attention query vectors. Experiments on the benchmark dataset show our approach can effectively improve the performance of relation extraction by incorporating the useful knowledge graph information.

Acknowledgments. This work is supported by the National Social Science Fund of China (15BTQ056).

References

1. Abujabal, A., Yahya, M., Riedewald, M., Weikum, G.: Automated template generation for question answering over knowledge graphs. In: WWW, pp. 1191–1200 (2017)
2. Auer, S., Bizer, C., Kobilarov, G., Lehmann, J., Cyganiak, R., Ives, Z.: DBpedia: a nucleus for a web of open data. In: Aberer, K., et al. (eds.) ASWC/ISWC -2007. LNCS, vol. 4825, pp. 722–735. Springer, Heidelberg (2007). https://doi.org/10.1007/978-3-540-76298-0_52
3. Bollacker, K., Evans, C., Paritosh, P., Sturge, T., Taylor, J.: Freebase: a collaboratively created graph database for structuring human knowledge. In: SIGMOD, pp. 1247–1250 (2008)
4. Bordes, A., Usunier, N., Garcia-Duran, A., Weston, J., Yakhnenko, O.: Translating embeddings for modeling multi-relational data. In: NIPS, pp. 2787–2795 (2013)
5. GuoDong, Z., Jian, S., Jie, Z., Min, Z.: Exploring various knowledge in relation extraction. In: ACL, pp. 427–434 (2005)
6. Hoffmann, R., Zhang, C., Ling, X., Zettlemoyer, L., Weld, D.S.: Knowledge-based weak supervision for information extraction of overlapping relations. In: ACL, pp. 541–550 (2011)
7. Ji, G., Liu, K., He, S., Zhao, J., et al.: Distant supervision for relation extraction with sentence-level attention and entity descriptions. In: AAAI, pp. 3060–3066 (2017)
8. Kambhatla, N.: Combining lexical, syntactic, and semantic features with maximum entropy models for extracting relations. In: ACL, p. 22 (2004)
9. Lin, Y., Liu, Z., Sun, M., Liu, Y., Zhu, X.: Learning entity and relation embeddings for knowledge graph completion. In: AAAI 2015, pp. 2181–2187 (2015)
10. Lin, Y., Shen, S., Liu, Z., Luan, H., Sun, M.: Neural relation extraction with selective attention over instances. In: ACL, pp. 2124–2133 (2016)
11. Mintz, M., Bills, S., Snow, R., Jurafsky, D.: Distant supervision for relation extraction without labeled data. In: ACL, pp. 1003–1011 (2009)
12. Riedel, S., Yao, L., McCallum, A.: Modeling relations and their mentions without labeled text. In: Balcázar, J.L., Bonchi, F., Gionis, A., Sebag, M. (eds.) ECML PKDD 2010. LNCS (LNAI), vol. 6323, pp. 148–163. Springer, Heidelberg (2010). https://doi.org/10.1007/978-3-642-15939-8_10
13. Riedel, S., Yao, L., McCallum, A., Marlin, B.M.: Relation extraction with matrix factorization and universal schemas. In: NAACL, pp. 74–84 (2013)
14. Srivastava, N., Hinton, G., Krizhevsky, A., Sutskever, I., Salakhutdinov, R.: Dropout: a simple way to prevent neural networks from overfitting. J. Mach. Learn. Res. **15**(1), 1929–1958 (2014)
15. Surdeanu, M., Tibshirani, J., Nallapati, R., Manning, C.D.: Multi-instance multi-label learning for relation extraction. In: EMNLP, pp. 455–465 (2012)
16. Xiao, H., Huang, M., Hao, Y., Zhu, X.: TransA: an adaptive approach for knowledge graph embedding. arXiv preprint arXiv:1509.05490 (2015)
17. Zeiler, M.D.: ADADELTA: an adaptive learning rate method. arXiv preprint arXiv:1212.5701 (2012)
18. Zeng, D., Liu, K., Chen, Y., Zhao, J.: Distant supervision for relation extraction via piecewise convolutional neural networks. In: EMNLP, pp. 1753–1762 (2015)
19. Zeng, D., Liu, K., Lai, S., Zhou, G., Zhao, J.: Relation classification via convolutional deep neural network. In: COLING, pp. 2335–2344 (2014)
20. Zhou, P., et al.: Attention-based bidirectional long short-term memory networks for relation classification. In: ACL, pp. 207–212 (2016)

Research on Construction and Automatic Expansion of Multi-source Lexical Semantic Knowledge Base

Siqi Zhu, Yi Li, and Yanqiu Shao[✉]

School of Information Science, Beijing Language and Culture University,
Beijing 100083, China
1231115@stu.blcu.edu.cn, blcu2014liyi@gmail.com,
yqshao163@163.com

Abstract. With the development of research on improving the performance of deep learning models in combination with the rich knowledge resources in traditional knowledge bases, more and more research on building knowledge bases has become a hot topic. How to use the rich semantic information of existing knowledge bases such as HowNet and Tongyici-Cilin to build a more comprehensive and higher quality knowledge graph has become the focus of scholars' research. In this work, we propose a way to integrate a variety of knowledge base information to build a new knowledge base, combined with deep learning techniques to expand the knowledge base. Successfully build a multi-source lexical semantic knowledge base through the steps of new ontology construction, data cleaning and fusion, and new knowledge expansion. Based on the establishment of the knowledge base, we use the graph database and JavaScript script to store and visualize the data separately. Through experiments, we obtained a lexical semantic knowledge base containing 153754 nodes, 1598356 triples and 137 relationships. It can provide accurate and convenient knowledge services, and can use a large number of semantic knowledge resources to support research on semantic retrieval, intelligent question answering system, semantic relationship extraction, semantic relevance calculation and ontology automatic construction [1].

Keywords: Lexicon semantic knowledge graph · Multiple source · Ontology build · Ontology-based data integration · Information extraction

1 Introduction

As the basic resource of natural language understanding and the medium and carrier of text content understanding, the semantic knowledge base collects, stores and expresses various words and concepts such as lexical, syntactic, semantic relations and background common sense. The main purpose of its establishment is to help Computers can understand natural language like humans. Semantic knowledge base is widely used in machine translation, word disambiguation, query expansion in information retrieval, text classification, question answering system, etc. In recent years, research on entity-based, fact-based semantic retrieval and information integration based on semantic

© Springer Nature Singapore Pte Ltd. 2019
X. Zhu et al. (Eds.): CCKS 2019, CCIS 1134, pp. 74–85, 2019.
https://doi.org/10.1007/978-981-15-1956-7_7

knowledge base has emerged. At the same time, along with the development of the Semantic Web, more and more linguists and Internet researchers are paying more and more attention to the research of semantics, especially the research on the construction of large-scale semantic knowledge base as the basic resource. At the same time, the combination of symbolism and connectionism has also achieved excellent results in some studies, making how to obtain a better knowledge base has become a research hotspot.

1.1 Existing Knowledge Base

In a series of studies, the researchers built a number of knowledge bases, and the established knowledge base has also been successful in a number of specific areas. The following is an introduction to representative work.

HowNet. As a large-scale language knowledge base marked by Mr. Dong Zhendong and Mr. Dong Qiang for 30 years, HowNet contains rich semantic information, which is based on the concept represented by Chinese and English words to reveal the relationship between concepts and the attributes of concepts. HowNet uses the most basic and indivisible semantic unit sememe to mark the semantic information of the vocabulary, and at the same time, the dynamic character information or semantic information is marked between the original, so that the vocabulary can be accurately described. In the structure of HowNet, words are composed of meaning items, and meaning items are defined by sememe and relationship. At present, HowNet contains more than 800 sememes, 212541 meanings and 118347 words [2].

Tongyici Cilin (Extended). Based on the original edition of Tongyici Cilin, HIT IR-Lab removed the rare words and stop words, and added some new common words from People Daily, and finally they finished this word and got this dataset which has a considerable number of words. The Tongyici Cilin (Extended) organizes all the collected terms according to the hierarchical structure of the tree, and divides the vocabulary into three categories: large, medium and small. There are 12 large classes, 97 intermediate classes, and 1,400 small classes. There are many words in each sub-category. These words are divided into several groups (paragraphs) according to the distance and relevance of the meaning of the words [3].

Semantic Knowledge-base of Contemporary Chinese (SKCC). The SKCC [4] is a large machine-readable dictionary developed by the Institute of Computation Linguistics and Chinese Department of Peking University. Through the continuous development for more than three years, the scale and quality of the knowledge-base have been improved remarkably. It can provide a large amount of semantic information such as semantic hierarchy and collocation features of 66539 Chinese words. The descriptions of semantic attributes are fairly thorough, comprehensive and authoritative [5].

The lexical semantic knowledge base mentioned above is constructed by hand and has a limited scale. In addition, there are also knowledge bases built on semi-structured resources (Wikipedia, Baidu, etc.), such as DBpedia and WikiNet, which extract information directly from Wikipedia. Also, the other way that combine the existing knowledge base and knowledge extracted by Wikipedia, such as YAGO, FreeBase.

For Chinese information processing, a number of Chinese semantic knowledge bases have been constructed that have been influential and have also played a practical role. However, there are also semantic knowledge bases built on the basis of linguistic research. It is not open enough and too complicated, thus limiting the scale of the dictionary and the prospects for large-scale applications. In addition, the construction of semantic knowledge bases is still in their own situation. Although the research objects and theoretical foundations of semantic knowledge bases are different, they are all defining and expressing the semantics of a concept/word and other concepts associated with it, focusing on the relationship between the semantics of words. Integrating existing resources and knowledge bases and building a large-scale Chinese vocabulary semantic knowledge base is an urgent task.

The difficulties during in the construction of the knowledge base are as follows: (1) The organizational structure and ontology level of different knowledge bases are different. How to combine the different forms of storage with the knowledge base of the ontology level is one of the difficulties in this research. At the same time, due to the huge amount of data, how to build a reasonable knowledge base onto massive data is the most important. (2) Due to the heterogeneity of the knowledge base, how to integrate, de-emphasize and disambiguate data from different sources will be the main point and core of this database construction. (3) Faced with the massive information and constantly updated knowledge of the Internet, how to maintain and update the constructed semantic vocabulary knowledge base, how to expand the size of the knowledge base to adapt to language changes is also a difficult problem to be solved.

2   The Process of Multi-source Knowledge Integration

Our knowledge base builds on HowNet, Tongyici-Cilin and SKCC. The entire fusion process is subdivided into noun part construction and verb noun connection. All of the process contains four steps: (1) Ontology construction of noun-part based on ontology reuse and fusion. (2) Data integration and structure construction for noun part. (3) Construction of verb structure and connection of verb and noun. (4) Data storage based on Graph Database and visualization.

2.1   The Ontology Construction for Multi-source Knowledge Base

The ontology was originally derived from philosophy and gradually extended to the aspect of information science [6]. The ontology of the knowledge map can be defined as a set of concepts and categories in this knowledge that shows their properties and the relations between them. The ontologies of different knowledge bases are very inconsistent [7]. The first step in our integration of the knowledge base is to build a suitable ontology for it. The ontology standardizes the structure of the knowledge base and the way the knowledge is organized. Through the construction of the ontology, we can integrate the structure of the three knowledge bases completely.

In HowNet, each concept is described by Knowledge System Description Language (KDML). Below we will illustrate the specific description structure of HowNet (see Fig. 1) and the information shown is from the 2008 version of HowNet data files.

As we can see, the words are described by sememes, the first sememe is basic sememe, which give a clear definition of the word. By extracting the first sememe of every word, and connecting these sememes according to their inclusion relationship, we can easily get the ontology of HowNet.

```
NO.=088214
W_C=苹果
G_C=N [ping2 guo3]
E_C=~源产哪国，山后是一片~，~什么时候结果，我们这里盛产~，~是栽植在山地好还是平原好
W_E=apple
G_E=N
E_E=
DEF={tree|树:{reproduce|生殖:PatientProduct={fruit|水果},agent={~}}}
```

Fig. 1. "NO" indicates the identifier number of the concept; "W_C" is the Chinese name of the concept; "G_C" defines the part of speech of the concept; "E_C" gives a concrete example of the concept (the example of the icon "apple" is not given "W_E" gives an English explanation of the concept; "G_E" indicates the part of speech in the English interpretation; "E_E" unified vacancy; "DEF" represents a detailed description of the concept by a combination of dynamic characters and meaning.

Tongyici Cilin organizes all the included terms together in a tree-like hierarchy. The terms are divided into three categories: large, medium and small. There are 12 major categories, 97 in the middle category, and 1,400 in the small category. There are many words in each subcategory. These words are divided into several groups based on the distance and relevance of the meaning of the words. The structure is shown (see Fig. 2).

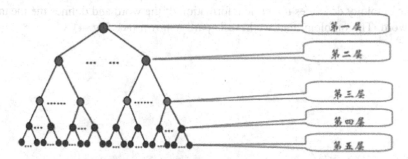

Fig. 2. The illustration shows the structure of the knowledge base. There are five layers of structure. The first layer is a large class with 12 major categories. The other layers are 95 intermediate classes, 1428 subclasses, 4229 word groups, and synonym data.

And the nouns of SKCC are also have its own format. Every noun in SKCC was given a series of information including class, subclass, meaning term, homomorphism, semantic class, direct upper position, valence number, reference body, object, etc. Above all, the structure will be shown (see Fig. 3).

词语	词类	子类	义项	词形	语义类	直接上位	配价数	参照体	对象
安全系数	n	LN			量化属性				
安全线	n				人工物				
安全性	n				物性				
安全员	n				职业				
安澜	n				处所				
安身之地	n				空间				
安史之乱	n				事件				
安顺	n				处所				
安庭	n				属性				
安慰赛	n				事件				
安阳	n				处所				
安详费	n				钱财				
桉树	n				树	树			
桉油	n				材料				
氨	n				材料|自然物				
氨基	n				构件(符号)	术语			
氨基酸	n				自然物				
氨气	n				自然物				
氨水	n				自然物				
鹌鹑	n				鸟				
桉钢	n				机构				
鞍马	n		3		人工物				

Fig. 3. The illustration shows a sample of the SKCC data.

Considering the structure and data organization of each knowledge base, we first extract the ontology of each knowledge base one by one from its data files, and then connect the ontology of other two knowledge bases through matching based on the ontology of HowNet. Finally, we manually check the constructed ontology, eliminate the error items and redundant items, and complete the lack of the ontology. In the actual construction process, because the ontology of Tongyici Cilin is divided into multiple layers, which makes it very redundant. We take noun part of the first layer (4 of 12 major categories) of its ontology structure as the elements of the new ontology construction. As for SKCC, we got a hierarchical ontology with 629 elements, in which there are duplicates with the HowNet ontology. So when we build the new ontology, we combine automatic and manual these two ways for integration and deduplication. Finally, we integrated the ontology of three databases with a hierarchy form of 1367 elements. This ontology defines a set of frameworks for the categories of words, and all `words can find their own classifications in the branches of the ontology. At the same time, the ontology describes the basic information of the word and defines the meaning of the word. The ontology that we have is partly shown (see Fig. 4).

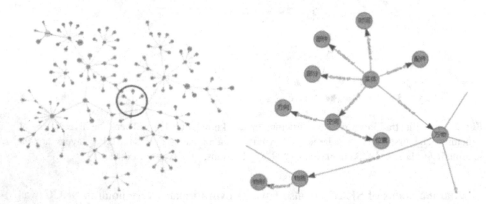

Fig. 4. The illustration shows part of the ontology we built in this experiment. The right picture shows the concrete representation of the red circle on the left. As shown in the figure, the ontology element is shown as a node, and the directed edge represents the category inclusion relationship between the elements.

2.2　Data Integration and Structure Construction for Noun Part

In this step, we will integrate, disambiguate and de-emphasize the data of the three knowledge bases. We first deal with the noun part which is extracted from the data files by its POS. The detailed processing steps are as follows.

Data Preprocessing. First, we preprocess the data so that the data is saved into the same structure. The whole data are represented as a collection of triples $\{(h, r, t)\}$, where h, t are the entity and r is the relation between them.

For HowNet, we design a structure analyzer to extract the information from the '*DEF*' part described by KMDL in data files shown in Fig. 1. Since the first sememe for every word give us a precise definition of it, we add a relation '*Is_Instance_of*' to describe this relation. For other sememes of the word, we can get the triples between them by reusing the event role and features as relations, so that we build triples by keeping its original relations.

For Tongyici Cilin, there is no precise definition for every word, but there are most relevant words for every word. We can easily use its knowledge by adding a relation '*SYN*' to link the synonyms. Since the relation between synonyms is reversible, we combine each of them to get the triples. And we just use the first layer in our ontology, the other four layers are also saved as triples with a tree hierarchy by adding a relation '*Is_Instance_of*'. Through this way, we can keep the layer information of synonyms.

As for SKCC, there already have the semantic class and direct upper word for every words. So we use their information directly to build triples. Defining the relation '*Is_Instance_of*' to link the word and its semantic class.

After this step is done, we get three triple datasets, which contain about 193349 words, 1736473 triples and 137 relations (see Fig. 5).

(部件,whole,交通工具) (部件,DESCRIB_OF,拴连) (拴连,instrument,~) (拴连,purpose,保护)
(文书,concerning,事务) (事务,CoEvent,保证) (事务,domain,保险)
(费用,domain,保险) (费用,DESCRIB_OF,保证) (保证,cost,~)
(费用,domain,保险) (费用,DESCRIB_OF,保证) (保证,cost,~)
(酬金,domain,保险) (酬金,DESCRIB_OF,付) (付,possession,~)
(场所,DESCRIB_OF,从事) (从事,agent,~) (从事,content,事务) (事务,CoEvent,保证) (事务,domain,保险)
(用具,DESCRIB_OF,保存) (保存,location,~) (保存,patient,钱财)
(用具,DESCRIB_OF,保存) (保存,location,~) (保存,patient,钱财)
(符号,RelateTo,保证) (保证,domain,保险) (保证,DESCRIB_OF,指代) (指代,isa,次序) (指代,relevant,~)
(用具,RelateTo,电) (用具,DESCRIB_OF,保护) (保护,instrument,~)
(多少,domain,保险) (多少,host,钱财) (钱财,DESCRIB_OF,保证) (保证,content,~)

Fig. 5. Part of the triple data is shown.

Data Integration and Data Structure Design. In this step, we use the ontology we designed to integrate the triples and design a proper structure to store our data. The steps are as follows:

By using the ontology to link our data, we can easily remove duplicate elements without doing additional similarity calculations. According to the relation between words and basic sememes in triples we get, we link every words in HowNet with the ontology elements. Since the first layer of Tongyici Cilin is integrated in our ontology, we also link its words with our ontology by using the hierarchy information saved in triples. What's more, we link the SKCC triples by using the inclusion relation triples. Also we keep the related triples from 'DEF' part of HowNet for every word as part of its properties. And we regard other knowledge bases' information as every word's attribution, such as examples, POS and so on, which are save into a single attribute file.

What's more, we link the words by using the relations. By doing this, we can make our knowledge base have a better quality.

2.3 Construct Verb Structure and Connection of Verb with Noun

This Step, we extract the verb from HowNet and SKCC, and build the structure that is integrated into ontology. What's more, we also connect the verb and noun for constructing a comprehensive knowledge base.

Construction of Verb Structure. In HowNet, every verb has its definition in 'DEF' part. And most of verb is described by a single basic sememe. So we can get a tree structure by linking the verb and its first sememe. Also in SKCC, every verb is given a sequence information including word class, subclass, meaning term, homomorphism, semantic class, valence number, subject, object and etc. So we extract the semantic class, and link every verb with its semantic class.

Since we have the verb from HowNet and SKCC, we consider to fuse the structures to remove duplicates and get a better classification criterion. We adding the classifications into the ontology in the last step manually. Meanwhile we maintain a vocabulary containing the verb only once to filter the similar. What's more, we link every word in this ontology (This step also removes a small part of the repetition).

Then we build the triples of verb, which links the verb with its basic sememe or semantic class. And save the other information given by knowledge bases as the properties of every verb.

What's more, we use the verb from Tongyici Cilin to improve the quality of our verb part. The verb in Cilin were used as synonym data to completing branches with fewer words. In this part, we have adopted a strategy: If the verb is redundant in our knowledge base, we just build triples with verbs and relation 'SYN', and link them in knowledge in graph. If the verb is not in knowledge, we define the missing verb as node and add it into the category branch where it belongs to.

Connect Verb with Noun. For this section, we will use the information supplied by SKCC. The subject/object from SKCC for every verb defines the types of noun that the verb should match. Considering this information, we propose two relations ('Subject_of', 'Object_of') to link every verb with noun through building triples. In actual situation, since the type of noun is given, we can match verb with the noun that belongs to this specific type. But there are still about 50000 verbs without any links with noun, we will complete later by using neural network to extract knowledge from our corpus.

2.4 Data Storage Based on Graph Database and Visualization

In building the lexical semantic knowledge base, we chose to use the graph database Neo4j j [8] to represent and store vocabulary and semantic relationships. Neo4 is a high-performance graph database that supports the storage of structured data in graphs.

It is increasingly popular among developers due to its advantages of embedded, high performance and lightweight. Neo4j uses nodes and relationships to represent and state knowledge in the diagram, supports each node to define its own attributes, and supports Cypher for querying and other operations. What's more, Neo4j officially announced an open source computing component that supports the combination of databases and neural networks, so that stored data can be applied to neural network models through components in the future.

First, we use five files storing separately the ontology, verb triples, noun triples, properties of verb, properties of noun.

Then we define ontology elements, nouns, and verbs as nodes in the Neo4j graph database, and import the elements of the verb and noun properties into the database as attributes of each node. At this point, the data storage is completed.

Then we use HTML, CSS, JavaScript to implement the query function and visualization in the form of web pages for project display (see Fig. 6).

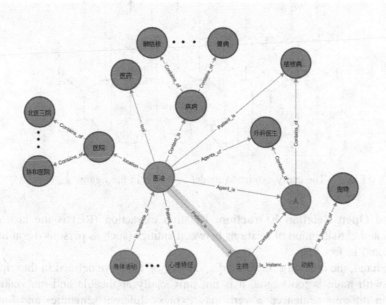

Fig. 6. The illustration shows an example of the verb 'healing' connected to the noun part. Different colors represent different parts, green is the ontology, yellow is the verb, pink is the noun. (Some nodes are omitted to facilitate understanding). (Color figure online)

3   Automatically Expand the Scale the Knowledge Graph

In this step, we consider the use of entity recognition, relationship extraction and other steps to extract the missing verbs, nouns and the relationship between them, the results obtained complement our knowledge base.

Entity Recognition. Since Google announced the pre-training model BERT on GitHub for everyone to download and use, fine-tuning on their own tasks can achieve very good results. We will use BERT to achieve the entity recognition [9].

In our work, firstly, we use BERT to generate a vector representation for every word in the text sequence.

Then the vectors will be used as input to the Bi-LSTM layer and encoded to model the input sequence in two-way information to capture context information, by doing feature extraction to obtain a vector.

The feature extracted from the Bi-LSTM layer is taken as input of CRF layer, and then the CRF is used as a decoder to calculate the label of each element in the sequence from these features.

By using this model, we can extract the entities in the free text (see Fig. 7).

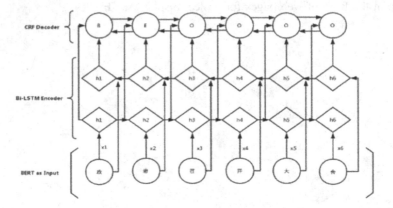

Fig. 7. The entity extraction model is shown in the figure.

Unsupervised Open Relation Extraction. Relation extraction (RE) is the task of identification and classification of relations between entities (such as persons, locations or organizations) in free text.

In the one hand, the relation ('*Subject_of*', '*Object_of*') that we defined in the triple to link verb with noun is too vague, it is not universally applicable and may cause errors. And in different sentences, a verb may express different semantics and form different semantic relations with different nouns. In the other hand, by using relation extraction to get knowledge in large scale text, we can supplement the knowledge base with information that is not included, and can further improve the quality of the data. In order to improve the accuracy of the inclusion knowledge and precisely describe the relationship between verbs and nouns, we consider to extract relations between entities from free text in an unsupervised setting. In this section, we used the methods that was designed by Elsahar, Demidova, Gottschalk, Gravier and Laforest [10].

In their work, they address a way to extract relation which is unsupervised. In addition to standard feature extraction, they develop a novel method to re-weight word embedding. Also they alleviate the problem of features sparsity using an individual feature reduction. Our approach exhibits a significant improvement by 5.8% over the state-of-the-art relation clustering scoring a F1-score of 0:416 on the NYT-FB dataset.

In this step, we use the model to extract the information in own data, the results are used to link verbs and nouns and add more information for noun. In experiment, firstly, we use the result from entity recognition, and use pyltp toolkit [11] to extract the lexicalized dependency path between each pair of entities. Then, we our own pre-trained word embedding and re-weight them according to the dependency path between the entities. After the whole process, we get the relation between entities from plain text (see Fig. 8).

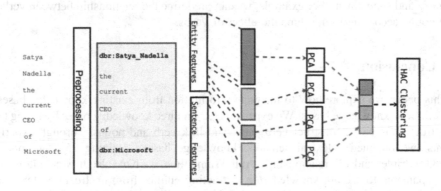

Fig. 8. System overview of relational extraction model.

4 Experimental Results and Analysis

After the process of multi-knowledge integration, we obtained a lexical semantic knowledge base containing 153754 nodes, 1598356 triples and 137 relationships. Compared with the verb part, the noun part of the knowledge base contains sufficient knowledge of words and words, and also describes the classification of words and the relationship between words. Due to the small size of the verb part and the insufficient quality of the verb knowledge, it is necessary to expand the verb part. At the same time, our approach to the connection of verbs and nouns is very rough and needs further improvement.

But there are also a large number of defects. Although the integration process of multi-source knowledge base has considerable data scale and good quality, the difference in structure makes it inevitably lose a considerable part of the information of the original knowledge base. Our build process tried to retain the original information, but still failed to fully utilize the knowledge from the three knowledge bases.

In response to the above problems, we conducted a preliminary exploration on the automatic expansion of the knowledge base. For entity recognition, we used the annotated MSRA corpus to train and test the model, and it score a F1-score of 0.9535 in average. And we use the trained model to extract entities in plain text. The result is used in next step of relation extraction. At the same time, our integration methods are very rough, and higher quality knowledge bases need to be better preprocessed, more representative relationships and data utilization. We will conduct research and manually construct the relation in our knowledge base. We will also explore better methods in the ontology classification of verbs and the connection of verbs and nouns.

In relation extraction, we extract the relation description words of given entities. This part is currently used by us to identify the relationship between nouns and to supplement the noun attributes. For the complementary aspects of the relationship between verb and nouns, we are unable to supplement by using the results of the relationship extraction. In the future, we will consider integrating more knowledge of the knowledge base to complement the missing parts. At the same time, consider to specific the definition the relationships and using a supervised neural network to identify and supplement. For example, we can predefine the relationship between verbs and nouns according to the semantic effect of verbs.

5   Conclusion

In this paper, we explore how to integrate information from existing knowledge bases to build new knowledge bases. We experimented on three knowledge bases by trying to construct noun parts, construct verb parts, and link verb and nouns. Through experiments, we obtained a lexical semantic knowledge base containing 153754 nodes, 1598356 triples and 137 relationships. At the same time, we have also tried to automate the expansion, to acquire knowledge by extracting entities from unstructured text for entity identification and relationships, and to improve the quality of the knowledge base and expand the volume of the knowledge base. The knowledge base we build this time will provide users with comprehensive and accurate semantic knowledge, which will help semantic analysis and semantic computing in natural language processing research, while supporting higher-level application research.

In the future, we will continue to expand the scale of the lexical semantic knowledge base, continue to research on the integration of more existing knowledge bases, and automatically expand the knowledge base, so that the entire knowledge base can not only expand in capacity, but also enhance the overall quality.

Acknowledgements. This research project is supported by the National Natural Science Foundation of China (61872402), the Humanities and Social Science Project of the Ministry of Education (17YJAZH068), Science Foundation of Beijing Language and Culture University (supported by "the Fundamental Research Funds for the Central Universities") (18ZDJ03), (supported by "the Fundamental Research Funds for the Central Universities", and "the Research Funds of Beijing Language and Culture University") (19YCX122).

References

1. Guo, H.: The Integration of Multiple Semantic Knowledge Bases. China Academic Journal Electronic Publishing House, HIT (2012)
2. Dong, Z., Dong, Q.: HowNet Homepage. http://www.keenage.com/. Accessed 14 May 2019
3. Mei, J., et al.: Tongyici-Cilin, 1st edn. Shanghai Dictionary Press, Shanghai (1996)
4. SKCC Homepage. http://ccl.pku.edu.cn/ccl_sem_dict/. Accessed 14 May 2019

5. Sun, D., Kang, S.: Development and application of modern Chinese verb semantic knowledge dictionary. J. Chin. Inf. Process. **32**(10), 19–27 (2018)
6. Wang, H., Yu, S., Zhan, W.: New progress of the semantic knowledgebase of contemporary Chinese (SKCC). In: The 7th National Joint Conference on Computational Linguistics, pp. 351–256. China Academic Journal Electronic Publishing House, Harbin (2003)
7. Xu, Z., Sheng, Y., He, L., Wang, Y.: Review on knowledge graph techniques. J. Univ. Electron. Sci. Technol. China **45**(04), 589–606 (2016)
8. Neo4j Homepage. https://neo4j.com. Accessed 14 May 2019
9. Devlin, J., Chang, M.-W., Lee, K., Toutanova, K.: BERT: pre-training of deep bidirectional transformers for language understanding. arXiv preprint arXiv:1810.04805, Google (2018)
10. Elsahar, H., Demidova, E., Gottschalk, S., Gravier, C., Laforest, F.: Unsupervised open relation extraction. In: Blomqvist, E., Hose, K., Paulheim, H., Ławrynowicz, A., Ciravegna, F., Hartig, O. (eds.) ESWC 2017. LNCS, vol. 10577, pp. 12–16. Springer, Cham (2017). https://doi.org/10.1007/978-3-319-70407-4_3
11. Che, W., Li, Z., Liu, T.: LTP: a Chinese language technology platform. In: Proceedings of the Coling 2010. Demonstrations, Beijing, pp. 13–16 (2010)

A Survey of Question Answering over Knowledge Base

Peiyun Wu[✉], Xiaowang Zhang[✉], and Zhiyong Feng

College of Intelligence and Computing, Tianjin Key Laboratory of Cognitive
Computing and Application, Tianjin University, Tianjin 300350, China
{wupeiyun,xiaowangzhang,zyfeng}@tju.edu.cn

Abstract. Question Answering over Knowledge Base (KBQA) is a
problem that a natural language question can be answered in knowledge
bases accurately and concisely. The core task of KBQA is to understand
the real semantics of a natural language question and extract it to match
in the whole semantics of a knowledge base. However, it is exactly a big
challenge due to variable semantics of natural language questions in a
real world. Recently, there are more and more out-of-shelf approaches
of KBQA in many applications. It becomes interesting to compare and
analyze them so that users could choose well. In this paper, we give a
survey of KBQA approaches by classifying them in two categories. Following the two categories, we introduce current mainstream techniques
in KBQA, and discuss similarities and differences among them. Finally,
based on this discussion, we outlook some interesting open problems.

Keywords: KBQA · Semantic parsing · Information retrieval

1 Introduction

Information technology is developing rapidly, how to accurately extract from
the large-scale information has become the goal of people, and question answer-
ing(QA) system is becoming one of the important research directions. In the
1960s, QA system was mainly expert system, which relied on lots of rules or
templates. With the development of technology, QA system turned to be the
research based on information retrieval. QA system based on retrieval relies on
keyword matching and information extraction to analyze shallow semantics and
extract answers from relevant documents. However, only the questions need to
be predefined can obtain the answers. In order to deal with this shortcoming,
large-scale commercial engines have been developed. This kind of community
QA system is based on keyword matching retrieval, relying on historical questions from netizens and recommendation answers to new questions. In recent
years, with the growth of the World Wide Web, a large number of high-quality
data have been accumulated and carefully designed, most large-scale knowledge
bases have emerged, such as Yago [1], Yago2 [2], DBpedia [3] and Freebase [4].
Knowledge base contains a large number of structured data, natural language

© Springer Nature Singapore Pte Ltd. 2019
X. Zhu et al. (Eds.): CCKS 2019, CCIS 1134, pp. 86–97, 2019.
https://doi.org/10.1007/978-981-15-1956-7_8

questions can be mapped to the structured queries on the knowledge base. Based on the knowledge base, how to correctly understand the semantics of user's questions and find the answers to the fact retrieval matching and reasoning in the knowledge base is the KBQA.

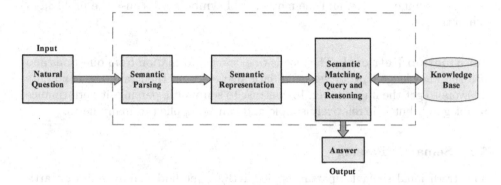

Fig. 1. The main process of KBQA.

The knowledge from knowledge base can be expressed in the form of interconnected triples like (subject, relation, object), this billions of triples are interconnected, which provides abundant resources for question answering system. Large-scale KBQA brings new opportunities and challenges to QA system. The main process of question answering in knowledge base is showed in Fig. 1. It gives natural language questions, which are first parsed into some kind of semantic representation, and then the corresponding answers are found and returned in the knowledge base through semantic matching, reasoning and query. From the perspective of application field, KBQA can be divided into open domain knowledge question answering, such as encyclopedic knowledge question answering, and specific domain knowledge question answering, such as question answering in the financial field. The traditional framework of KBQA system can be roughly divided into four modules: Question Analysis, Phrase Mapping, Disambiguation and Query Construction. At present, there are two main methods to solve the question answering over knowledge base: semantic parsing and information retrieval. In fact, there is no strict division between those two methods, they can even be used together. In coming section, we will focus on those two kinds of methods to analyze the related research and achievements in recent years.

2   Methods for KBQA

The critical problem of KBQA is to understand natural language questions and convert them into computer-understandable formal languages. The main methods of existing KBQA problem can be divided into two categories.

Semantic Parsing. It is a higher level analysis better than grammatical analysis. The main idea behind it is transform unstructured natural language questions into a series of logical forms. Through bottom-up analysis of the logical forms, the logical forms that can express semantics, i.e. expressions without ambiguity can be obtained by querying the knowledge base. But these methods are based on symbolic logic, and the matching of symbols will cause the problem of semantic gap.

Information Retrieval. The idea is to extract information from questions and use the knowledge base to get candidate answers, and then rank the candidate answers to get the final answer. In contrast to senmantic parsing, it performance is not good, but it is relatively simple and can be applied in many fields.

2.1 Semantic Parsing

The traditional semantic parsing styled KBQA method mainly relies on artificial construction rules [5], supervised learning [6], grammatical level based on classical combination category grammar (CCG) [7–14], lexical tree-adjoint grammars (LTAG) [15], etc., transforms natural language questions into logical expressions and query for knowledge base. For example, the logical language lambda calculus converts 'number of dramas starring Tom Cruise' into $count(\lambda x.Genre(x, Drama) \land \exists y.Performance(x, y) \land Actor(y, TomCruise))$, Berant et al. [6] uses the logical language Lambda Dependency-Based Compositional Semantics($\lambda - DCS$) [16] to convert natural language questions. Most of these traditional methods are not scalable and require manual labeling.

Most of the traditional semantic parsing styled methods are largely separated from the knowledge base, lexical mapping is also based on statistical methods. Yih et al. [17] proposed a novel semantic parsing framework for KBQA. The query graph is defined as a logical form that can be directly mapped to a lambda-calculus logic form. Then the semantic parsing is applied to simplify the query graph generation. Convolutional neural network(CNN) is used to improve the mapping of natural language to knowledge base relationship. This approach leverages the knowledge base in an early stage to prune the search space and thus simplifies the semantic matching problem. On the basis of advanced entity chain finger system and deep convolution neural network, the performance is state-of-the-art.

With the application and development of deep learning in many fields, such as sentiment analysis [18], machine translation [19], syntactic analysis [20], KBQA based on deep learning has gradually become one of the important research directions. In addition to Yih et al. [17] using CNN to promote traditional semantic parsing methods, seq2seq and attention mechanisms are also applied to KBQA problems. Dong et al. [21] considers that traditional methods depend on high-quality dictionaries, manually constructed templates and language features. A method based on attention-enhanced encoder-decoder model is proposed, which converts semantic analysis into seq2seq problem. The encoder-decoder model with attention mechanism is used to input natural language to obtain logical form. This paper proposes two variants of the model. The first is the Sequence-to-Sequence Model, which regards semantic analysis as a task of sequence transformation. The second is the Sequence-to-Tree Model, which is equipped with a hierarchical tree decoder, which clearly captures the structure of the logical form for translation. The main contribution of this paper is propose a data reorganization method, a new framework for injecting such prior knowledge into the model, and obtain a high-precision generation model from the training set. Dong et al. [21]'s method is mainly on the decoder side, and Xu et al. [22] thinks that syntactic features are very important for encoder. Xu et al. [22] uses a syntactic graph to represent word-order, dependency, and constituency features, and uses the graph2seq model, firstly encoding the syntactic graph using the graph encoder, and then decoding it using RNN and Attention to get the Logical Form.

All of the above methods use semantic parsing to convert natural language questions into logical forms. In addition, there are other effective methods. For example, Cui et al. [23] uses templates to represent natural language questions and solve BFQ (binary factoid questions) problems, it learns automatic learning templates from QA corpus rather than manually annotating templates. Based on these templates, their QA system KBQA effectively supports binary factoid questions, as well as complex questions which are composed of a series of binary factoid questions. The system architecture of Cui et al. [23] is mainly divided into two parts: offline procedure and online procedure. The goal of offline procedure is to learn the mapping from template to attribute. The online procedure is used for parsing, predicate inference and answer retrieval. The whole process from natural language question to generating answer can be modeled as a probability graph model. Cui et al. [23]'s QA system has two distinct differences from the previous system: first, it uses templates to understand problems; second, it learns semantic parsing from a very large QA corpus. There are other novel and interesting methods for KBQA based on semantic parsing, such as Neural symbolic machines: Learning semantics parsers on freebase with weak supervision (Liang et al. [24]) proposes Neural Symbolic Machines (see Fig. 2), first, it contains a neural programmer, such as an end-to-end model by mapping language to programs. Second, it includes a symbolic computer, such as an interpreter for Lisp that can execute programs. Experiments show that NSM only requires QA pairs for training, and does not require any feature engineering and domain knowledge

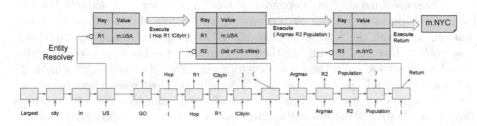

Fig. 2. Semantic parsing with neural symbolic machines.

to exceed the state-of-the-art approach on the WebQuestionsSP dataset. Talmor et al. [25] proposes to evaluate semantic parsing-based question answering models by comparing them to a question answering baseline that queries the web and extracts the answer only from web snippets, without access to the target knowledge-base. Andreas et al. [26] dynamic composite neural network module is suitable for question answering model. Firstly, different neural network modules are defined to parse the semantics, then these modules are combined for questions, and the composite model is used to answer questions.

2.2 Information Retrieval

After introducing the method based on semantic parsing, the next step is to study the KBQA based on Information Retrieval.

Simple Information Extraction. Information Extraction over Structured Data: Question Answering with Freebase (Yao et al. [27]), a representative paper of information extraction methods, regards knowledge base Freebase as a set of interrelated topics, extracts subject words in question sentences, finds neighboring hop nodes and edges centered on the corresponding entities of the subject words in the knowledge base, and extracts them as sub-graphs (subject graphs) of knowledge base. Each node and edge in the graph is regarded as a candidate answer, and then information is extracted according to some artificial rules or templates. The feature vectors representing the characteristics of the question and candidate answer are obtained. The classifier is established and the feature vectors are input to filter the candidate answer, and the correct answer is obtained.

The process of extracting information from natural language questions is the transformation from dependency tree to problem,three operations are carried out.

(1) Add question word (qword), question focus (qfocus), question verb (qverb) and question topic (qtopic) as corresponding nodes.
(2) If the node is a named entity, then the node is changed into a named entity form.
(3) Delete unimportant leaf nodes, such as punctuation marks.

The transformation from dependency tree to question is to extract the feature of the question related to the answer and delete the unimportant information. Although the method in this paper has great advantages in knowledge base such as Freebase, it still has the disadvantage of being unable to deal with complex questions. With the rapid development of word embedding technology, the research on KBQA has been greatly improved. Most researchers have conducted deep research on the introduction of word embedding [28–30], such as Bordes et al. uses subgraph embedding (see Fig. 3) to solve KBQA problems. The following are all methods that incorporate word embedding techniques with different ways'.

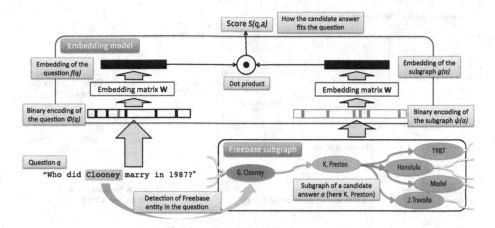

Fig. 3. Subgraph embedding model.

Seq2Seq with CNN. Dong et al. [31] proposed an automatic question-and-answer model based on Freebase, using multi-column convolutional neural networks (MCCNNs) to extract features and classifications without using any manual features and vocabulary. The model considers the matching degree between questions and answers from different aspects. One is the type of answer, the other is the context of the answer, and the other is the path between the answer and the main entity. In the expression of questions, three convolutional neural networks are used to learn the semantic representation of questions separately. At the same time, the information of answer type, answer context and answer path of candidate answers are presented separately in the knowledge base, and their distributed representations are learned. The similarity between the three convolutional neural networks and the vector representation of questions is calculated, and the scores are provided. The error analysis of the model is also carried out, which is mainly caused by Candidate Generation, Time-Aware Questions and Ambiguous Questions. The model takes full account of all kinds of information of candidate answers and achieves good results based on deep learning. Some breakthroughs can be made in error analysis for the author later's work.

Seq2Seq with Attention. The use of the attention mechanism has become an effective method to solve the KBQA problem. Golub et al. [32] not only introduces the attention mechanism but also solves the KBQA problem from character-level. Golub et al. [32] is different from the previous method, it no longer uses the word-level encoder and decoder, but starts with character-level, proposes a character-level encoder-decoder framework, and introduces the attention mechanism to effectively improve the OOV (out-of-vocabulary) problem in QA system. The entire framework (see Fig. 4) is divided into three parts: Question encoder, Entity and Predicate encoder and KB query decoder. The core of the information retrieval styled method lies in the distributed expression of

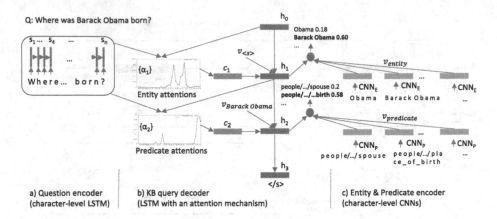

Fig. 4. Character-level encoder-decoder framework.

the learning problem and the candidate answer. The idea of Zhang et al. [33] is that for different answers, the focus of the problem is different. According to the information of the candidate answers, the candidate answers are converted into distributed expressions, the natural language problems are transformed into distributed expressions, and attention is introduced in the score function.

Hao et al. [34] believes that the previous work did not emphasize the problem expression, and the question, regardless of its candidate answer, will be converted into a fixed-length vector. This simple expression is difficult to express the information inside the problem. Therefore, Hao et al. [34] proposes an end-to-end neural network model to dynamically express problems and their scores from the level of problem candidate answers through the cross-attention mechanism. Experiments on WebQuestions demonstrate the effectiveness of the proposed algorithm.

Information Retrieval with Memory. Using more complex memory network is a promising way to solve KBQA based on deep learning. Memory network [35] has a strong expansibility. Each module of memory network has a lot of room for improvement. It is a very suitable framework for deep learning of KBQA. Bordes et al. [36] initially tried to apply memory network to KBQA problem. Simple Question Answering is a problem that only depends on one knowledge triple. Bordes et al. [36] considered that the present KBQA method still has difficulties in solving Simple Question Answering. Therefore, a larger simple problem data set SimpleQuestions was constructed, and each problem of the data set depends on the knowledge triple. According to a knowledge triple knowledge, it constructs the problem manually. This method first stores the knowledge in the knowledge base into the memory network. Secondly, QA-pairs is used to train the memory network. The input module processes the data and transforms the questions into distributed expressions. The output module chooses a supporting memory with the highest relevance to the questions. The answer module outputs the object corresponding to the triple as the final answer. Finally, the generalization module is used to test the generalization ability of the network.

Based on the work of Bordes et al. [36], Jain [37] has designed a new framework of memory-based network, using QA-pairs as training set for end-to-end training, instead of strong supervision in the form of (question, associated facts in KB) pairs. The system of Jain [37] generate distributed representation of questions and KB in same word vector space, extract a subset of initial candidate facts, then try to find a path to answer entity using multi-hop reasoning and refinement.

There are many other ideas for solving KBQA problems based on vector modeling methods. For example, Türe et al. [38] represents tasks as two machine learning problems:detecting entities in the question, and classifying the question as one of the relation types in the KB, Türe et al. [38] trains a recurrent neural network to solve each problem. Qu et al. [39] proposed an attentive recurrent neural network with similarity matrix based convolutional neural network (AR-SMCNN) model, which is able to capture comprehensive hierarchical information utilizing the advantages of both Recurrent Neural Network and Convolutional Neural Network. Yu et al. [40] proposed a text matching relationship detection model (HR-BiLSTM, Hierarchical Residual-BiLSTM) based on different granularity and applied to KBQA problem. Serban et al. [41] uses GRU recurrent neural network combined with attention mechanism to automatically generate questions, etc.

3 Discussion

Through the research and discussion of the above work, we can discover that KBQA still faces many difficulties and challenges.

Semantic Gap. To complete the mapping from natural sentences to knowledge base, entity links and relationships extraction are the key steps. If the quality of entity links stage is not high, errors may be transmitted to the relationship extraction stage, resulting in the mismatch between sentences and knowledge base, which has a great impact on the final results. For example, Yih et al. [17] pointed out the importance of entity link and relationship extraction in error analysis. Although there are many ways to alleviate the semantic gap, the research on the basic steps of entity link and relationship extraction is still not deep enough.

Complex Problem. Complex problems generally contain two or more relationships or constraints, e.g, "From what country is the winner of the Australian Open women's singles 2008?". The existing knowledge base question answering system is simple in question. A lot of progress has been made in the answer, but the study of complex issues remains a challenge. Bao et al. [42] releases a new data-set ComplexQuestions to tackle 'multi-constraint' questions. Abujabal et al. [43] tries to solve the parallel complex questions, but still can't answer most of the complex questions. Research and processing of complex issues requires researchers and scholars to continue deeping.

Data Set. At present, the data sets used are simple fact questions, such as artificial knowledge base Freebase or knowledge base acquired by automatic extraction, such as Chen et al. [44] using Wikipedia as knowledge source for KBQA, but the corpus of these knowledge bases is not rich enough. How to acquire or build a higher quality and richer knowledge base is a difficult problem.

The construction of question answering system in knowledge base is a difficult problem, which involves various techniques in natural language processing, such as relation extraction, parsing, etc. With the deepening and continuous optimization of machine learning and deep learning, there is still a long way to go to build a mature question answering system and give high accuracy answers to natural language questions. Vectorization is an effective way to solve natural language processing. Through the research and analysis of KBQA two kinds of methods, it can be found that by introducing word embedding vectorization, knowledge base question answering has been significantly improved. By transforming natural language into computer processable vector, combining deep learning, network and so on, the field of knowledge base question answering will have more far-reaching development.

4   Conclusion

This paper gives an overview about question answering over knowledge base, introduces the advanced methods of semantic parsing and information retrieval, and analysis the difficulties and shortcomings of these methods, which highlight the future direction. Although the existing knowledge base question answering is still weak in dealing with complex problems, and there are some problems such as mismatch between sentences and contents of knowledge base. With the development of technology and the unremitting research of scientific researchers, it is full of hope to solve the problem of knowledge base question answering.

Acknowledgments. This work is supported by the National Key Research and Development Program of China (2017YFC0908401) and the National Natural Science Foundation of China (61672377). Xiaowang Zhang is supported by the program of Peiyang Young Scholars in Tianjin University (2019XRX-0032).

References

1. Suchanek, F.M., Kasneci, G., Weikum, G.: YAGO: a core of semantic knowledge. In: Proceedings of WWW, pp. 697–706. ACM, Alberta (2007)
2. Hoffart, J., Suchanek, F.M., Berberich, K., Weikum, G.: YAGO2: a spatially and temporally enhanced knowledge base from Wikipedia. Artif. Intell. **194**, 28–61 (2013)

3. Auer, S., Bizer, C., Kobilarov, G., Lehmann, J., Cyganiak, R., Ives, Z.: DBpedia: a nucleus for a web of open data. In: Aberer, K., et al. (eds.) ASWC/ISWC -2007. LNCS, vol. 4825, pp. 722–735. Springer, Heidelberg (2007). https://doi.org/10.1007/978-3-540-76298-0_52
4. Bollacker, K.D., Evans, C., Paritosh, P., Sturge, T., Taylor, J.: Freebase: a collaboratively created graph database for structuring human knowledge. In: Proceedings of SIGMOD, pp. 1247–1250. ACM, Vancouver (2008)
5. Tunstall-Pedoe, W.: True knowledge: open-domain question answering using structured knowledge and inference. AI Mag. **31**(3), 80–92 (2010)
6. Berant, J., Chou, A., Frostig, R., Liang, P.: Semantic parsing on freebase from question-answer pairs. In: Proceedings of EMNLP, pp. 1533–1544. ACL, Seattle (2013)
7. Reddy, S., Lapata, M., Steedman, M.: Large-scale semantic parsing without question-answer pairs. TACL **2**, 377–392 (2014)
8. Kwiatkowski, T., Zettlemoyer, L.S., Goldwater, S., Steedman, M.: Lexical generalization in CCG grammar induction for semantic parsing. In: Proceedings of EMNLP, pp. 1512–1523. ACL, Edinburgh (2011)
9. Zettlemoyer, L.S., Collins, M.: Learning to map sentences to logical form: structured classification with probabilistic categorial grammars. CoRR abs/1207.1420 (2012)
10. Hakimov, S., Unger, C., Walter, S., Cimiano, P.: Applying semantic parsing to question answering over linked data: addressing the lexical gap. In: Biemann, C., Handschuh, S., Freitas, A., Meziane, F., Métais, E. (eds.) NLDB 2015. LNCS, vol. 9103, pp. 103–109. Springer, Cham (2015). https://doi.org/10.1007/978-3-319-19581-0_8
11. Zettlemoyer, L.S., Collins, M.: Online learning of relaxed CCG grammars for parsing to logical form. In: Proceedings of EMNLP, pp. 678–687. ACL, Prague (2013)
12. Zettlemoyer, L.S., Collins, M.: Learning context-dependent mappings from sentences to logical form. In: Proceedings of ACL, pp. 976–984. The Association for Computer Linguistics, Singapore (2009)
13. Krishnamurthy, J., Mitchell, T, M.: Weakly supervised training of semantic parsers. In: Proceedings of EMNLP, pp. 754–765. ACL, Jeju Island (2012)
14. Cai, Q., Yates, A.: Large-scale semantic parsing via schema matching and lexicon extension. In: Proceedings of ACL, pp. 423–433. The Association for Computer Linguistics, Sofia (2013)
15. Unger, C., Bühmann, L., Lehmann, J., Ngomo, A.N., Gerber, D., Cimiano, P.: Template-based question answering over RDF data. In: Proceedings of WWW, pp. 639–648. ACM, Lyon (2012)
16. Liang, P.: Lambda dependency-based compositional semantics. CoRR abs/1309.4408 (2013)
17. Yih, W., Chang, M., He, X., Gao, J.: Semantic parsing via staged query graph generation: question answering with knowledge base. In: Proceedings of ACL, Beijing, China, pp. 1321–1331 (2015)
18. Socher, R., et al.: Recursive deep models for semantic compositionality over a sentiment treebank. In: Proceedings of EMNLP, pp. 1631–1642. ACL, Seattle (2013)
19. Cho, K., et al.: Learning phrase representations using RNN encoder-decoder for statistical machine translation. In: Proceedings of EMNLP, Doha, Qatar, pp. 1724–1734 (2014)
20. Socher, R., Manning, C.D., Ng, A.Y.: Learning continuous phrase representations and syntactic parsing with recursive neural networks. In: Proceedings of NIPS-2010 Deep Learning and Unsupervised Feature Learning Workshop, pp. 1–9 (2010)

21. Dong, L., Lapata, M.: Language to logical form with neural attention. In: Proceedings of ACL, Berlin, Germany (2016)
22. Xu, K., Wu, L., Wang, Z., Yu, M., Chen, L., Sheinin, V.: Exploiting rich syntactic information for semantic parsing with graph-to-sequence model. In: Proceedings of EMNLP, Brussels, Belgium, pp. 918–924 (2018)
23. Cui, W., Xiao, Y., Wang, H., Song, Y., Hwang, S., Wang, W.: KBQA: learning question answering over QA corpora and knowledge bases. PVLDB **10**(5), 576–576 (2017)
24. Liang, C., Berant, J., Le, Q.V., Forbus, K.D., Lao, N.: Neural symbolic machines: learning semantic parsers on freebase with weak supervision. In: Proceedings of ACL, Canada, pp. 23–33 (2017)
25. Talmor, A., Geva, M., Berant, J.: Evaluating semantic parsing against a simple web-based question answering model. In: Proceedings of STARSEM, Vancouver, Canada, pp. 161–167 (2017)
26. Andreas, J., Rohrbach, M., Darrell, T., Klein, D.: Learning to compose neural networks for question answering. In: Proceedings of NAACL, San Diego, California, USA, pp. 1545–1554 (2016)
27. Yao, X., Durme, B.V.: Information extraction over structured data: question answering with freebase. In: Proceedings of ACL, MD, USA, pp. 956–966 (2014)
28. Bordes, A., Chopra, S., Weston, J.: Question answering with subgraph embeddings. In: Proceedings of EMNLP, Doha, Qatar, pp. 615–620 (2014)
29. Bordes, A., Weston, J., Usunier, N.: Open question answering with weakly supervised embedding models. In: Calders, T., Esposito, F., Hüllermeier, E., Meo, R. (eds.) ECML PKDD 2014. LNCS (LNAI), vol. 8724, pp. 165–180. Springer, Heidelberg (2014). https://doi.org/10.1007/978-3-662-44848-9_11
30. Yang, M., Duan, N., Zhou, M., Rim, H.: Joint relational embeddings for knowledge-based question answering. In: Proceedings of EMNLP, Doha, Qatar, pp. 645–650 (2014)
31. Dong, L., Wei, F., Zhou, M., Xu, K.: Question answering over freebase with multi-column convolutional neural networks. In: Proceedings of EMNLP, Doha, Qatar, pp. 645–650 (2014)
32. Golub, D., He, X.: Character-Level question answering with attention. CoRR abs/1604.00727 (2016)
33. Zhang, Y., et al.: Question answering over knowledge base with neural attention combining global knowledge information. CoRR abs/1606.00979 (2016)
34. Hao, Y., et al.: An end-to-end model for question answering over knowledge base with cross-attention combining global knowledge. In: Proceedings of ACL, Vancouver, Canada, pp. 221–231 (2017)
35. Weston, J., Chopra, S., Bordes, A.: Memory networks. In: Proceedings of ICLR, San Diego, USA (2015)
36. Bordes, A., Usunier, N., Chopra, S., Weston, J.: Large-scale simple question answering with memory networks. CoRR abs/1506.02075 (2015)
37. Jain, S.: Question answering over knowledge base using factual memory networks. In: Proceedings of NAACL, pp. 109–115, San Diego, California, USA (2016)
38. Türe, F., Jojic, O.: No need to pay attention: simple recurrent neural networks work! In: Proceedings of EMNLP, Copenhagen, Denmark, pp. 2866–2872 (2017)
39. Qu, Y., Liu, J., Kang, L.: Question answering over freebase via attentive RNN with similarity matrix based CNN. CoRR abs/1506.02075 (2018)
40. Yu, M., Yin, W., Hasan, K.S., Santos, C.N., Xiang, B., Zhou, B.: Improved neural relation detection for knowledge base question answering. In: Proceedings of ACL, Vancouver, Canada, pp. 571–581 (2017)

41. Serban, I.V., et al.: Generating factoid questions with recurrent neural networks: the 30M factoid question-answer corpus. In: Proceedings of ACL, Berlin, Germany (2016)
42. Bao, J., Duan, N., Yan, Z., Zhou, M., Zhao, T.: Constraint-based question answering with knowledge graph. In: Proceedings of COLING, Osaka, Japan, pp. 2503–2514 (2016)
43. Abujabal, A., Yahya, M., Riedewald, M., Weikum, G.: Automated template generation for question answering over knowledge graphs. In: Proceedings of WWW, Perth, Australia, pp. 1191–1200 (2017)
44. Chen, D., Fisch, A., Weston, J., Bordes, A.: Reading Wikipedia to answer open-domain questions. In: Proceedings of ACL, Vancouver, Canada, pp. 1870–1879 (2017)

Fast Neural Chinese Named Entity Recognition with Multi-head Self-attention

Tao Qi[1]([✉]), Chuhan Wu[1], Fangzhao Wu[2], Suyu Ge[1], Junxin Liu[1], Yongfeng Huang[1], and Xing Xie[2]

[1] Department of Electronic Engineering,
Tsinghua University, Beijing 100084, China
{qit16,wuch15,gesy17,ljx16,yfhuang}@mails.tsinghua.edu.cn
[2] Microsoft Research Asia, Beijing 100080, China
fangzwu@microsoft.com, xing.xie@microsoft.com

Abstract. Named entity recognition (NER) is an important task in natural language processing. It is an essential step for many downstream tasks, such as relation extraction and entity linking which are important for knowledge graph building and application. Existing neural NER methods are usually based on the LSTM-CRF framework and its variants. However, since the LSTM network has high time complexity to compute, the efficiency of these LSTM-CRF based NER methods is usually unsatisfactory. In this paper, we propose a fast neural NER model for Chinese texts. Our approach is based on the CNN-SelfAttention-CRF architecture, where the convolutional neural network (CNN) is used to learn contextual character representations from local contexts, the multi-head self-attention network is used to learn contextual character representations from global contexts, and the conditional random fields (CRF) is used to jointly decode the labels of characters in a sentence. Since both CNN and self-attention network can be computed in parallel, our approach can have higher efficiency than those LSTM-CRF based methods. Extensive experiments on two benchmark datasets validate that our approach is more efficient than existing neural NER methods and can achieve comparable or even better performance on Chinese NER.

Keywords: Named entity recognition · Neural network · Multi-head self-attention

1 Introduction

Named entity recognition (NER) aims to extract named entities from the texts and classify them into different categories, such as person, location and organization. For example, in the sentence "阿里准备去阿里工作" (Ali plans to work for Alibaba), NER task aims to recognize the first "阿里" as a person entity and the second "阿里" as an organization entity. NER is an important task in natural

X. Zhu et al. (Eds.): CCKS 2019, CCIS 1134, pp. 98–110, 2019.
https://doi.org/10.1007/978-981-15-1956-7_9

language processing field and a prerequisite for many downstream applications, such as entity linking [9] and relation extraction [16], both of which are very important for building and applying knowledge graphs. Thus, NER task has attracted increasing attentions in recent years [5,12,29]. In this paper we focus on named entity recognition for Chinese texts.

In recent years, deep learning based approaches have been widely used in NER [3,8,14,17,22]. These methods are usually based on the LSTM-CRF architecture and its variants. For example, Lample et al. [14] proposed a neural NER approach based on LSTM-CRF, where LSTM was used to learn contextual word representations from sentences and CRF was used to capture the dependencies between word labels for jointly label decoding. Chiu et al. [3] proposed an approach based on CNN-LSTM-CRF architecture, where the CNN network was used to learn word representations from characters. Peters et al. [22] proposed a semi-supervised NER approach named TagLM based on the CNN-LSTMs-CRF architecture. They propose to incorporate the contextual word vectors from a pre-trained language model into their model to enhance the word representations. Different from English texts, there is no explicit delimiter such as space to separate words in Chinese texts. Thus, Chinese NER is usually modeled as a character-level sequence tagging problem [1,2,21,29]. For example, Peng et al. [21] proposed a neural Chinese NER approach based on LSTM-CRF architecture, where the LSTM network was used to learn contextual character representations from sentences and the CRF was used to capture the dependencies between neighbouring labels for label decoding. However, the time complexity of computing LSTM network is very high. In addition, it cannot be computed in parallel and is difficult to benefit from the acceleration via GPU [10]. Thus, the efficiency of these LSTM-CRF based NER methods is usually unsatisfactory [24].

In this paper, we propose a fast neural NER approach for Chinese texts which is based on the CNN-SelfAttention-CRF architecture. The CNN network in our approach is used to capture local contexts to learn contextual character representations, since local contexts are very important for Chinese NER. For example, we can easily infer that the character "中" is a location entity in "中美关系很重要" (The relationship between China and America is very important) and is not an entity in "我在两楼中间" (I am in the middle of two buildings) according to its local contexts such as "美" and "间". The multi-head self-attention network in our approach is used to capture global contexts to learn contextual character representations, since global contexts also have important influence on NER. For example, in the two sentences "阿里是一个有名的公司" (Ali is a famous company) and "阿里是一个有名的拳击手" (Ali is a famous boxer), only by capturing the global contexts can we infer that "阿里" is an organization entity in the first sentence and is a person entity in the second sentence. The CRF in our approach is used to jointly decode the labels of characters in the same sentence, since there are strong dependencies between neighbouring character labels. In our approach, both the CNN network and the multi-head self-attention network can be computed in parallel. Thus, our NER model can be computed efficiently.

We conduct extensive experiments on two benchmark datasets. The experimental results validate that our approach can effectively improve the efficiency of Chinese named entity recognition, and can achieve comparable or even better performance than existing methods.

The rest of this paper is organized as follows.In the Sect. 2, we present a literature review on NER methods. In the Sect. 3, we introduce our fast neural Chinese NER model in detail.In the Sect. 4, we present the experimental results and analysis. In the Sect. 5, we make a conclusion for this paper.

2   Related Work

Named entity recognition is an important task in natural language field and has attached increasing attentions in recent years [5,7,8]. Traditional NER methods are usually based on machine learning methods, such as Support Vector Machine (SVM) [13], Hidden Markov Models (HMM) [23,26] and Conditional Random Fields (CRF) [19,23,27]. SVM based approaches usually model NER task as a multi-classification problem. For example, Kudoh [13] proposed to use SVM with n-grams, part-of-speech (POS) tags and previous labels as features. However, SVM cannot capture global contextual information and model the dependencies between neighbouring labels. HMM and CRF usually model NER task as sequence tagging problem. For example, Ratinov et al. [23] proposed to use HMM with n-grams, gazetteers and word semantic classification results as features. Passos et al. [19] proposed a NER approach based on CRF. They combined n-grams, lexicon features and word types as input features. However, the performance of these machine learning based methods are usually influenced by the qualities of the input features, which are usually very time-consuming and expensive to design.

With the development of deep learning, many neural network based approaches are proposed for NER [6,8,20,26]. For example, Lample et al. [14] proposed an LSTM-CRF based approach. They used the LSTM network to learn contextual word representations from global contexts and CRF layer to jointly decode labels in a sentence. Chiu et al. [3] proposed a neural NER approach based on CNN-LSTM-CRF architecture, where the network was used to learn word representations from characters. Peters et al. [22] proposed the TagLm based on CNN-LSTMs-CRF architecture with contextual word representations generated by the pre-trained language model. However, different from English texts, there is no explicit delimiter in the Chinese texts. Thus, Chinese NER is usually modeled as a sequence tagging problem [1,2,21,28,29]. For example, Peng et al. [21] proposed a neural Chinese NER approach based on LSTM-CRF architecture, where the LSTM network was used to learn contextual character representations from global contexts and the CRF layer was used to jointly decode labels. These popular neural NER methods are usually based on the LSTM-CRF architecture. However, the LSTM network cannot be computed efficiently and the efficiency of these models are usually unsatisfactory [10,24]. Different from existing neural approaches, our approach is based on CNN-SelfAttention-CRF architecture, where the CNN network is used to capture local contexts to learn contextual character representations, the multi-head self-attention network is used to capture global contexts to learn contextual character representations and the CRF layer is used to capture the dependencies between labels to jointly decode labels in a sentence. In this way, our model can be computed efficiently since the CNN network and the self-attention network can be computed in parallel. Extensive experiments on two benchmark datasets validate that our approach is efficient for Chinese NER task and can outperform many baseline methods.

3   Our Approach

In this section, we introduce our approach for fast Chinese named entity recognition based on the CNN-SelfAttention-CRF architecture (named *CSAC*). The framework of our approach is illustrated in Fig. 1. There are three major modules in our *CSAC* model, i.e., *local contexts extractor*, *global contexts extractor*, and *label decoder*. Next we introduce each module in detail.

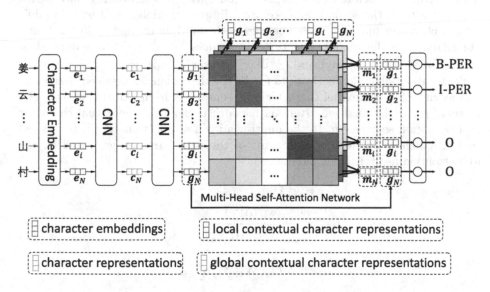

Fig. 1. The architecture of our *CSAC* model for Chinese NER.

The first module is *local contexts extractor*. It is used to learn local contextual character representations from local contexts. There are two components in this module. The first one is a character embedding layer. Denote the input sentence s as $[q_1, q_2, ..., q_N]$, where q_i denotes the i-th character and N is the length of the sentence. It is transformed into a low-dimensional dense vector sequence $[e_1, e_2, ..., e_N]$ via a character embedding matrix $E \in R^{D_c \times V_c}$, where D_c is the dimension of character embeddings and V_c is the size of character vocabulary. The second component is a two-layer convolutional neural network (CNN) [15], which is used to capture local contextual information. Local contextual information is very important for Chinese NER. For example, given two sentences, "中美关系很重要" (The relationship between China and America is very important) and "我站在两栋楼中间" (I am in the middle between two buildings), we can easily infer "中" is a location entity in the first sentence according to its local context, i.e., "美" but not in the second sentence according to its local context, i.e., "'间". Thus, we employ a two-layer CNN network to learn local contextual character representations in our approach. The input of the CNN network is the sequence of character embeddings and the output of the CNN network is the sequence of local contextual character representations, denoted as $\mathbf{g} = [\mathbf{g}_1, \mathbf{g}_2, ..., \mathbf{g}_N]$.

The second module is *global contexts extractor*. It is a multi-head self-attention network, which is used to learn global contextual character representations from global contexts. Usually, global contexts are very useful for Chinese NER. For example, given two similar sentences, "阿里是一个有名的公司" (Ali is a famous company) and "阿里是一个有名的拳击手" (Ali is a famous boxer), "阿里" (Ali) is recognized as an organization entity in the first sentence and a person entity in the second sentence according to its global contexts. In addition, a character may have dependencies with multiple characters in the texts. For example, in the two aforementioned sentences, "阿里" (Ali) have dependencies with "公司" (company) and "拳击手" (boxer). Thus, we propose to use a multi-head self-attention network to model the dependencies between characters and learn global contextual character representations from global contexts. The input of the multi-head self-attention network is the local contextual character representation sequence $\mathbf{g}$. In the multi-head self-attention network, the global contextual character representation $\mathbf{m}_j^i$ of the j-th character generated by the i-th attention head, is formulated as:

$$\hat{\alpha}_{j,k}^i = \mathbf{g}_j^T \mathbf{U}_i \mathbf{g}_k,$$
$$\alpha_{j,k}^i = \frac{\exp(\hat{\alpha}_{j,k}^i)}{\sum_{n=1}^N \exp(\hat{\alpha}_{j,n}^i)}, \tag{1}$$
$$\hat{\mathbf{m}}_j^i = ReLU(\mathbf{W}_i(\sum_{n=1}^N \alpha_{j,n}^i \mathbf{g}_n)),$$

where $\alpha_{j,k}^i$ denotes the relative importance of the k-th character to the j-th character according to the i-th self-attention head, and $\mathbf{U}_i$ and $\mathbf{W}_i$ are the trainable parameters of the i-th attention head. The global contextual character representation of the j-th character is the concatenation of the representation vectors generated by K separate self-attention heads, denoted as $\mathbf{m}_j = [\mathbf{m}_j^1; \mathbf{m}_j^2; ...; \mathbf{m}_j^K]$. In this way, the global contextual information can be incorporated into our model through modeling the dependencies between characters. The output of the multi-head self-attention network is the sequence of global contextual character representations, denoted as $\mathbf{m} = [\mathbf{m}_1, \mathbf{m}_2, ..., \mathbf{m}_N]$.

The third module is *label decoder*. There are two major components in this module. The first one is a feature concatenation layer. The output of this layer is a contextual character representation sequence **h** which is the concatenation of the local contextual character representations and global contextual character representations and denoted as $\mathbf{h} = [\mathbf{h}_1, \mathbf{h}_2, ..., \mathbf{h}_N]$, where $\mathbf{h}_i = [\mathbf{g}_i; \mathbf{m}_i]$. In this way, both local and global contextual information is extracted and incorporated into our *label decoder*. The second component is a CRF layer. There usually exist dependencies between neighbouring labels. For example, the label "I-PER" cannot be the succeed of the label "B-LOC", where "I-PER" denotes the inside of the person entity, "B-LOC" denotes the beginning of the location entity. Thus, we employ a CRF layer to capture these dependencies. Denote Y_s as the set of all possible label sequences and **y** as a possible label sequence which belongs to Y_s. Then the score of the label sequence **y** with the input contextual character representation sequence **h** is formulated as:

$$m(\mathbf{y}, \mathbf{h}) = \sum_{i=1}^{N} \mathbf{L}_{i,y_i} + \sum_{i=1}^{N-1} \mathbf{T}_{y_i, y_{i+1}},$$

$$\mathbf{L}_i = \mathbf{W}_C \mathbf{h}_i + \mathbf{b}_C, \tag{2}$$

where $m(\mathbf{y}, \mathbf{h})$ is the overall score of label sequence **y** corresponding to **h**, $\mathbf{L}_{i,y_i}$ is the local score of assigning label y_i to the i-th character, $\mathbf{T}_{y_i, y_{i+1}}$ is the transition score of two neighbouring labels, and $\mathbf{W}_C, \mathbf{b}_C, \mathbf{T}$ are trainable parameters of the CRF layer. The probability of label sequence **y** is formulated as:

$$p(\mathbf{y}|s) = \frac{\exp(m(\mathbf{y}, \mathbf{h}_s))}{\sum\limits_{\mathbf{y}' \in Y_s} \exp(m(\mathbf{y}', \mathbf{h}_s))}, \tag{3}$$

where $\mathbf{h}_s$ is the contextual character representation sequence of the input sentence s. The loss function of our NER model is formulated as:

$$\mathcal{L}_{NER} = -\sum_{s \in \mathcal{S}} \log p(\mathbf{y}|s), \tag{4}$$

where $\mathcal{S}$ is the labeled dataset. In this way, our approach can effectively capture both local and global contexts and recognize entities from Chinese texts effectively. In addition, since both the CNN network and the multi-head self-attention network can be computed in parallel, our approach can also recognize entities in an efficient way.

4   Experiment

4.1   Dataset and Experimental Settings

Our experiments were conducted on two benchmark datasets. The first one is the *Bakeoff-3* released by the third SIGHAN Chinese language processing bakeoff[1].

---

[1] http://sighan.cs.uchicago.edu/bakeoff2006/download.html.

This dataset contains 50,729 sentences which are divided into a training dataset including 46,364 sentences and a test dataset including 4,365 sentences. The second one is the *Bakeoff-4* released by the fourth SIGHAN Chinese language processing bakeoff[2]. *Bakeoff-4* contains 23,181 sentences in the training set and 4,636 sentences in the test set. Both of the two datasets contain three different entity categories, i.e., person, location and organization.

Following previous works [2], we employ BIOE tagging scheme in our experiments. In this scheme, B, I, E and O represent the beginning, inside, end, and outside of an entity respectively. In order to evaluate the effectiveness of our approach in recognizing entities, we employ micro precision, recall and F1 score as the evaluation metrics in our experiments. In order to evaluate the efficiency of our approach in recognizing entities, we employ the time of training models and predicting labels as the evaluation metrics.

In our experiments, the character embeddings were pre-trained on Sogou CA corpus[3] via word2vec [18], whose dimension is 200. Both of the two CNN networks contain 512 filters. Our multi-head self-attention network contains 4 self-attention head and the dimension of the output vector of each self-attention head is set to 128. In order to reduce over-fitting, we employ dropout technique [25] on the output of the character embedding layer, the CNN network and the multi-head self-attention network with 0.2 dropout probability. We use Adam optimizer [11] to train our model and the learning rate is set to 0.0001. The batch set is set to 64. All these the hyper-parameters are selected on validation set. We repeat each experiment four times and report the average results.

4.2 Performance Evaluation

We compare our approach with several baseline methods to evaluate the effectiveness and efficiency of our approach in recognizing entities. The baseline methods are listed as follows:

- *CNN-Softmax*: using the CNN network to learn local contextual character representations and softmax to decode labels.
- *CNN-CRF* [4]: using the CNN network to learn local contextual character representations and CRF layer to jointly decode labels.
- *LSTM-Softmax*: using the LSTM network to learn global contextual character representations and softmax to decode labels.
- *LSTM-CRF* [21]: using the LSTM network to learn global contextual character representations and CRF layer to jointly decode labels.

We conduct extensive experiments on two benchmark datasets. The experimental results are listed in the Tables 1 and 2. According to the experimental results, we have several observations.

First, the baseline methods based on the LSTM network outperform the baseline methods based on the CNN network with the same layer to decode

---

[2] https://www.aclweb.org/mirror/ijcnlp08/sighan6/chinesebakeoff.htm.
[3] https://www.sogou.com/labs/resource/ca.php.

Table 1. Performance of different methods on two benchmark datasets.

	Bakeoff-3			Bakeoff-4		
	P	R	F1	P	R	F1
CNN-Softmax	38.56 ± 1.41	56.87 ± 2.45	45.96 ± 1.8	40.81 ± 0.39	59.21 ± 1.0	48.31 ± 0.06
CNN-CRF	83.62 ± 0.14	79.98 ± 0.74	81.76 ± 0.32	85.22 ± 0.11	83.55 ± 0.10	84.37 ± 0.10
LSTM-Softmax	78.38 ± 0.17	82.46 ± 0.11	80.37 ± 0.04	79.38 ± 0.33	85.51 ± 0.71	82.33 ± 0.51
LSTM-CRF	**88.77 ± 0.67**	81.80 ± 0.70	85.14 ± 0.07	**87.01 ± 1.01**	86.12 ± 0.64	86.57 ± 0.16
CSAC	87.59 ± 0.36	**86.37 ± 0.28**	**86.97 ± 0.09**	86.56 ± 0.41	**88.12 ± 0.11**	**87.34 ± 0.16**

Table 2. The time complexity of different methods in training and prediction on two benchmark datasets.

	Bakeoff-3		Bakeoff-4	
	LSTM-CRF	CSAC	LSTM-CRF	CSAC
Training time (min)	133	**38**	66	**19**
Predicting time (ms)	714.07	**405.99**	734.92	**417.49**

label. For example, *LSTM-CRF* outperforms *CNN-CRF* and *LSTM-Softmax* outperforms *CNN-Softmax*. This is because the CNN network can only capture local contextual information. However, the LSTM network can capture both local and global contextual information. This result validates that global contextual information is very important for Chinese NER task.

Second, the baseline methods based on the CRF layer outperform the baseline methods based on Softmax with the same network to capture contextual information. For example, *LSTM-CRF* outperforms *LSTM-Softmax*. This is because there exist dependencies between labels. The CRF layer can effectively capture the dependencies between labels and decode labels jointly. This result validates the effectiveness of CRF layer for Chinese NER.

Third, our approach can consistently outperform all baseline methods and needs much less time than methods based on the LSTM-CRF architecture to train and predict. Different from these baseline methods, our approach is based on the CNN-SelfAttention-CRF architecture. In this way, our approach can capture local contextual information via the CNN network and global contextual information via the LSTM network, and model the dependencies between neighbouring labels via the CRF layer, all of which are very critical for Chinese NER task. In addition, the CNN network and the self-attention network can be computed in parallel. Thus, our approach can recognize entities in a more efficient way. These experimental results validate the effectiveness of our approach in Chinese NER and show that our approach is more efficient than other neural methods based on the LSTM-CRF architecture in Chinese NER.

4.3 Module Effectiveness

In this section, we conduct several experiments to evaluate the influence of each component in our approach. The experiments are conducted on *Bakeoff-3* and *Bakeoff-4*. We independently remove each component from our model to verify their influence. The experimental results are shown in Fig. 2. From the Fig. 2, we have several observations. First, after removing the multi-head self-attention network, the performance of our approach declines. This is because global contextual information is crucial for Chinese NER. After removing the multi-head self-attention network, our approach cannot capture global contextual information. This result also validates the effectiveness of the multi-head self-attention network in capturing global contextual information. Second, after removing the local contextual character representations $\mathbf{g}_i$ from the contextual character representations $\mathbf{h}_i = [\mathbf{g}_i; \mathbf{m}_i]$, the performance of our approach also declines. This is because our approach explicitly captures the local contextual information via the CNN network and encodes it in the $\mathbf{g}_i$. After removing $\mathbf{g}$ from $\mathbf{h}$, our approach loses much local contextual information when decoding labels in the CRF layer. This result also validates the usefulness of local contextual information for Chinese NER. Third, after removing the CRF layer, the performance of our approach declines significantly. This is because there exist dependencies between neighbouring labels. After removing the CRF layer, our approach cannot effectively capture the dependencies between neighbouring labels. This result validates the effectiveness of the CRF layer in capturing dependencies between labels, which is very important for NER task. In conclusion, these experimental results show that each component in our approach is useful.

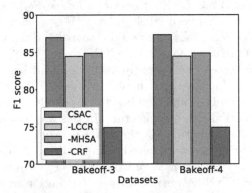

Fig. 2. The effectiveness of different components in our approach. "-LCCR" denotes removing local contextual character representations from contextual character representations, "-MHSA" denotes removing multi-head self-attention network from our model, "-CRF" denotes removing CRF layer from our model, and "CSAC" denotes our model.

4.4   Influence of Hyper-parameters

In this section, we conduct further experiments to evaluate the influence of an important hyper-parameter in our approach, i.e., the number of self-attention heads K. Our experiments are conducted on *Bakeoff-3* dataset and *Bakeoff-4* dataset. We evaluate the performance of our approach with different K. The experiments results are shown in Fig. 3. According to Fig. 3, the performance of our approach first improves with the increase of K. This is because a character may have dependencies with multiple characters in the texts. When K is too small, the multi-head self-attention network cannot model these dependencies effectively. However, when K becomes too large, the performance of our approach starts to decline. This maybe because there are too many parameters in our model and our model is easier to become overfitting. Thus, a moderate value of K is suitable for our approach, i.e., 4.

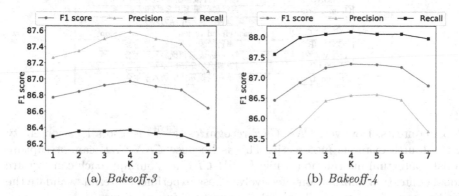

(a) *Bakeoff-3*   (b) *Bakeoff-4*

Fig. 3. The influence of hyper-parameter K on the performance of our approach.

4.5   Case Study

In this section, we conduct several case studies to explore the effectiveness of our approach in capturing local and global contextual information. We compare our approach with other baseline methods, i.e., *CNN-CRF* and *LSTM-CRF*. The prediction results of these methods are listed in Table 3. In the first and second examples, we explore the effectiveness of our approach in capturing local contextual information. In the two sentences, we can infer "中" is a location entity in the first sentence according to its local context, i.e., "美" and a non-entity in the second sentence according to its local context "其" . According to Table 3, *CNN-CRF*, *LSTM-CRF* and our approach can label the two sentences correctly. These experimental results validate the effectiveness of our approach in capturing local contextual information. In the third and fourth examples, we explore the effectiveness of our approach in capturing global contextual information. *LSTM-CRF* and our approach correctly recognize "阿里" is a location entity in the third example and a person entity in the fourth example according to its

Table 3. Several Chinese named entity recognition examples. We use different colors to represent different kinds of entities, i.e., person and location.

Example	Method	Sentence and prediction result
1	Sentence	中美贸易争端 (The trade conflict between China and America)
	CNN-CRF	中美贸易争端
	LSTM-CRF	中美贸易争端
	CSAC	中美贸易争端
	Ground Truth	中美贸易争端
2	Sentence	其中美好的时光令人怀念 (The beautiful time in it is nostalgic)
	CNN-CRF	其中美好的时光令人怀念
	LSTM-CRF	其中美好的时光令人怀念
	CSAC	其中美好的时光令人怀念
	Ground Truth	其中美好的时光令人怀念
3	Sentence	每年都有很多游客来到阿里 (Many tourists visit Ali every year)
	CNN-CRF	每年都有很多游客来到阿里
	LSTM-CRF	每年都有很多游客来到阿里
	CSAC	每年都有很多游客来到阿里
	Ground Truth	每年都有很多游客来到阿里
4	Sentence	阿里曾经表示拒绝加入学生会 (Ali has refused to join the student union)
	CNN-CRF	阿里曾经表示拒绝加入学生会
	LSTM-CRF	阿里曾经表示拒绝加入学生会
	CSAC	阿里曾经表示拒绝加入学生会
	Ground Truth	阿里曾经表示拒绝加入学生会

global contexts. However, *CNN-CRF* recognizes "阿里" is also a location entity in the fourth example incorrectly. This is because *CNN-CRF* cannot capture global contextual information, while *LSTM-CRF* and our approach can capture global contextual information effectively. These experimental results validate the effectiveness of our approach in global contextual information.

5 Conclusion

In this paper, we propose a fast neural named entity recognition approach for Chinese texts. Our approach is based on the CNN-SelfAttention-CRF architecture, where the CNN network is used to learn contextual character representations from local contexts, the multi-head self-attention network is used to learn contextual character representations from global contexts, and the CRF is used to jointly decode character labels to capture the dependencies between neighbouring labels. Since both CNN and multi-head self-attention networks can be computed in parallel, our NER model is efficient to train and predict. Experiments on two benchmark datasets show our approach can improve the efficiency of Chinese NER and can achieve better performance than existing methods.

Acknowledgments. This work was supported by Tsinghua University Initiative Scientific Research Program, the National Key Research and Development Program of China under Grant number 2018YFC1604002, and the National Natural Science Foundation of China under Grant numbers U1836204, U1705261, and U1636113.

References

1. Cao, P., Chen, Y., Liu, K., Zhao, J., Liu, S.: Adversarial transfer learning for Chinese named entity recognition with self-attention mechanism. In: EMNLP, pp. 182–192 (2018)
2. Chen, A., Peng, F., Shan, R., Sun, G.: Chinese named entity recognition with conditional probabilistic models. In: Proceedings of the Fifth SIGHAN Workshop on Chinese Language Processing, pp. 173–176 (2006)
3. Chiu, J.P., Nichols, E.: Named entity recognition with bidirectional LSTM-CNNs. Trans. Assoc. Comput. Linguist. **4**, 357–370 (2016)
4. Collobert, R., Weston, J., Bottou, L., Karlen, M., Kavukcuoglu, K., Kuksa, P.: Natural language processing (almost) from scratch. J. Mach. Learn. Res. **12**, 2493–2537 (2011)
5. Ekbal, A., Saha, S.: Stacked ensemble coupled with feature selection for biomedical entity extraction. Knowl.-Based Syst. **46**, 22–32 (2013)
6. Gregoric, A.Z., Bachrach, Y., Coope, S.: Named entity recognition with parallel recurrent neural networks. In: ACL, pp. 69–74 (2018)
7. Gridach, M.: Character-level neural network for biomedical named entity recognition. J. Biomed. Inform. **70**, 85–91 (2017)
8. Habibi, M., Weber, L., Neves, M., Wiegandt, D.L., Leser, U.: Deep learning with word embeddings improves biomedical named entity recognition. Bioinformatics **33**(14), i37–i48 (2017)
9. Han, X., Sun, L., Zhao, J.: Collective entity linking in web text: a graph-based method. In: SIGIR, pp. 765–774 (2011)
10. Hwang, K., Sung, W.: Single stream parallelization of generalized LSTM-like RNNs on a GPU. In: ICASSP, pp. 1047–1051 (2015)
11. Kingma, D.P., Ba, J.: Adam: a method for stochastic optimization. arXiv preprint arXiv:1412.6980 (2014)
12. Konkol, M., Brychcín, T., Konopík, M.: Latent semantics in named entity recognition. Expert Syst. Appl. **42**(7), 3470–3479 (2015)
13. Kudoh, T., Matsumoto, Y.: Use of support vector learning for chunk identification. In: Fourth Conference on Computational Natural Language Learning and the Second Learning Language in Logic Workshop (2000)
14. Lample, G., Ballesteros, M., Subramanian, S., Kawakami, K., Dyer, C.: Neural architectures for named entity recognition. In: NAACL, pp. 260–270 (2016)
15. LeCun, Y., Bottou, L., Bengio, Y., Haffner, P., et al.: Gradient-based learning applied to document recognition. Proc. IEEE **86**(11), 2278–2324 (1998)
16. Lin, Y., Shen, S., Liu, Z., Luan, H., Sun, M.: Neural relation extraction with selective attention over instances. In: ACL, pp. 2124–2133 (2016)
17. Ma, X., Hovy, E.: End-to-end sequence labeling via bi-directional LSTM-CNNs-CRF. In: ACL, pp. 1064–1074 (2016)
18. Mikolov, T., Sutskever, I., Chen, K., Corrado, G.S., Dean, J.: Distributed representations of words and phrases and their compositionality. In: NIPS, pp. 3111–3119 (2013)
19. Passos, A., Kumar, V., McCallum, A.: Lexicon infused phrase embeddings for named entity resolution. In: CoNLL, pp. 78–86 (2014)
20. Peng, N., Dredze, M.: Named entity recognition for Chinese social media with jointly trained embeddings. In: EMNLP, pp. 548–554 (2015)
21. Peng, N., Dredze, M.: Multi-task domain adaptation for sequence tagging. In: Proceedings of the 2nd Workshop on Representation Learning for NLP, pp. 91–100 (2017)

22. Peters, M., Ammar, W., Bhagavatula, C., Power, R.: Semi-supervised sequence tagging with bidirectional language models. In: ACL, pp. 1756–1765 (2017)
23. Ratinov, L., Roth, D.: Design challenges and misconceptions in named entity recognition. In: CoNLL, pp. 147–155 (2009)
24. Shen, Y., Yun, H., Lipton, Z.C., Kronrod, Y., Anandkumar, A.: Deep active learning for named entity recognition. arXiv preprint arXiv:1707.05928 (2017)
25. Srivastava, N., Hinton, G., Krizhevsky, A., Sutskever, I., Salakhutdinov, R.: Dropout: a simple way to prevent neural networks from overfitting. J. Mach. Learn. Res. **15**(1), 1929–1958 (2014)
26. Tran, Q., MacKinlay, A., Yepes, A.J.: Named entity recognition with stack residual LSTM and trainable bias decoding. In: IJCNLP, pp. 566–575 (2017)
27. Tran, V.C., Nguyen, N.T., Fujita, H., Hoang, D.T., Hwang, D.: A combination of active learning and self-learning for named entity recognition on twitter using conditional random fields. Knowl.-Based Syst. **132**, 179–187 (2017)
28. Wu, F., Liu, J., Wu, C., Huang, Y., Xie, X.: Neural Chinese named entity recognition via CNN-LSTM-CRF and joint training with word segmentation. In: WWW, pp. 3342–3348 (2019)
29. Zhang, Y., Yang, J.: Chinese NER using lattice LSTM. In: ACL, pp. 1554–1564 (2018)

A Practical Framework for Evaluating the Quality of Knowledge Graph

Haihua Chen[1], Gaohui Cao[2], Jiangping Chen[1], and Junhua Ding[1(✉)]

[1] University of North Texas, Denton, TX 76203, USA
{haihua.chen,jiangping.chen,junhua.ding}@unt.edu
[2] Central China Normal University, Wuhan 430079, Hubei, China
bolue@qq.com

Abstract. Knowledge graphs have become much large and complex during past several years due to its wide applications in knowledge discovery. Many knowledge graphs were built using automated construction tools and via crowdsourcing. The graph may contain significant amount of syntax and semantics errors that great impact its quality. A low quality knowledge graph produce low quality application that is built on it. Therefore, evaluating quality of knowledge graph is necessary for building high quality applications. Many frameworks were proposed for systematic evaluation of knowledge graphs, but they are either too complex to be practical or lacking of scalability to large scale knowledge graphs. In this paper, we conducted a comprehensive study of existing frameworks and proposed a practical framework for evaluating quality on "fit for purpose" of knowledge graphs. We first selected a set of quality dimensions and their corresponding metrics based on the requirements of knowledge discovery based on knowledge graphs through systematic investigation of representative published applications. Then we recommended an approach for evaluating each metric considering its feasibility and scalability. The framework can be used for checking the essential quality requirements of knowledge graphs for serving the purpose of knowledge discovery.

Keywords: Knowledge graph · Knowledge discovery · Quality dimension · Quality metric · Fit for purpose · Machine learning

1 Introduction

Knowledge Graph (KG) is a graph representation of knowledge in entities, edges and attributes, where the entity represents something in real world, the edge represents relationship, and the attribute defines an entity [6,14]. "A knowledge graph allows for potentially interrelating arbitrary entities with each other, and covers various topical domains" [14]. Many large scale knowledge graphs were

This research is partially supported by United States NSF award #1852249, China NSSFC 2019–2022 project 19BTQ075.

X. Zhu et al. (Eds.): CCKS 2019, CCIS 1134, pp. 111–122, 2019.
https://doi.org/10.1007/978-981-15-1956-7_10

built recently such as Freebase, Wikidata, DBpedia, Google KG, and Microsoft KG. Many large companies including Google, Facebook, LinkedIn, Amazon, and Microsoft also built large scale knowledge graphs for building knowledge discovery or intelligent systems. Since a knowledge graph better captures the context of individual entities than separated individual entities in a traditional database, it is getting more attention recently for building more intelligent systems. For examples, knowledge graphs have been used for building knowledge-based information retrieval systems, conversation systems, question and answer (Q&A) systems, topic recommendation systems, and many others [6]. However, the quality of knowledge graph can great impact the performance of knowledge based systems that are built on the it.

The quality of knowledge graph mainly concerns about the "fitness of purposes" to an application that is built on the graph. A high quality knowledge graph shall be correct, comprehensive and fresh [6]. Many frameworks have been developed for evaluating the quality in term of the correctness, freshness and comprehensiveness of knowledge graph. Zaveri et al. conducted a systematic literature review of quality frameworks of knowledge graphs and propose one that includes 18 quality dimensions/criteria in four categories and 69 metrics for measuring the criteria [24]. The metrics are classified according to the their common properties into four categories: accessibility, intrinsic, contextual and representational [24], which were first defined in the widely cited data quality paper authored by Wang and Strong [22]. Zaveri et al. also summarized 12 tools for evaluating the quality of knowledge graph [24]. Although the framework proposed by Zaveri et al. in [24] provides a comprehensive way for evaluating the quality of knowledge graph, some of these quality criteria are not necessary for evaluating the quality regarding "fit for purpose" of knowledge graph or not practical to be evaluated. For example, some quality criteria can be validated in application development phases, and some quality problems can be handled by the application directly. Knowledge graph especially a large scale knowledge graph is supposed to contain low quality items such as incorrect relations, erroneous entities and literals. An application developer shall be aware the potential problem in a knowledge graph and ensure the application can handle the problem in some degree. Therefore, quality evaluation of knowledge graph is to check whether a knowledge graph meets basic quality standard and to ensure it fits for the purpose. We need a quality framework for knowledge graph that can well balance between ensuring "fit for purpose" of knowledge graph and being practical for evaluation. In this research, we first identify a group of quality requirements of knowledge graph that were developed on representative publications of applications of knowledge graphs. The quality requirements are essential to the effectiveness of a knowledge based system built on the knowledge graph. We then map quality criteria that defined in [24] to quality requirements to select a subset of the criteria that can be used for evaluating basic quality standard of a knowledge graph. Each criterion is evaluated by one or more metrics, and each metric is measured by one or more approaches. We investigated existing evaluation approaches and tools to propose one practical approach for evaluating each metric or an alternative version of a metric if its evaluation is infeasible. The ultimate goal of this research is to provide a practical quality evaluation framework that can easily used for ensuring basic quality standard of knowledge graph.

This paper is organized as follows: Sect. 2 provides a background introduction of quality of knowledge graph. Section 3 presents a recommended framework for evaluating quality of knowledge graph. Section 4 presents related work and state-of-the-art research on quality of knowledge graphs. Summary and future work are briefly discussed in Sect. 5.

2 Quality of Knowledge Graph

In this section, we discuss basic representation of knowledge graph and concept of quality of knowledge graph.

2.1 Knowledge Graph

The term of Knowledge Graph was used by Google in 2012 to call its new searching strategy that searches for things but not strings [17]. The definition of knowledge graph could be significantly different, which could produce knowledge graphs in different representation, size and content. The definition of knowledge graph in this research is developed based on the definition of knowledge graph proposed by Paulheim in [14]. A knowledge graph is a graph, which includes entities as nodes, edges as relations among entities, and attributes are used for describing entities. It can be represented as a group of triples. A triple defines a relation among two entities, and each entity is described by its attributes. A knowledge graph usually is a large network including thousands of entities and millions of edges among the entities. For example: the last version of Free-base contains around 50 million entities, 1.9 billion triples, roughly 27,000 entity types and 38,000 relation types [4,14]. A knowledge graph normally is constructed using automated tools through crowdsourcing, errors including syntax and semantic errors do exist in knowledge graph. These errors may impact the performance of knowledge-based applications built on the knowledge graph since "garbage in, garbage out" still applies to knowledge graph. Therefore, it is necessary to evaluate the quality especially "fit for purpose" of a knowledge graph for building an application. Evaluation of the quality of knowledge graph includes two tasks: one is the identification of quality criteria for measuring the quality of knowledge graph, and the other is the approaches and tools for measuring each criterion.

2.2 Quality Metrics for Knowledge Graph

Wang and Strong proposed a comprehensive framework for data quality in 1996 [22], which has been widely used for evaluating data quality. Stvilia et al. conducted a theoretic research of information quality assessment focusing on linking roots of information quality problems and information activity types, and then proposed a framework for information quality assessment [18]. Many frameworks for evaluating data quality including the quality of knowledge graph were developed based on the two frameworks. Zaveri et al. proposed a quality assessment framework for linked data, which can be looked at a general format of knowledge graph. The framework is essentially similar to the framework proposed by Wang and Strong and the framework proposed by Stivilia. For example, Zaveri's framework categories quality dimensions into four categories: Accessibility, Intrinsic, Contextual, and Representational. Stvilia's framework has three categories of quality dimensions: Intrinsic, Contextual, and Reputational. Accessibility and Representational dimensions in Zaveri's framework are categorized into Contextual, and Reputational dimensions in Stvilia's framework are included in Contextual category as Trustworthiness dimension. Zaveri's framework includes more dimensions and metrics for evaluating the quality dimensions. The framework can be directly used for systematically evaluating the quality of knowledge graph. Therefore, the framework we develop in this research is built based on the framework proposed by Zaveri et al. in [24].

Zaveri et al. conducted a systematic literature review of quality assessment of linked data and analyzed 30 data quality evaluation approaches. They identified 18 quality dimensions that are classified into four categories: Accessibility, Intrinsic, Contextual, and Representational [24]. 69 quality metrics were developed for evaluating the 18 quality dimensions, whose measurability is defined as the ability to assess the variation along a dimension [18]. A quality metric is a procedure for measuring a data quality dimension [24]. Accessibility category includes dimensions: availability, licensing, interlinking, security, and performance. Intrinsic category includes dimensions: syntactic validity, semantic accuracy, consistency, conciseness, and completeness. Contextual category includes dimensions: relevancy, trustworthiness, understandability, and timeliness. Representational category includes dimensions: representational conciseness, interoperability, interpretability and versatility. Each quality dimension is evaluated by several quality evaluation metrics. For example, The metrics for dimension availability include "accessibility of the RDF dumps", "dereferenceability of the URI, and others. The metrics for dimension security include "usage of digital signatures", and "authenticity of the dataset". The metrics for dimension semantic accuracy include "no outliers", "no inaccurate values", "no misuse of properties", "no inaccurate annotations, labellings or classifications", and "detection of value rules". The metrics for evaluating each quality dimension is not complete but are important properties that are closely related to the dimension. It is infeasible to define a complete set of general metrics for adequately evaluating each dimension of data quality. But the metrics can be extended for a special domain or an application. For example, metric "usage of digital signature" is not necessary important for evaluating the security of knowledge graph, but many quality metrics such as privacy should be used for evaluating security dimension. Metrics for measuring security dimension should be defined on access control, flow control, inference control and cryptographic control. It is also same difficult to define metrics for evaluating other complex quality dimensions such as semantic accuracy and completeness.

2.3 Approaches and Tools for Evaluating Quality of Knowledge Graph

Most of quality dimensions such as Licensing and Availability in accessibility category are easily manually evaluated. Evaluation of dimension Interlinking is not difficult and several approaches and tools are available. Dimension Performance can be checked using the data management system that stores the knowledge graph, or it is not important if the knowledge graph is stored in files since performance should be concerned by the system that is built on the knowledge graph. A knowledge graph should be treated as shared resource that could be used by many different applications. Therefore, performance requirements from a special application is not a concern of construction of knowledge graph. Evaluation of dimension Security could be very difficult, but we don't think security is closely related to "fit for purpose" of knowledge graph. Security including privacy should be just evaluated for whether appropriate protection mechanisms are used for protecting the data for meeting security requirements.

Quality dimensions in representational category are also easy to be evaluated or they should be left for evaluation by the application that is built on the knowledge graph. For example, dimension Representation conciseness is a subjective dimension and it can be manually evaluated through sampling, and interoperability and versatility can be evaluated through checking related readme documents. Evaluation of dimension Interpretability can be implemented through parsing knowledge graph against standard documents.

Zaveri et al. conducted a systematic review of published approaches and tools for quality evaluation of linked data, and reviewed 30 selected approaches and 12 tools [24]. Each of the approach covers at least one quality dimension, and the 30 approaches together cover all 18 dimensions. Dimension Versatility, Performance and Security was only covered by one article, and Representation conciseness, Licensing, and Interoperability was covered by two articles. It confirms our observation that some dimensions are easy to be validated or not so important to quality regarding "fit for purpose". Dimensions such as Syntactic validity and Semantic accuracy that are more important for evaluating the fitness for purpose of knowledge graph are getting more attention. Dimensions Syntactic validity and Semantic accuracy was covered by 7 and 11 articles, respectively [24]. Paulheim conducted a survey of knowledge graph refinement, which includes adding missing knowledge or identifying and removing errors [14]. The approaches for knowledge refinement especially the one for identifying errors can be directly used for evaluating the quality of knowledge graph.

Some general approaches for evaluating knowledge quality were also developed. For example, Kontokostas et al. proposed a test driven evaluation for linked data quality. In the approach, test cases can be generated by solving constraints on data schemas, test patterns, and test requirements [9]. The test cases are queries for retrieving the linked data and queried results are checked for specific quality metrics. The approach provide an elegant and effective approach for evaluating most quality dimensions of knowledge graph. Recently, Gao et al. introduced a sampling approach for efficiently evaluating the accuracy of knowledge graph. The approach can "provide quality accuracy evaluation with strong statistical guarantee while minimizing human efforts [5]."

3   A Recommended Framework for Quality Evaluation of Knowledge Graph

A quality evaluation framework for knowledge graph is designed for evaluating "fit for purpose" of a knowledge graph for building knowledge based application. Therefore, a quality evaluation dimension in a framework should be linked to specific quality requirements of knowledge based applications that are built on the knowledge graph. For example, in knowledge graph-based question answering [7], dimensions Syntactic validity and Semantic accuracy of triples are critical while dimension Conciseness might not be necessary. In this section, we first review publications on knowledge based applications developed on knowledge graphs and develop a group of quality requirements, and then map the quality requirements to quality dimensions. Each dimension is measured by suggested quality metrics and evaluation approaches. We begin with a systematic analysis of major activities related to knowledge graph in each system, and link each activity to quality requirements of knowledge graph with considering the activity system context. Then each quality requirement is linked to a set of quality dimensions.

In order to analyze quality requirements of typical knowledge based applications built on knowledge graphs, we conducted a systematic analysis related literature of knowledge graph applications. We use "knowledge graph" as keyword to search digital libraries Google Scholar, Microsoft Academic, ISI Web of Science, ACM Digital Library, IEEE Xplore Digital Library, Springer Link, Science Direct, and PubMed. 80 articles from last five years were selected as potentially relevant primary studies. Then two Ph.D. students read the title and abstract of each article to identify potentially eligible articles. 41 articles were finally selected for this research. We summarize five categories of the applications of knowledge graph: 1. semantic search; 2. decision making; 3. knowledge management; 4. data mining; and 5. prediction. According to the literature, semantic search is the most popular application of knowledge graph, tasks such as recommendation, information retrieval, question answering are also popular applications of knowledge graphs.

In the recommendation case, knowledge graphs should contains three aspects of information: 1. semantic relatedness among items to help find their latent connections and improve the precision of recommended items; 2. relations with various types to extend a user's interests reasonably and increasing the diversity of recommended items; 3. users' historical records and the recommended ones to ensure explainability of recommender systems [19]. While in question answering case, knowledge graphs are composed of vast amounts of facts with various expressions [10]. The ambiguity of entity names and partial names is also an important component since many entities in a large knowledge graph may share same names and end users could use partial names in their utterances [27]. Besides, knowledge graphs for question answering should be robust to expand so that new entities and relations can be easily added to them [8], or new relations for non-neighbor entity pairs can be created [25]. However, in the application of information retrieval, especially text retrieval, entities in the knowledge graphs are typically associated with different names.

The central function of knowledge graph for decision making is to automatically generate practical knowledge for a given task in different fields such as medical and agriculture. Knowledge graphs are often used for knowledge management because the ability to connect different types of data in meaningful ways and support richer data services. The applications of knowledge graph in prediction can be used in industry and in academia. Except for accuracy, trustworthiness,consistency, relevancy, timeliness acts as an important factor to enhance the prediction performance [2].

Data mining becomes a hot topic with the development of machine learning and deep learning. Recently, knowledge graph proved to be useful in data mining. The accuracy of the entities and relation extraction is the precondition for mining. Meanwhile, if the constructed knowledge graph is incompleteness, the performance will also be affected.

Based on the analysis of the works mentioned above related to knowledge graph applications, we summarize 18 requirements on knowledge graph quality:

1. Triples should be concise [2, 26].
2. Contextual information of entities should be captured [2].
3. Knowledge graph does not contain redundant triples [2].
4. Knowledge graph can be updated dynamically [12].
5. Entities should be densely connected [11, 16, 26].
6. Relations among different types of entities should be included [21].
7. Data source should be multi-field [8, 10, 21].
8. Data for constructing a knowledge graph should in different types and from different resources [15, 21].
9. Synonyms should be mapped and ambiguities should be eliminated to ensure reconcilable expressions [8, 10, 21].
10. Knowledge graph should be organized in structured triples for easily processed by machine [21].
11. The scalability with respect to the KG size [20].
12. The attributes of the entities should not be missed [13].
13. Knowledge graph should be publicly available and proprietary [3].
14. Knowledge graph should be authority [26].
15. Knowledge graph should be concentrated [26].
16. The triples should not contradict with each other [8, 20].
17. For domain specific tasks, the knowledge graph should be related to that field [1, 2, 26].
18. Knowledge graph should contain the latest resources to guarantee freshness [6, 27].

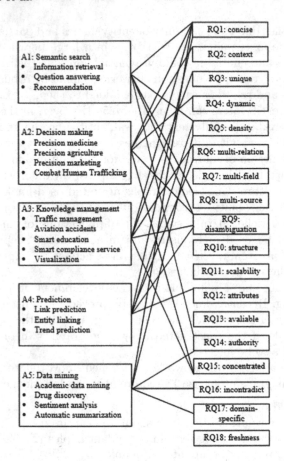

Fig. 1. Knowledge graph requirements produced from representative applications

The mapping between knowledge graph applications and the essential quality requirements is shown in Fig. 1.

Also, to incorporate with the knowledge graph quality evaluation dimensions mentioned in [24], we map the knowledge graph quality requirements mentioned above to the corresponding quality evaluation dimensions, as shown in Fig. 2. We do not take all of the dimensions since some of them didn't co-related with any requirements, for example, licensing, security, and representational-conciseness, interoperability, and versatility. In the meanwhile, we add two new dimensions robust and diversity to the representational and contextual categories respectively. Robust means that the knowledge graph should be easily expanded without affect the original knowledge graph too much, while diverse means the data for constructing a knowledge graph should be multi-source and multi-type. The metrics and tools proposed in [24] can be used for measuring the proposed dimensions here.

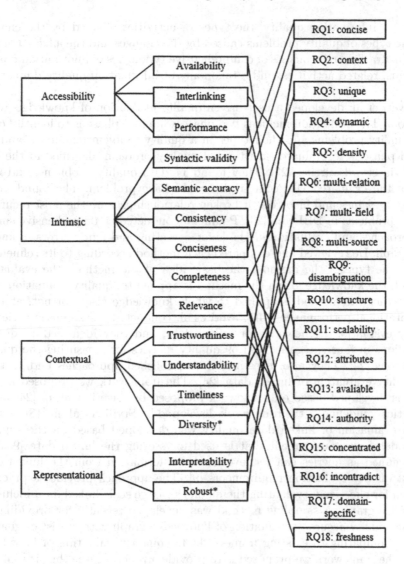

Fig. 2. Mapping knowledge graph requirements quality dimensions

4   Related Work

Wang and Strong [22] developed a hierarchical framework for defining data quality dimensions into four categories: which are intrinsic data quality, contextual data quality, representational data quality and accessibility data quality. They concluded that "high quality data should be intrinsically good, contextually appropriate to the task, clearly represented, and accessible to the data consumer" [22]. Stvilia et al. proposed a framework for information quality assessment [18]. They conducted a theoretical study to investigate root causes of change of information quality, the types of activities affected by the change, and the types of quality problems caused by the changes and the affected activities. The framework "consists of comprehensive typologies of information quality problems, related activities, and a taxonomy of information quality dimensions [18]".

Zaveri et al. developed a user-driven quality evaluation of knowledge graph DBPedia. The evaluation includes two phases: the first phase is to identify common quality problems and their types in a quality problem taxonomy, and the second phase is to evaluate each type of quality problem identified in the first phase via crowdsourcing [23]. They found 17 data quality problems, and near 12% of the evaluated DBPedia triples could have problem. The found incorrect entity values and incorrect or broken relationships were the most recurring quality problems in DBPedia [23]. Paulheim conducted a comprehensive survey of approaches and evaluation methods for detecting and fixing errors in knowledge graph. He reviewed and compared each method according to its refinement target, the type of the method, the basic idea of the method, the evaluation method, the knowledge graph the method is applied to, quality evaluation metric, whether the method is applied to whole knowledge graph or not, and the computational performance [14]. Zaveri et al. conducted a systematic review of quality evaluation frameworks for linked data, and they identified 18 quality dimensions in four categories and 69 quality metrics for measuring the quality dimensions [24]. They also investigated 30 published approaches and 12 tools for quality evaluation of linked data [24]. The framework we proposed in this paper is developed based on framework proposed by Zaveri et al. in [24] under theoretical guideline of the framework developed by Stvilia et al. in [18]. A test-driven evaluation of linked data quality was developed based on the support of the database management that is used for storing the linked data [9]. The tests defined as queries can retrieve needed information from the linked data against quality evaluation requirements [9]. The approach provides a practical solution for effectively evaluating the quality of large scale linked data including knowledge graph. A sampling method was developed recently for providing an efficient quality accuracy evaluation of knowledge graph with statistics guarantee [5]. Comparing to existing frameworks for quality evaluation of knowledge graph, the framework we proposed is to provide a practical one that is well balanced between evaluation comprehensiveness and evaluation efficiency so that the framework can be easily used for measuring the quality of knowledge graph for the basic level quality for building knowledge based applications.

5   Summary and Future Work

Knowledge graphs may contain significant amount of syntax and semantics errors that could great impact its quality of the knowledge based applications built on it. Existing frameworks for systematic evaluation of knowledge graphs are either too complex to be practical or lacking of scalability to large knowledge graphs. We conducted a comprehensive study of the proposed frameworks and proposed a practical framework for evaluating quality on "fit for purpose" of knowledge graphs. We selected a set of quality dimensions and their corresponding metrics based on the requirements of knowledge discovery applications built on a knowledge graph. Then we d an approach for evaluating each metric considering its feasibility and scalability. The framework can be used for checking the basic quality requirements of knowledge graphs for serving the purpose of knowledge discovery. In the future, we will evaluate the effectiveness of the framework on large knowledge graphs and conduct surveys from domain specialists including application developers, business analysts and knowledge graph researchers to evaluate and improve the framework.

References

1. Chen, Y., Kuang, J., Cheng, D., Zheng, J., Gao, M., Zhou, A.: AgriKG: an agricultural knowledge graph and its applications. In: Li, G., Yang, J., Gama, J., Natwichai, J., Tong, Y. (eds.) DASFAA 2019. LNCS, vol. 11448, pp. 533–537. Springer International Publishing, Cham (2019). https://doi.org/10.1007/978-3-030-18590-9_81
2. Deng, S., Zhang, N., Zhang, W., Chen, J., Pan, J.Z., Chen, H.: Knowledge-driven stock trend prediction and explanation via temporal convolutional network. In: Companion Proceedings of The 2019 World Wide Web Conference, WWW 2019, pp. 678–685. ACM, New York (2019). https://doi.org/10.1145/3308560.3317701
3. Dietz, L., Kotov, A., Meij, E.: Utilizing knowledge graphs for text-centric information retrieval. In: The 41st International ACM SIGIR Conference on Research & #38; Development in Information Retrieval, SIGIR 2018, pp. 1387–1390. ACM, New York (2018). https://doi.org/10.1145/3209978.3210187
4. Freebase: Data Dumps, June 2013. https://developers.google.com/freebase/
5. Gao, J., Li, X., Xu, Y.E., Sisman, B., Dong, X.L., Yang, J.: Efficient knowledge graph accuracy evaluation. Technical Report (2019). https://users.cs.duke.edu/~jygao/KG_eval_vldb_full.pdf. Accessed 25 May 2019
6. Gao, Y., Liang, J., Han, B., Yakout, M., Mohamed, A.: Building a large-scale, accurate and fresh knowledge graph. In: KDD-2018, Tutorial T39, August 2018. https://kdd2018tutorialt39.azurewebsites.net/
7. Hixon, B., Clark, P., Hajishirzi, H.: Learning knowledge graphs for question answering through conversational dialog. In: HLT-NAACL (2015)
8. Huang, X., Zhang, J., Li, D., Li, P.: Knowledge graph embedding based question answering. In: Proceedings of the Twelfth ACM International Conference on Web Search and Data Mining, WSDM 2019, pp. 105–113. ACM, New York (2019). https://doi.org/10.1145/3289600.3290956
9. Kontokostas, D., et al.: Test-driven evaluation of linked data quality. In: Proceedings of the 23rd International Conference on World Wide Web, WWW 2014, pp. 747–758 (2014)
10. Lukovnikov, D., Fischer, A., Lehmann, J., Auer, S.: Neural network-based question answering over knowledge graphs on word and character level. In: Proceedings of the 26th WWW, pp. 1211–1220 (2017). https://doi.org/10.1145/3038912.3052675
11. Keller, R.M.: Building a knowledge graph for the air traffic management community. In: Companion Proceedings of The 2019 WWW, pp. 700–704 (2019). https://doi.org/10.1145/3308560.3317706

12. Muppalla, R., Lalithsena, S., Banerjee, T., Sheth, A.: A knowledge graph framework for detecting traffic events using stationary cameras. In: Proceedings of WebSci 2017, pp. 431–436 (2017). https://doi.org/10.1145/3091478.3162384
13. Ostapuk, N., Yang, J., Cudre-Mauroux, P.: ActiveLink: deep active learning for link prediction in knowledge graphs. In: The World Wide Web Conference, WWW 2019, pp. 1398–1408. ACM, New York (2019). https://doi.org/10.1145/3308558.3313620
14. Paulheim, H.: Knowledge graph refinement: a survey of approaches and evaluation methods. Semant. Web **8**, 489–508 (2016)
15. Ping, P., Watson, K., Han, J., Bui, A.: Individualized knowledge graph: a viable informatics path to precision medicine. Circ. Res. **120**(7), 1078–1080 (2017). https://doi.org/10.1161/CIRCRESAHA.116.310024
16. Radhakrishnan, P., Talukdar, P., Varma, V.: ELDEN: improved entity linking using densified knowledge graphs. In: Proceedings of the 2018 Conference of NACCAL: Human Language Technologies, Volume 1, pp. 1844–1853, June 2018. https://doi.org/10.18653/v1/N18-1167
17. Singhal, A.: Introducing the knowledge graph: things, not strings. Google Blog, August 2012. https://www.blog.google/products/search/introducing-knowledge-graph-things-not/
18. Stvilia, B., Gasser, L., Twidale, M.B., Smith, L.C.: A framework for information quality assessment. J. Am. Soc. Inf. Sci. Technol. **58**(12), 1720–1733 (2007)
19. Wang, H., et al.: Ripple network: propagating user preferences on the knowledge graph for recommender systems. CoRR abs/1803.03467 (2018). http://arxiv.org/abs/1803.03467
20. Wang, H., et al.: Knowledge graph convolutional networks for recommender systems with label smoothness regularization. arXiv preprint arXiv:1905.04413 (2019)
21. Wang, R., et al.: AceKG: a large-scale knowledge graph for academic data mining. CoRR abs/1807.08484 (2018), http://arxiv.org/abs/1807.08484
22. Wang, R.Y., Strong, D.M.: Beyond accuracy: what data quality means to data consumers. J. Manag. Inf. Syst. **12**, 5–33 (1996)
23. Zaveri, A., et al.: User-driven quality evaluation of DBpedia. In: Proceedings of the 9th International Conference on Semantic Systems, I-SEMANTICS 2013, pp. 97–104 (2013)
24. Zaveri, A., Rula, A., Maurino, A., Pietrobon, R., Lehmann, J., Auer, S.: Quality assessment for linked data: a survey. Semant. Web **7**, 63–93 (2016)
25. Zhang, Y., Dai, H., Kozareva, Z., Smola, A.J., Song, L.: Variational reasoning for question answering with knowledge graph. CoRR abs/1709.04071 (2017). http://arxiv.org/abs/1709.04071
26. Zhao, Q., Li, Q., Wen, J.: Construction and application research of knowledge graph in aviation risk field. In: MATEC Web of Conferences, vol. 151, p. 05003, January 2018. https://doi.org/10.1051/matecconf/201815105003
27. Zheng, W., Yu, J.X., Zou, L., Cheng, H.: Question answering over knowledge graphs: question understanding via template decomposition. Proc. VLDB Endow. **11**(11), 1373–1386 (2018). https://doi.org/10.14778/3236187.3236192

Entity Subword Encoding for Chinese Long Entity Recognition

Changyu Hou, Meiling Wang, and Changliang Li[✉]

AI Lab, KingSoft Corporation, Beijing, China
{houchangyu,wangmeiling1,lichangliang}@kingsoft.com

Abstract. Named entity recognition (NER) is a fundamental and important task in natural language processing area, which jointly predicts entity boundaries and pre-defined categories. For Chinese NER task, recognition of long entities has not been well addressed yet. When character sequences of entities become longer, Chinese NER becomes more difficult with existing character-based and word-based neural methods. In this paper, we investigate Chinese NER methods that operate on subword units and propose to recognize Chinese long entities based on subword encoding. Firstly, our method generates subword units on known entities, which prevents noisy information brought by Chinese word segmentation and eases the determination of long entity boundaries. Then subword-character mixed sequences of sentences are served as input into character-based methods to perform Chinese NER. We apply our method on iterated dilated convolutional neural networks (ID-CNNs) and conditional random fields (CRF) for entity recognition. Experimental results on the benchmark People's Daily and Weibo datasets show that our subword-based method achieves significant performance on long entity recognition.

Keywords: Chinese NER · Chinese long entity · Entity subword encoding · BPE algorithm · ID-CNNs

1 Introduction

Named entity recognition (NER) is a fundamental and important task for information extraction (IE), which has traditionally been solved as a sequence labeling problem to jointly predict entity boundaries and pre-defined categories. NER plays an essential role in downstream IE tasks, such as relation extraction [2] and event extraction [4], and meanwhile it can also be used in many other natural language processing (NLP) tasks, such as question answering [17] and machine translation [1].

In recent years, numerous neural network architectures have been carefully studied, and great improvements have been achieved on Chinese NER task. Character-based models apply architectures such as bi-directional long short-term memory (BiLSTM) [6] and iterated dilated convolutional neural networks

© Springer Nature Singapore Pte Ltd. 2019
X. Zhu et al. (Eds.): CCKS 2019, CCIS 1134, pp. 123–135, 2019.
https://doi.org/10.1007/978-981-15-1956-7_11

(ID-CNNs) [13] on Chinese character sequences, where explicit word sequence information is not fully exploited but can be potentially useful. Based on the correlation between Chinese NER task and word segmentation task [3,19], word-based models leverage word boundary information by ways such as pipeline from word segmentation to NER and joint word segmentation and NER [11, 14]. However, these methods can be affected by segmented training data and segmentation errors, which results that word-based methods may achieve worse performance than character-based methods [19]. To prevent the noise brought by Chinese word segmentation task, recently Zhang and Yang propose Lattice LSTM [19], which integrates latent word information into character-based long short-term memory (LSTM) with a large automatically-obtained lexicon, and Cao et al. incorporate adversarial training into transfer learning [3].

Recognition of Chinese entities with long character sequences has not been well addressed yet. As shown in Fig. 1, more than 10% of entities have more than six characters in People's Daily NER dataset, and about 6% of entities have more than six characters in Weibo NER dataset. When character sequences of entities become longer, such as exceed 6 characters, it is more difficult to determine entity boundaries accurately. Generally long entities are composed of more words. As shown in Fig. 2, entity '中国共产党第七次全国人民代表大会' (The seventh National People's Congress of the Communist Party of China) is divided into three words by Chinese word segmentor jieba[1]. With word-based neural NER methods, boundaries between more words bring more noise to the determination of long entity boundaries. In character-based neural NER methods, it is hard for BiLSTM and ID-CNNs to conduct direct connections between arbitrary two characters to determine entity boundaries, although they can learn long-distance dependencies. For entity '中国共产党第七次全国人民代表大会' (The seventh National People's Congress of the Communist Party of China), NER models should explicitly capture the dependencies among all the characters and assign them into a single organization entity.

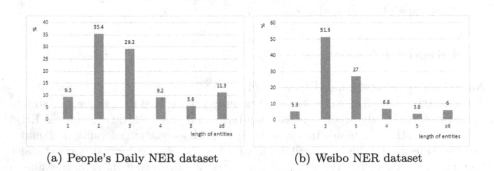

(a) People's Daily NER dataset   (b) Weibo NER dataset

Fig. 1. Distribution of length of entities.

---

[1] https://github.com/fxsjy/jieba.

Entity	中　国　共　产　党　第　七　次　全　国　人　民　代　表　大　会 The Seventh National People's Congress of the Communist Party of China		
Segmentation	中　国　共　产　党 B　 I 　I 　I 　E Communist Party of China	第　七　次 B　 I 　E the seventh	全　国　人　民　代　表　大　会 B　 I 　I 　I 　I 　I 　E National People's Congress

Fig. 2. An example of Chinese long entity and Chinese word segmentation.

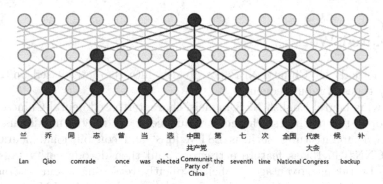

Fig. 3. An example of ID-CNNs on subword-character mixed sequences.

In this paper, we investigate neural Chinese NER methods that operate on subword units and propose to recognize Chinese long entities based on subword encoding. Firstly, our method generates subword units on known entities instead of on sentences to prevent noisy information brought by Chinese word segmentation. Character sequences of input sentences are transformed into subword-character mixed sequences, which shortens sequence length and eases the determination of long entity boundaries. As shown in Fig. 3, sequence length of the input sentence is decreased from 23 to 15 by regarding subword units as single symbols. Then vector representations for subword-character mixed sequences are computed and served as input into character-based neural NER methods. We apply our method on ID-CNNs and conditional random fields (CRF) for Chinese NER. We conduct experiments on the benchmark People's Daily and Weibo datasets and compare our subword-based method with outstanding character ID-CNNs model and Lattice LSTM model. Experimental results show that our method significantly outperforms the baseline models in Chinese long entity recognition.

The contributions of this paper are threefold.

(1) We explore Chinese NER based on entity subword encoding. In our knowledge, this is the first work that perform Chinese NER on entity subword level.

(2) Our method of subword encoding on known entities prevents noisy information brought by Chinese word segmentation effectively, and meanwhile sequence length is shortened to ease the determination of long entity boundaries.

(3) We serve subword-character mixed sequences as input into character-based model to explicitly exploit word sequence information and improve Chinese NER.

2   Related Work

Neural methods for Chinese NER are divided into character-based and word-based by types of input sequences.

Following neural English NER models, character-based neural Chinese NER models operate on Chinese character sequences, and they generally use neural network architectures such as LSTM [6,8] and convolutional neural networks (CNNs) [5,13] as feature extractors, and then decode entity tags with CRF [9] by taking advantage of their explicitly reasoning about interactions among neighboring tags. Although architectures such as BiLSTM [6] and ID-CNNs can learn long-distance dependencies, they cannot conduct direct connections between arbitrary two characters to determine boundaries of Chinese long entities.

Word boundaries may provide richer information for Chinese NER [3,11,19], and studies on word-based neural Chinese NER explore various ways to leverage word boundary information. The initial choices are pipelined approaches that perform word segmentation first before applying word sequence labeling. However pipelined approaches usually suffer from error propagation problems and incorrectly segmented entity boundaries lead to NER errors. Joint word segmentation and NER is a better way to incorporate word boundary information into Chinese NER. Xu et al. [14] build a joint model that performs joint word segmentation and NER using the dual decomposition algorithm for inference to boost the performance. Peng and Dredze [11] combine Chinese word segmentation system and NER model by joint training word boundary representations with NER. However, the joint models can also be affected by segmented training data and segmentation errors from segmentor. To address these issues, Zhang and Yang propose Lattice LSTM [19], which integrates latent word information into character-based LSTM by matching a sentence with a large automatically-obtained lexicon. Cao et al. propose adversarial transfer learning framework [3] to incorporate shared boundary information from Chinese word segmentation and to prevent the noisy boundary information brought by segmentor. For Chinese long entities, word segmentation brings more noise to the determination of entity boundaries. We perform Chinese long entity recognition on entity subword level to prevent noisy information brought by Chinese word segmentation.

Subword encoding generally helps addressing the rare word problem and enlarging vocabulary [12,16], and byte pair encoding (BPE) algorithm [7] is used as the standard subword splitting method. BPE is an originally simple data compression algorithm, which iteratively merges the most frequent pair of bytes in a sequence as a new byte. In NLP domains, BPE algorithm is used to merge characters in the text corpus rather than bytes, constructing the subwords that represent the most frequent character compositions in corpus level. It has been successfully used in neural machine translation task by capturing the most frequent subwords to solve the problem of OOV (Out of Vocabulary) [12]. It has also been adapted for Chinese word segmentation to utilize subword information and it has given better segmentation performance [16].

Dilated convolution [18], which extends traditional convolution operation, is first described for pixel classification in computer vision and has the ability to incorporate global context without losing important local information. The architecture of ID-CNNs [13] is presented as an application of dilated convolutions for sequence labeling in NLP. ID-CNNs demonstrate better capacity for large context and structured prediction and meanwhile permitting fixed-depth convolutions to run in parallel across entire documents.

3 Proposed Method

This section explains our subword-based Chinese NER method. Our method consists of three parts: subword encoding, subword-level NER and tag decoding. We first describe subword encoding, which encodes each sentence as subword-character mixed sequence. Following that, we describe subword-level NER that generates entity tags for subwords and characters, and finally entity tags are transformed into character-level.

3.1 Subword Encoding

We first encode each character sequence as subword-character mixed sequence, where subword units are generated by merging characters of known entities with BPE algorithm [7] here. The algorithm runs as following steps.

(1) Get all the known entities and calculate frequency for each entity;
(2) Initialize the symbol vocabulary with the character vocabulary, and represent each entity as a sequence of characters, plus a special end-of-entity symbol </w>, which allows to restore the original entity after operation;
(3) Iteratively count all symbol pairs and replace each occurrence of the most frequent pair (for example 'A', 'B') with a new symbol (for example 'AB'), where frequent character n-grams (or whole entities) are eventually merged into a single symbol;
(4) The final symbol vocabulary size is equal to the size of the initial vocabulary, plus the number of merge operations.

The final symbol vocabulary size is decided by the number of merge operations, which is the only hyperparameter of the algorithm. For efficiency, we do not consider pairs that cross entity boundaries.

Table 1. Example of BPE merge operations. Blue represents the most frequent pairs.

Iterations	New subwords	Entities
0		中/国/共/产/党/第/七/次/全/国/人/民/代/表/大/会< /w > 中/国/人/民/保/险/公/司< /w > 中/国/共/产/党/第/十/三/次/代/表/大/会< /w >
1	中国	中国/共/产/党/第/七/次/全/国/人/民/代/表/大/会< /w > 中国/人/民/保/险/公/司< /w > 中国/共/产/党/第/十/三/次/代/表/大/会< /w >
2	共产 人民 代表 大会< /w >	中国/共产/党/第/七/次/全/国/人民/代表/大会< /w > 中国/人民/保/险/公/司< /w > 中国/共产/党/第/十/三/次/代表/大会< /w >
3	共产党 代表大会< /w >	中国/共产党/第/七/次/全/国/人民/代表大会< /w > 中国/人民/保/险/公/司< /w > 中国/共产党/第/十/三/次/代表大会< /w >

Table 1 shows an example of BPE merge operations. In the table, three known entities are initially split into sequences of characters and then represented as subword-character mixed sequences after BPE operations. In each iteration, characters or subwords in blue denote the most frequent pairs to be merged as subwords. For example, in the first iteration, '中/国' (China) is the most frequent pair of characters and '中' (China) and '国' (Country) are merged as a subword '中国' (China), and then '中国' (China) is regarded as a new symbol in each entities. After executing BPE merge operations, sequence length of sentences are shortened especially for the ones containing long entities. For example, '中国共产党第七次全国人民代表大会' (The seventh National People's Congress of the Communist Party of China) which contains 16 characters becomes '中国/共产党/第/七/次/全/国/人民/代表大会' which only has 9 symbols.

3.2 Subword-Level NER

Let $x = [x_1, x_2, ..., x_T]$ be our input sequence where each token x_i represents a subword or a character, and let $y = [y_1, y_2, ..., y_T]$ be per-token output tags. Our task is to predict the most likely y, given a conditional model $P(y|x)$. We solve the task by serving subword-character mixed sequences as input into character-based models. Here we apply character ID-CNNs-CRF, and note that all the character-based NER models can be applied, such as BiLSTM-CRF and lattice LSTM.

Vector Representation. We transform input sequences into low-dimensional vectors, which are fed as input into ID-CNNs. We employ word2vec to train character embeddings. Subword embeddings are computed as average of embeddings of characters contained in subwords.

ID-CNNs. Dilated convolutions are the basic operations of ID-CNNs [13]. The dilated convolutional operator applied to each token x_t with output c_t is defined as:

$$c_t = W_c \oplus_{k=0}^r x_{t\pm k\gamma} \tag{1}$$

where $\oplus$ is vector concatenation. The dilated convolutional operator means applying an affine transformation, W_c to a sliding window of width r tokens on either side of each token in the sequence, where tokens of dilation width γ are skipped over at a time. Here, we do not explicitly write the bias terms in affine transformation. Dilation-1 convolution, which is a dilated convolution with $\gamma = 1$, is equivalent to a traditional convolution, and dilation-γ convolution with $\gamma > 1$ incorporates broader context into the representation of a token than the traditional convolution with same number of parameters.

The architecture of ID-CNNs applies the same block of dilated convolutions repeatedly, where each iterate takes as input the result of the last application. In each block, layers of dilated convolutions of exponentially increasing dilation width are stacked. Formally, let $D_\gamma^{(j)}$ denote the jth dilated convolutional layer of dilation width γ.

Firstly, to ensure that no tokens within the effective input width of any token are excluded, the first layer is a dilation-1 convolution $D_1^{(0)}$ that transforms a sequence of T vectors x into a representation i.

$$i = D_1^{(0)} x \tag{2}$$

Next, L_c layers of dilated convolutions of exponentially increasing dilation width are stacked with the following recurrence:

$$c^{(j)} = r(D_{2^{j-1}}^{(j-1)} c^{(j-1)}) \tag{3}$$

where $1 \leq j \leq L_c$ and $r(\cdot)$ denote the ReLU activation function. Let $c^{(0)} = i$, and the second layer also is a dilation-1 convolution.

Finally, a dilation-1 convolution layer is added to the stack:

$$c^{(L_c+1)} = r(D_1^{L_c} c^{L_c}) \tag{4}$$

Let $B(\cdot)$ denote this stack of dilated convolutions and iteratively apply B L_b times with $b^{(1)} = B(i)$:

$$b^{(k)} = B(b^{(k-1)}) \tag{5}$$

and a simple affine transformation W_o is applied to $b^{(k)}$ to output a sequence of per-class scores $h^{(k)}$ of block k for x:

$$h^{(k)} = W_o(b^{(k)}) \tag{6}$$

where $2 \leq k \leq L_b$. In the architecture, blocks of stacked layers easily incorporate broader information from a whole sequence and the iteration of small blocks and parameter sharing among blocks prevent overfitting.

Table 2. Statistics of People's Daily and Weibo datasets.

	People's Daily			Weibo		
	Training	Development	Testing	Training	Development	Testing
Sentences	20864	2318	4636	1350	270	270
All Entities	33992	7707	3819	1391	320	304
Entities L ⩾ 6	3832	892	399	81	15	24

Training. We follow the training strategy of [13], which minimizes the average of the losses for each application of blocks:

$$\frac{1}{L_b} \sum_{k=1}^{L_b} P(y|\boldsymbol{h}^{(k)}) \tag{7}$$

where $P(y|\boldsymbol{h}^{(k)})$ is computed by applying a standard CRF model [9] on $\boldsymbol{h}^{(k)}$, the output of block k of ID-CNNs.

3.3   Tag Decoding

We get entity BIO tags for subword-character mixed sequences with subword-level NER. In addition, we need transform tags for subwords into tags for characters.

- If the tag of a subword is 'B', then the first character of the subword is labeled with 'B' and the other characters are labeled with 'I';
- For other situations, all the characters of the subword have the same tag with the subword.

4   Experiment

To evaluate our method, we conduct experiments on the benchmark People's Daily and Weibo [10] datasets and compare our subword-based method with character ID-CNNs-CRF model and lattice LSTM model.

4.1   Experimental Setting

Data. Comparison between People's Daily and Weibo datasets is shown in Table 2. People's Daily dataset contains People's Daily news reports annotated with three entity types (person, organization and location). There are 27,818 sentences in total, divided into 20,864 sentences in training set, 2318 sentences in development set and 4636 sentences in testing set. There are 33992, 7707 and 3819 entities in training set, development set and testing set respectively, where 3832, 892 and 399 entities have more than six characters respectively.

Weibo dataset contains Sina Weibo messages annotated with four entity types (person, organization, location and geo-political entity). There are 1890 sentences in total, divided into 1350 sentences in training set, 270 sentences in development set and 270 sentences in testing set. There are 1391, 320 and 304 entities in training set, development set and testing set respectively, where 81, 15 and 24 entities have more than six characters respectively.

People's Daily news reports have standard expression and are mainly about political topics such as national leaders' activities and social news, while the Weibo messages have non-standard expression and cover more diverse topics.

Hyperparameters. For each BiLSTM in the models, one layer is contained, and the hidden size is set to 200. Embeddings sizes are set to 100. Dropout rate is set to 0.5. Adam is used for optimization with learning rate of 0.001. BPE vocabulary size is set to 1000 for the People's Daily dataset and 400 for the Weibo dataset.

4.2 Baselines

The compared baselines include character ID-CNNs-CRF [13] and lattice LSTM [19][2], and they are both outstanding models for neural Chinese NER. For lattice LSTM, we follow Zhang and Yang [19] and use the neural word segmentor of Yang et al. [15][3] to automatically obtain lexicon.

4.3 Experimental Results

We evaluate Chinese NER using standard precision (P), recall (R) and F1-score (F1) as metrics. We refer to the implementation of our method in Sect. 3.2 as Subword ID-CNNs-CRF. To compare with lattice LSTM, we apply our method on lattice LSTM, which is referred to as Subword Lattice LSTM.

Results for Long Entities. Table 3 displays the evaluation results for entities with length larger than 6 in People's Daily and Weibo datasets.

(1) Subword ID-CNNs-CRF outperforms ID-CNNs-CRF and Subword Lattice LSTM outperforms Lattice LSTM in both datasets on almost all metrics, demonstrating that subword-based methods can benefit Chinese long entity recognition effectively.
(2) Especially, Subword ID-CNNs-CRF and Subword Lattice LSTM achieve significant performance on recall (R) in both datasets, and probable reason is that sequence length is shorten by subword-based methods, which improves the recall of long entity boundaries.

---

[2] https://github.com/jiesutd/LatticeLSTM.
[3] https://github.com/jiesutd/RichWordSegmentor.

Table 3. NER performance for long entities in two datasets.

Model	People's Daily			Weibo		
	P	R	F1	P	R	F1
ID-CNNs-CRF	**20.05**	22.42	22.23	8.16	11.11	9.41
Subword ID-CNNs-CRF	14.32	**83.48**	24.45	**9.43**	**14.29**	**11.36**
Lattice LSTM	13.60	74.86	23.02	**7.69**	3.7	5.00
Subword Lattice LSTM	**14.48**	81.36	**24.58**	4.55	**6.25**	**5.26**

Table 4. NER performance for all entities in two datasets.

Model	People's Daily			Weibo		
	P	R	F1	P	R	F1
ID-CNNs-CRF	88.40	85.35	86.85	41.61	**40.66**	41.13
Subword ID-CNNs-CRF	**91.37**	**88.77**	**90.07**	52.31	37.05	**43.38**
Lattice LSTM	92.07	**90.06**	91.06	**69.80**	34.55	46.22
Subword Lattice LSTM	**92.65**	89.61	**91.10**	65.32	**37.54**	**47.68**

(3) Subword ID-CNNs-CRF and Subword Lattice LSTM achieve slightly better performance in People's Daily dataset, and probable reason is the more standard expression of People's Daily news reports.

(4) Subword ID-CNNs-CRF has a lower precision on long entity recognition. By analyzing experimental results, we find that some noise may be introduced when subwords are generated on entities. For example, '德国' (Germany) is generated as a subword and regarded as a symbol in '哈立德国王' (King Khalid), resulting that '哈立德国' (Harry Germany) is recognized as a person.

Results for All Entities. Table 4 displays the evaluation results for all entities in People's Daily and Weibo datasets. As shown in Table 4, Subword ID-CNNs-CRF outperforms ID-CNNs-CRF and Subword Lattice LSTM outperforms Lattice LSTM in both datasets on almost all metrics, which demonstrates that the subword-based methods can benefit Chinese entity recognition effectively.

Selection of BPE Vocabulary Size. Figure 4 displays F1-score of Subword ID-CNNs-CRF for increasing BPE vocabulary size in the People's Daily dataset. As shown in Fig. 4, F1-score is affected by BPE vocabulary size and gets a maximal value when BPE vocabulary size is about 1000, which is determined by dataset features such as size and word frequency.

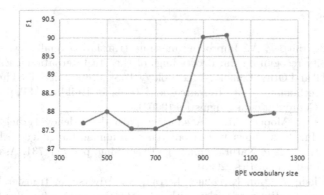

Fig. 4. F1-score for increasing BPE vocabulary size in the People's Daily dataset.

Table 5. Examples for recognizing a long location entity. Blue represents correct entities and red represents incorrect entities.

Sentence	在索非亚大学生体育馆里
	in the Sofia University Gymnasium
Correct entity	在 索菲亚大学生体育馆 里
Lattice LSTM	在 索菲亚 大学生体育馆里
Subword Lattice LSTM	在/ 索/菲/亚/大学/生/体育/馆/ 里

4.4 Case Study

Table 5 shows a case for recognizing a long location entity '索菲亚大学生体育馆' (the Sofia University Gymnasium) to compare Lattice LSTM and Subword Lattice LSTM. As shown in Table 5, Subword Lattice LSTM recognizes the location entity correctly with subword information of '大学' (University) and '体育' (sports), but Lattice LSTM only recognizes a part of the long entity, i.e. '索菲亚' (Sofia).

5 Conclusion

We propose a Chinese long entity recognition method based on entity subword encoding. Our method of subword encoding on known entities prevents noisy information brought by Chinese word segmentation and meanwhile shortens sequence length. We serve subword-character mixed sequences as input into character-based model to explicitly exploit word sequence information, and we apply our method on ID-CNNs-CRF model for Chinese NER. Experimental results reveal that our method significantly outperforms existing outstanding Chinese NER models with respect to long entity recognition. In the future, we plan to evaluate our method on more datasets.

References

1. Babych, B., Hartley, A.: Improving machine translation quality with automatic named entity recognition. In: Proceedings of the 7th International EAMT Workshop on MT and Other Language Technology Tools, Improving MT Through Other Language Technology Tools: Resources and Tools for Building MT, pp. 1–8. Association for Computational Linguistics (2003)
2. Bunescu, R.C., Mooney, R.J.: A shortest path dependency kernel for relation extraction. In: Proceedings of the Conference on human Language Technology and Empirical Methods in Natural Language Processing, pp. 724–731. Association for Computational Linguistics (2005)
3. Cao, P., Chen, Y., Liu, K., Zhao, J., Liu, S.: Adversarial transfer learning for Chinese named entity recognition with self-attention mechanism. In: Proceedings of the 2018 Conference on Empirical Methods in Natural Language Processing, pp. 182–192 (2018)
4. Chen, Y., Xu, L., Liu, K., Zeng, D., Zhao, J.: Event extraction via dynamic multi-pooling convolutional neural networks. In: Proceedings of the 53rd Annual Meeting of the Association for Computational Linguistics and the 7th International Joint Conference on Natural Language Processing (Volume 1: Long Papers), vol. 1, pp. 167–176 (2015)
5. Chiu, J.P., Nichols, E.: Named entity recognition with bidirectional LSTM-CNNs. Trans. Assoc. Comput. Linguist. **4**, 357–370 (2016)
6. Dong, C., Zhang, J., Zong, C., Hattori, M., Di, H.: Character-based LSTM-CRF with radical-level features for Chinese named entity recognition. In: Lin, C.-Y., Xue, N., Zhao, D., Huang, X., Feng, Y. (eds.) ICCPOL/NLPCC -2016. LNCS (LNAI), vol. 10102, pp. 239–250. Springer, Cham (2016). https://doi.org/10.1007/978-3-319-50496-4_20
7. Gage, P.: A new algorithm for data compression. C Users J. **12**(2), 23–38 (1994)
8. Hammerton, J.: Named entity recognition with long short-term memory. In: Proceedings of the Seventh Conference on Natural Language Learning at HLT-NAACL 2003-Volume 4, pp. 172–175. Association for Computational Linguistics (2003)
9. Lafferty, J.D., McCallum, A., Pereira, F.C.: Conditional random fields: probabilistic models for segmenting and labeling sequence data. In: Proceedings of the Eighteenth International Conference on Machine Learning, pp. 282–289. Morgan Kaufmann Publishers Inc. (2001)
10. Peng, N., Dredze, M.: Named entity recognition for Chinese social media with jointly trained embeddings. In: Proceedings of the 2015 Conference on Empirical Methods in Natural Language Processing, pp. 548–554 (2015)
11. Peng, N., Dredze, M.: Improving named entity recognition for Chinese social media with word segmentation representation learning. In: The 54th Annual Meeting of the Association for Computational Linguistics, p. 149 (2016)
12. Sennrich, R., Haddow, B., Birch, A.: Neural machine translation of rare words with subword units. In: Proceedings of the 54th Annual Meeting of the Association for Computational Linguistics (Volume 1: Long Papers), vol. 1, pp. 1715–1725 (2016)
13. Strubell, E., Verga, P., Belanger, D., McCallum, A.: Fast and accurate entity recognition with iterated dilated convolutions. In: Proceedings of the 2017 Conference on Empirical Methods in Natural Language Processing, pp. 2670–2680 (2017)
14. Xu, Y., et al.: Joint segmentation and named entity recognition using dual decomposition in chinese discharge summaries. J. Am. Med. Inform. Assoc. **21**(e1), e84–e92 (2013)

15. Yang, J., Zhang, Y., Dong, F.: Neural word segmentation with rich pretraining. In: Proceedings of the 55th Annual Meeting of the Association for Computational Linguistics (Volume 1: Long Papers), pp. 839–849 (2017)
16. Yang, J., Zhang, Y., Liang, S.: Subword encoding in lattice LSTM for Chinese word segmentation. arXiv preprint arXiv:1810.12594 (2018)
17. Yao, X., Van Durme, B.: Information extraction over structured data: question answering with freebase. In: Proceedings of the 52nd Annual Meeting of the Association for Computational Linguistics (Volume 1: Long Papers), vol. 1, pp. 956–966 (2014)
18. Yu, F., Koltun, V.: Multi-scale context aggregation by dilated convolutions. In: Proceedings of the 2016 International Conference on Learning Representations (2016)
19. Zhang, Y., Yang, J.: Chinese NER using lattice LSTM. In: Proceedings of the 56th Annual Meeting of the Association for Computational Linguistics (Volume 1: Long Papers), pp. 1554–1564 (2018)

AliMe KBQA: Question Answering over Structured Knowledge for E-Commerce Customer Service

Feng-Lin Li[✉], Weijia Chen, Qi Huang, and Yikun Guo

Alibaba Group, Hangzhou 311100, China
{fenglin.lfl,yikun.gyk}@alibaba-inc.com

Abstract. With the rise of knowledge graph (KG), question answering over knowledge base (KBQA) has attracted increasing attention in recent years. Despite much research has been conducted on this topic, it is still challenging to apply KBQA technology in industry because business knowledge and real-world questions can be rather complicated. In this paper, we present AliMe-KBQA, a bold attempt to apply KBQA in the E-commerce customer service field. To handle real knowledge and questions, we extend the classic "subject-predicate-object (SPO)" structure with property hierarchy, key-value structure and compound value type (CVT), and enhance traditional KBQA with constraints recognition and reasoning ability. We launch AliMe-KBQA in the *Marketing Promotion* scenario for merchants during the "Double 11" period in 2018 and other such promotional events afterwards. Online results suggest that AliMe-KBQA is not only able to gain better resolution and improve customer satisfaction, but also becomes the preferred knowledge management method by business knowledge staffs since it offers a more convenient and efficient management experience.

Keywords: Knowledge representation · Property hierarchy · Key-value type · Compound Value Type (CVT) · Knowledge reasoning

1 Introduction

AliMe [13] is an intelligent assistant that offers *after-sales service* in the E-commerce customer service field. With question-answer pair (QA[1]) knowledge representation and deep learning (DL) based text matching, AliMe has achieved remarkable success in the consumer community: it currently serves millions of customer questions per day and is able to address 90%+ of them. However, there is still room for improvement in the merchant community, where customer questions are more scattered and complicated.

In our observation, there are still several challenges in knowledge management and for AliMe to better understand customer questions. First, our

---

[1] We use "QA" to refer to "question answering" and "question-answer" interchangeably.

© Springer Nature Singapore Pte Ltd. 2019
X. Zhu et al. (Eds.): CCKS 2019, CCIS 1134, pp. 136–148, 2019.
https://doi.org/10.1007/978-981-15-1956-7_12

knowledge is organized as QA pairs, which are widely used as index for knowledge, rather than true knowledge. The treatment of **knowledge as QA pairs** introduces redundancy (a piece of knowledge has to be enumerated as to deal with real life scenarios, for example, the two QA pairs "一个账号可以绑定几个手机号? how many phone numbers can be bound to a Taobao account" and "为什么我的账号绑定手机时说超出限制? why the system shows that the number of phone numbers exceeds the limit when binding a phone to my account?" actually refers to the same piece of knowledge "一个账号可以绑定6个手机号码 a Taobao account can associate with at most 6 phone numbers"), not to mention sometimes questions can not be exhaustively listed, especially for instance-level and compositional knowledge (for example, knowledge staffs have to maintain such a question "how to register for a promotion program" for at least dozens of programs in AliMe).

Second, with QA representation, business knowledge staffs have to constantly analyse regulations and elicit frequently asked questions (FAQs) for similar and even repeated scenarios like promotional programs, which can be largely alleviated by defining a common schema structure for customer questions. Third, QA pairs do not support reasoning, which is indeed needed in customer service where regulations are of key importance. For example, we have a regulation "店铺级优惠和店铺级优惠不能同时使用 (In-store and in-store discount can not be applied at the same time)", but do not index a specific instance-level knowledge like "优惠券和店铺红包不能同时使用 (Coupon and in-store red packet can not used at the same time)", where "优惠券 (Coupon)" and "店铺红包 (In-store Red Packet)" are both of type "In-store Discount".

To address these challenges, we launched **Knowledge Cloud** project, aiming at constructing a systematically structured knowledge representation and enabling AliMe to better understand customer questions instead of simply matching questions to knowledge items based on text or semantic similarity.

In this paper, we present AliMe-KBQA, a knowledge graph based bot application, and introduce its underlying knowledge representation and supporting techniques. To the best of our knowledge, this is the first attempt to apply KBQA techniques in customer service industry on a large scale. Our paper makes the following contributions:

- Extends the classic SPO structure to capture practical knowledge and questions: (1) we use property hierarchy instead of flatten properties to organize knowledge, and guide vague questions; (2) we adopt key-value structure and Compound Value Type (CVT) to characterize complicated answer for precise question answering.
- Empower traditional KBQA with constraints recognition and reasoning ability based on our structured knowledge representation in support of complicated and regulation-oriented QA in the E-commerce customer service field.
- Launch AliMe-KBQA as a practical QA bot in the *Marketing Promotion* scenario. Online results suggestion that KBQA is able to not only gain better resolution rate and degree of satisfaction from customer side, but also be

preferred by business knowledge staffs since it offers better knowledge management experience.

The rest of the paper is structured as follows: Sect. 2 presents our structured knowledge representation; Sect. 3 discusses the extended KBQA approach; Sect. 4 demonstrates system features; Sect. 5 reviews related work, Sect. 6 concludes the paper and sketches directions for future work.

2   Knowledge Representation

In general, a knowledge graph $\mathcal{K}$ is organized in terms of nodes and links, and defined as a set of triples $(e_h, p, e_t) \in \mathcal{E} \times \mathcal{P} \times \mathcal{E}$ (e.g., "Beijing, capital_of, China"), where $\mathcal{E}$ denotes a set of entities/classes/literals, and $\mathcal{P}$ denotes a set of properties.

Not surprisingly, this general triple representation is insufficient in capturing practical knowledge and questions. One can see the examples shown in Table 1. The piece of knowledge k_1 is very general and need to be further specified, otherwise its answer will be too complicated to maintain and read. The problem with the k_2 is that it includes two entities "淘抢购 (Tao Flash Sale)" and "双十一 (Double 11)", and the former modifies the latter. Similarly, the entity "Double 11" in k_3 is a modifier of "floor price", which is also an entity as merchants often ask what it is and how to calculate it. In k_4 "优惠券 (Coupon)" and "单品宝 (SKU-Bao)" are specific instances of "In-store Discount", and such combination of different kinds of discount is hard to enumerate and maintain for business knowledge staffs.

Table 1. Example QA-style knowledge items

k_1. 店铺宝优惠规则
The discount regulation of Store-Bao
k_2. 怎么参加淘抢购的双十一?
How join in the Double 11 event of Tao Flash Sale?
k_3. 淘抢购是否计入双十一最低活动价?
Whether Tao Flash Sale is counted in Double 11's floor price?
k_4. 优惠券和单品宝能不能一起使用?
Can coupon and SKU-Bao can be used in conjunction?

To capture real business knowledge, we present our extended knowledge representation in Fig. 1, where colored rectangles denote our extension: (1) a property can be decomposed into sub-properties; (2) value type is extended with key-value structure and Compound Value Type (CVT). In our ontology, a property is treated as a mapping function that maps an entity of type "Class" (domain) to a value that has a type "Value_Type" (range). An entity reifies a property of its class when the value of that property is configured. Our CVT is adopted from

Freebase [5], treated as self-defined class and captured as table. For simplicity, we define for each CVT table a main (answer) column that will be queried, and take the other columns as conditions or constraints.

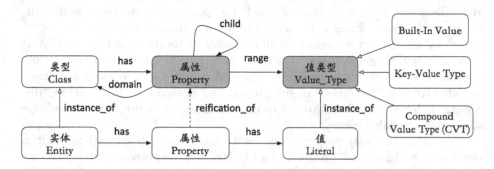

Fig. 1. The ontology of our structured knowledge representation (Color figure online)

We show an excerpt of the schema of "Promotion_Tool" in Fig. 2. Nodes are entities $e \in \mathcal{E}$ (e.g., "店铺宝 Store-Bao"), classes $c \in \mathcal{C}$ (e.g., "营销工具 Promotion_Tool"), literals $l \in \mathcal{L}$ (e.g., "三星级 3-star"). Links are properties $p \in \mathcal{P}$ (e.g., "定义 definition"). Moreover, the entity "Store-Bao" is an instance of "Promotion_Tool", and reifies its properties through associating corresponding values.

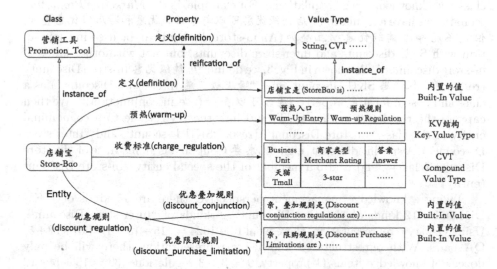

Fig. 2. An excerpt of our extended knowledge representation

A property, if composite, can be decomposed into sub-properties according to business knowledge. The resulting hierarchical structure, instead of flatten properties, offers better understandability and knowledge management experience. A path from root property to leaf property constitutes a property chain that links an entity to a corresponding value. For example, the root property "discount_regulation" in Fig. 2 is decomposed into "discount_conjunction" and "discount_purchase_limitation"; and, the path "discount_regulation - discount_conjunction" forms a property chain that maps "Store-Bao" to a text string value. An extra benefit of hierarchical property structure is that it enables a bot to guide vague[2] customer questions through recommendation. For example, if a customer merely mention "discount", we can guide customers to either entities "Store-Bao" or sub-properties "'discount_conjunction" or "discount_purchase_limitation" through recommendation according to the knowledge structure and dialog context.

The value of (leaf) property can be a simple value (captured as built-in types such as String and Integer), or a block of text (captured as String or key-value segmented wiki-style document), or a composite value (captured as CVT). The key-value structure allows to segment a long answer text on demand, is able to support tabbed UI representation of the answer and bring about better reading experience. The use of CVT to characterize multiple-fields of a property, allows us to capture multi-constraints of a knowledge item (e.g., the value of "charge_regulation" depends on not only "Business Unit" but also "Merchant Rating"), and enables us to perform precise question answering (e.g., if we know the "Business Unit" and "Merchant Rating", we can get the precise answer instead of output the whole table).

Our knowledge representation is able to capture not only instance-level but also class-level knowledge (e.g., regulations). For example, in the *Marketing Promotion* scenario, we have a regulation: "店铺级优惠可以与单品级优惠和跨店级优惠叠加, 但是不能和店铺级优惠相互叠加 (An in-store discount can be used in conjunction with SKU discounts and inter-store discounts, but not with other kinds of in-store discounts)". As shown in Fig. 3, we define "店铺级优惠 In-store Discount" (resp. "单品级优惠 SKU Discount" and "跨店级优惠 Inter-store Discount") as a class and design for it a property "是否可以叠加 (use_in_conjunction)". We then capture the regulation with a CVT, and link the CVT table to a cognominal entity of the class "In-store Discount" (resp. "SKU Discount" and "Inter-store Discount"). A specific discount, e.g., "优惠券 Coupon", is an instance of "In-store Discount (class)", and is also a member of the special entity "In-store Discount (entity)".

Taking a knowledge management perspective, there are 15 kinds of "SKU Discount", 12 kinds of "In-store Discount", 5 kinds of "Inter-store Discount". Using QA style representation, there would be $1024 = (15+12+5)*(15+12+5)$ QA pairs. With our structured knowledge representation, there will be only dozens of knowledge items (1 property, $9 = 3 \times 3$ regulations, $32 = 15 + 5 + 12$ "instance_of" and "member_of" tuples). That is, the structured representation largely reduces the number of knowledge items, enabling convenient knowledge

---

[2] It is worth to mention that nearly a quarter of questions are vague or incomplete in practice.

單品級優惠 SKU Discount (15): 單品宝(SKU Bao), 预售(Pre-sale), 秒杀(SecKill) ······
店铺级优惠 In-store Discount (12): 优惠券 (Coupon) , 店铺红包 (In-store Red Packet) ······
跨店级优惠 Inter-store Discount (5):购物津贴 (Shopping allowance) , 品类券(Category Coupon) ······

Fig. 3. An example of regulation knowledge

management and better model matching performance (large number of similar QA pairs are difficult for model to distinguish).

With the defined schema, given a new promotion program, business knowledge staffs only need to fill in the answer of defined properties that represent customer questions, and do not need to elicit frequently asked questions any more. More than that, the training samples for the properties of a schema can be highly, or even totally reused (only entity mentions need to be substituted). That is, the cold-start cost can be largely reduced. In fact, it only took us one working day to launch AliMe-KBQA in the *Marketing Promotion* scenario for the "Double 12" day after its application in the "Double 11" period.

3   KBQA Approach

We base our KBQA approach on staged query graph generation [19] which uses knowledge graph to prune the search space, and multi-constraint query graph [2] that focuses on constraint recognition and binding [2]. We focus on how to utilize the structured knowledge representation for KBQA applications, and employ state-of-the-art DL models (CNN, Bi-GRU, attention, label embedding, etc.) to perform our task.

In this line of research, the KBQA problem can be defined as follows: given a question q and a knowledge base $\mathcal{K}$, q is translated to a set of query graphs $\mathcal{G}$ according to $\mathcal{K}$, then a feature vector $f(q, g)$ is extracted for each graph $g \in \mathcal{G}$ and used for ranking, the graph with the highest score will be chosen and executed to obtain the answer a.

We show an overview of our approach in Fig. 4. Given a question, we at first generate a set of basic query graphs in the form of (e, p, v), where e denotes a topic entity, p denotes a property and v denotes a variable node. Specifically, we identify entities from the question through a *trie*-based rule engine[3], substitute the mentioned entities with a special symbol, and then map the masked question to candidate (leaf) properties of the classes of identified entities through a tailored CNN [10] classification model.

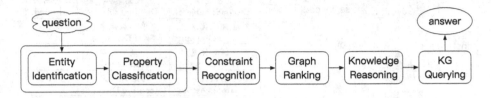

Fig. 4. An overview of our KBQA approach

In the case v is a CVT node, a basic query graph will have the form of (e, p, v_{cvt}, r, x), where r denotes the answer column of the CVT table, and x stands for a specific value in a CVT cell. One can refer to the bottom right corner of Fig. 5 for an example, where the entity is "Double 11" and the property is "registration_process". Further, we use rule-based and similarity-based string matching to identify constraints and link them to the CVT node. As shown at the rightmost part of Fig. 5, the recognized constraint $(Tao\_Flash\_Sale, =, y_1)$ is linked to the CVT node through $(v_{cvt}, promo\_method, y_1)$.

Note that Fig. 5 shows only one possible query graph for the given question. As we usually have multiple query graphs, simple or complicated, we at last employ a ranking model based on LambdaRank [8] to rank candidate graphs and reply with the answer of Top-K graphs ($K = 1$ for question answering and $K = 3$ for recommendation).

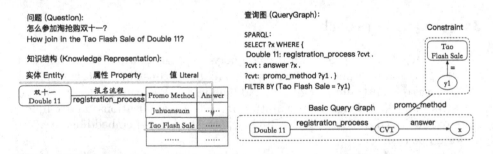

Fig. 5. Question answering over structured knowledge representation: an example

Last but not least, we need to perform reasoning (when needed) on the ranked Top-K graphs in order to obtain the answer, especially for class-level

---

[3] Entity linking is not performed as disambiguation is not necessary in our current scenario.

regulations in the E-commerce customer service field. As in Fig. 6, given the question "优惠券和单品宝能不能一起使用 (Can coupon and SKU-Bao be used at the same time?)", we first form the basic graph (e, p, v_{cvt}, r, x), where e indicates "Coupon", p stands for "use_in_conjunction", r represents "answer". On observing that the domain and the range of p need to be inferred[4], we generalize "Coupon" (resp. "SKU-Bao") as a kind of "In-store Discount" (resp. "SKU Discount") by following the "member_of" property shown in Fig. 3. After that, we are able to query the CVT table whether "In-store Discount" can be used together with "SKU Discount", and obtain the explicit and precise answer "NO".

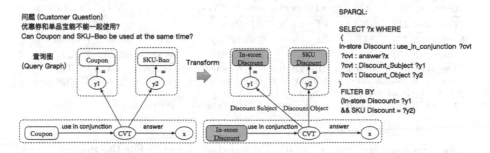

Fig. 6. Knowledge reasoning over structured representation: an example

4   KBQA System

We first launched our KBQA system in the *Marketing Promotion* scenario in AliWanxiang (a product of the AliMe family) for Tmall merchants. Our schema includes 121 properties, 73 out of which are associated with CVTs, and covers 320 original QA pairs. During the "Double 11" period in 2018, our bot served more than one million customer questions, and achieved a resolution rate[5] of 90%+, which is 10-percent higher than traditional QA-style representation and question to question text matching. Moreover, it also won a 10% increase of satisfaction degree according to our user survey.

We further applied our structured knowledge representation and KBQA approach in three other scenarios, and found that our representation is adequate in capturing practical knowledge and our KBQA approach is able to deal with real-world customer questions. The statistics in Table 2 show that the number

---

[4] We use an indicator to denote whether the domain (resp. range) of a property need to be inferred (yes:1, no:0), and how it will be inferred (e.g., by following the "member_of" property).

[5] The resolution rate rr is calculated as follows: $rr = 1 - U/T$, where U denotes the number of unsolved sessions, which includes disliked sessions, no-answer sessions, and sessions that explicitly requests for staff service, and T stands for the number of total sessions.

of QA pairs can be largely reduced (we are more concerned about the compression ratio regarding QA pairs and properties $Compr_1$ because the number of properties indicates how many knowledge items need to label training samples for and perform model matching on), and the resolution rate gains an absolute increase of 5% on average. It also show that CVT is of importance, even essential (e.g., CVT accounts for 62.5% of the properties in scenario-3), in representing practical knowledge.

Table 2. Statistics of knowledge before and after structuration

Scenarios	#QA[a]	#Entity	#Property	$Compr_1$ $(Compr_2)$[b]	#CVT	$CVTr$[c]	Resolution
Scenario-1	232	35	78	2.97 (2.04)	9	11.54%	↑ 7.88%
Scenario-2	776	111	73	10.63 (4.22)	27	36.99%	↑ 4.9%
Scenario-3	870	367	72	12.08 (1.98)	45	62.5%	↑ 3.24%

[a]The symbol '#' represents the number of QA pairs, entities, properties or CVTs.
[b]The compression ratio is defined as $Compr_1 = \#QA \div \#Property$ and $Compr_2 = \#QA \div (\#Entity + \#Property)$.
[c]The CVT ratio is defined as $CVTr = \#CVTProperty \div \#Property$.

We demonstrates precise question answering in Fig. 7. For the first example, given the question "优惠券和单品宝能不能一起使用 (Can coupon and SKU Bao be used at the same time?)", our bot replies with a precise and interpretable answer "Coupon is a kind of In-store Discount, SKU-Bao is a kind of SKU Discount, In-store Discount and SKU Discount can be used in conjunction". For the second example, one asks "淘抢购是否计入双十一最低价 (Whether the Tao Flash Sale is counted in the floor price of Double 11)", our bot answers with a precise "计入 (Yes)" in the concise and explicit table through identifying the "Subject Event", "Object Event" and "Promotion Means" slots[6], and further gives tips that help customers to understand relevant regulations. The third example shows how the structured representation is used to guide customers when questions are vague: when a customer merely mention "618", our bot generates several probable questions based on the candidate properties of "Promotion_Program", the class of "618". The forth example demonstrates how our key-value structure can be used to segment long text answer and support tabbed knowledge representation.

5 Related Work

In this section, we review related work on knowledge representation, KBQA, and knowledge reasoning, which are closely related to the techniques employed in this paper.

Knowledge Representation. The key of knowledge graphs (KG) is to understand real world entities and their relationships in terms of nodes and links,

---

[6] Note that the slot "participated goods" is defaulted as "Yes".

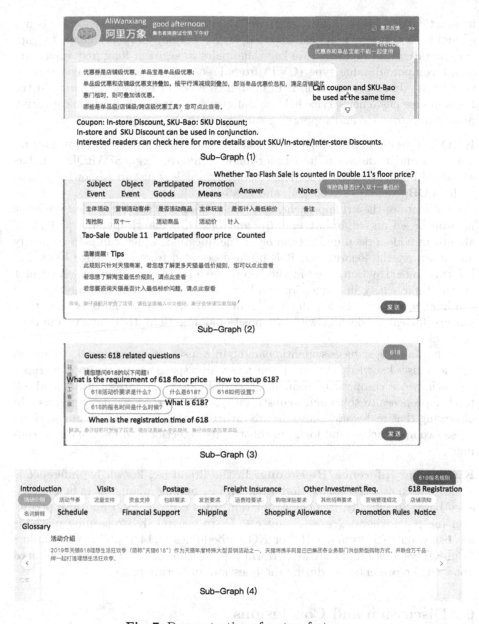

Fig. 7. Demonstration of system features

i.e., things, not strings. To the best of our knowledge, most of the studies on KBQA treat knowledge graphs as a set of subject-predicate-object (SPO) triples, build their approaches on ready-made knowledge graphs such as Freebase [5], YAGO [16] and DBpedia [1], and evaluate them on benchmark data-sets e.g., WebQuestions [3]). Few researchers have tried to apply the classic triple structure in practical scenarios. In fact, not surprisingly, this triple representation is not enough in capturing practical knowledge. We employ property chain to capture hierarchical properties, use key-value pairs to segment long text value, and adopt compound value type (CVT) from Freebase [5] to capture constraints. Our knowledge representation is evaluated in a set of realistic scenarios in the E-commerce customer service field, and it turns out to be adequate in capturing practical knowledge and supporting subsequent KBQA applications.

KBQA. Question answering over knowledge base, which takes as input natural language and translate it into tailor-made language (e.g., SPARQL [5]), has attracted much attention since the rise of large scale structured knowledge base such as DBpedia [1], YAGO [16], and Freebase [5].

The state-of-the-art approaches can be classified into two categories: *semantic parsing* based and *information extraction* based. Semantic parsing [3,4,11] is able to provide a deep understanding of the question, which can help to justify and interpret the answer, but it is often decoupled from knowledge base [19]. Information extraction based methods retrieve a set of candidate answers center on the topic entity in a question, and extract features from the question and candidates to rank them [6,9]. One limitation of such methods is that they are insufficient in dealing with compositional questions that involve multiple constraints.

Yih et al. [19] reduces semantic parsing into a staged query graph generation problem, uses knowledge base to prune the search space when forming the graph, and achieves a competitive result on the WebQuestions dataset. Bao et al. [2] further proposes to solve multi-constraint questions based on query graphs. On observing that real-world questions are rather complicated, we base our work on these two approaches, and focus on constraints detection and knowledge reasoning.

Knowledge Inference/Reasoning. In the literature, knowledge inference is usually taken as a KB completion problem, i.e., finding missing facts in a knowledge base. Specifically, it includes relation inference $(e_h, ?, e_t)$ and link prediction $(e_h, p, ?)$, where $e_h, e_t \in \mathcal{E}$ and $r \in \mathcal{P}$. In general, KB reasoning methods are based on path formulas [12] or KG embeddings [7,14,18]. Our work differs from KB completion in that we perform type reasoning based on our structured knowledge representation during the question answering process.

6   Discussion and Conclusions

To our knowledge, this is the first attempt to apply KBQA in customer service industry. To deal with complicated knowledge and questions, we propose a novel structured knowledge representation, and accordingly introduce our approach about how to support multi-constraint and reasoning.

The benefits of our structured knowledge representation are many-fold: (1) it is able to capture class-level, rather than instance-level knowledge, hence largely reducing the number of knowledge items and making it more convenient for human management and easier for model-based text matching; (2) it defines a common structure for repetitive scenarios, with which business knowledge staffs do not need to repeatedly eliciting FAQs and training samples can be highly reused for scenarios of the same type; (3) it supports multi-constraint and reasoning, which contribute to performing precise question answering and offering better user experience; (4) it allows to guide vague or incomplete customer questions based on knowledge structure and dialog context; (5) Last but not least, it enables diversified UI representation of knowledge (e.g., key-value structured for tabbed representation, CVT for table representation), which brings about better readability and understandability, hence better customer satisfaction.

Several problems remain open. One interesting problem is how to lower the cost of manual schema construction through utilizing information extraction [15] techniques. We are also interested in investigating TableQA [17] for systematically addressing constraints recognition in our CVT knowledge structure.

References

1. Auer, S., Bizer, C., Kobilarov, G., Lehmann, J., Cyganiak, R., Ives, Z.: DBpedia: a nucleus for a web of open data. In: Aberer, K., et al. (eds.) ASWC/ISWC -2007. LNCS, vol. 4825, pp. 722–735. Springer, Heidelberg (2007). https://doi.org/10.1007/978-3-540-76298-0_52
2. Bao, J., Duan, N., Yan, Z., Zhou, M., Zhao, T.: Constraint-based question answering with knowledge graph. In: Proceedings of COLING 2016, The 26th International Conference on Computational Linguistics: Technical Papers, pp. 2503–2514 (2016)
3. Berant, J., Chou, A., Frostig, R., Liang, P.: Semantic parsing on freebase from question-answer pairs. In: Proceedings of the 2013 Conference on Empirical Methods in Natural Language Processing, pp. 1533–1544 (2013)
4. Berant, J., Liang, P.: Semantic parsing via paraphrasing. In: Proceedings of the 52nd Annual Meeting of the Association for Computational Linguistics (Volume 1: Long Papers), vol. 1, pp. 1415–1425 (2014)
5. Bollacker, K., Evans, C., Paritosh, P., Sturge, T., Taylor, J.: Freebase: a collaboratively created graph database for structuring human knowledge. In: Proceedings of the 2008 ACM SIGMOD International Conference on Management of Data, pp. 1247–1250. ACM (2008)
6. Bordes, A., Chopra, S., Weston, J.: Question answering with subgraph embeddings. arXiv preprint arXiv:1406.3676 (2014)
7. Bordes, A., Usunier, N., Garcia-Duran, A., Weston, J., Yakhnenko, O.: Translating embeddings for modeling multi-relational data. In: Advances in Neural Information Processing Systems, pp. 2787–2795 (2013)
8. Burges, C.J.: From ranknet to lambdarank to lambdamart: an overview. Learning 11(23–581), 81 (2010)
9. Dong, L., Wei, F., Zhou, M., Xu, K.: Question answering over freebase with multi-column convolutional neural networks. In: Proceedings of the 53rd Annual Meeting of the Association for Computational Linguistics and the 7th International Joint Conference on Natural Language Processing (Volume 1: Long Papers), vol. 1, pp. 260–269 (2015)

10. Kim, Y.: Convolutional neural networks for sentence classification. arXiv preprint arXiv:1408.5882 (2014)
11. Kwiatkowski, T., Choi, E., Artzi, Y., Zettlemoyer, L.: Scaling semantic parsers with on-the-fly ontology matching. In: Proceedings of the 2013 Conference on Empirical Methods in Natural Language Processing, pp. 1545–1556 (2013)
12. Lao, N., Mitchell, T., Cohen, W.W.: Random walk inference and learning in a large scale knowledge base. In: Proceedings of the Conference on Empirical Methods in Natural Language Processing, pp. 529–539. Association for Computational Linguistics (2011)
13. Li, F.L., et al.: Alime assist: an intelligent assistant for creating an innovative e-commerce experience. In: Proceedings of the 2017 ACM on Conference on Information and Knowledge Management, pp. 2495–2498. ACM (2017)
14. Lin, Y.-., Liu, Z., Sun, M., Liu, Y., Zhu, X.: Learning entity and relation embeddings for knowledge graph completion. In: Twenty-Ninth AAAI Conference on Artificial Intelligence (2015)
15. Niklaus, C., Cetto, M., Freitas, A., Handschuh, S.: A survey on open information extraction. arXiv preprint arXiv:1806.05599 (2018)
16. Suchanek, F.M., Kasneci, G., Weikum, G.: Yago: a core of semantic knowledge. In: Proceedings of the 16th International Conference on World Wide Web, pp. 697–706. ACM (2007)
17. Sun, Y., et al.: Semantic parsing with syntax-and table-aware SQL generation. arXiv preprint arXiv:1804.08338 (2018)
18. Wang, Z., Zhang, J., Feng, J., Chen, Z.: Knowledge graph embedding by translating on hyperplanes. In: Twenty-Eighth AAAI Conference on Artificial Intelligence (2014)
19. Yih, S.W.T., Chang, M.W., He, X., Gao, J.: Semantic parsing via staged query graph generation: Question answering with knowledge base. In: Proceedings of the Joint Conference of the 53rd Annual Meeting of the ACL and the 7th International Joint Conference on Natural Language Processing of the AFNLP (2015)

CN-StartEnd: A Chinese Event Base Recording Start and End for Everything

Hualong Zhang, Liting Liu, Shuzhi Cheng, and Wenxuan Shi[✉]

Nankai University, Tianjin, China
nankaizhl@gmail.com, nkliuliting826@mail.nankai.edu.cn,
shuzhichengspace@163.com, shiwx@nankai.edu.cn

Abstract. Start and end are very important attributes in knowledge graphs. The entities or relations in a knowledge graph often have their validity periods represented by start timestamps and end timestamps. For example, Obama's birthday is the start time of his life and the departure time is the end of his president's career. We need to refer to the start timestamps or end timestamps when dealing with temporal tasks such as temporal question answering. The existing Chinese knowledge graphs, with popular examples including CN-DBpedia, Zhishi.me and PKU-PIE, contain some unprocessed start timestamps and end timestamps for their entities. While in Chinese, a large number of descriptions about the beginning or end of entities, relations and states lie in events. In this paper we introduce our work in constructing a Chinese event base which focus on start-events and end-events. We extract more than 3 million event-temporal cases from infoboxes and natural texts of Chinese encyclopedias. After selection and matching, these event-temporal cases are reconstructed into a large-scale knowledge base that incorporates over 2.3 million start-events and 700 thousand end-events. Events describing the same object and match our start-end templates are merged into more than 150 thousand start-end pairs. Dumps for CN-StartEnd are available at: http://eventkg.cn/cn_StartEnd.

Keywords: Event base · Chinese event · Temporal knowledge graph

1 Introduction

In a knowledge graph, a certain state of an entity is often accompanied by a time attribute. The relations between entities also sometimes have their validity periods. Start time and end time are very important attributes for both entities and relations. In event-centric knowledge graphs like EventKG [1], a start timestamp means a certain event starts, a certain state of an entity starts or a certain relation exists. For example, Obama's birthday is the beginning time of his life and the time he took office is the start of his president's career. When dealing with temporal tasks such as temporal question answering and timeline generation, well-organized event-temporal cases are necessary.

The existing Chinese knowledge graphs are mainly entity-centric while pay less attention on events and temporal data. In practice, the triples in Chinese entity-centric graphs such as CN-DBpedia, Zhishi.me and PKU-PIE are mainly extracted from

© Springer Nature Singapore Pte Ltd. 2019
X. Zhu et al. (Eds.): CCKS 2019, CCIS 1134, pp. 149–157, 2019.
https://doi.org/10.1007/978-981-15-1956-7_13

semi-structured infobox of encyclopedias like Wikipedia. While in Chinese, a large number of descriptions about event with temporal expressions lie in natural texts.

Table 1. Typical types of begin-events and end-events.

Begin or End	Event
Begin	入学 / school entrance
	出生 / birth
	出版 / publishment
	创建 / establishment
End	毕业 / graduation
	去世 / death
	停刊 / stop publication
	倒闭 / bankruptcy

In this paper, we collect as many event cases with temporal expressions and actors as possible from existing Chinese encyclopedias including Baidu baike, Hudong baike and Wikipedia-zh. A rule-based approach is used to collect event candidates and a distant supervision method is used to build templates. Then we focus on finding the cases which can be used to represent beginning or ending for entities, relations and certain states. Birthdays and deaths are the most obvious and easiest to get. However, for general event cases, it is difficult to judge whether they have the meaning of start or end. We choose to learn patterns from existing Chinese texts with time ranges to find typical event types that match our target. Examples of some typical events and corresponding categories are shown in Table 1. Finally, we build a knowledge base with millions of start-events and end-events. If a start-event and end-event describe the same object and match a start-end template, they will be merge into a start-end pair. Over 150 thousand start-end pairs are found out.

2 Related Work

EventKG [1] is a multilingual event-centric knowledge graph which extract events from existing entity-centric knowledge graphs including Wikidata, YAGO and DBPedia. EventKG models events and relations with SEM (Simple Event Model) [2]. In EventKG, a core event instance can be assigned an existence time denoted via a hasBeginTimeStamp property and a hasEndTimeStamp property. However, due to the imbalance of data in Wikidata, YAGO and DBPedia, there are very few Chinese entities and relations. We are unable to build a usable Chinese event graph via the multilingual framework of EventKG. This inspires us to build a Chinese event base using more localized data sources. As for how to extract events from open knowledge bases and web pages, some available solutions have been given. Hienert et al. provide a multi-granularity framework for extracting events from Wikipedia [3]. Yubo et al.

propose to automatically label training data for event extraction via world knowledge and linguistic knowledge [4]. Faced with our task we also generate training data for temporal tagging in a similar way.

For Chinese, researchers have developed some entity-centric knowledge graphs like CN-DBpedia [5] which introduces event cases into graph in its recent versions. We are inspired by this to develop a different Chinese event base focus on start and end.

Table 2. Structure of a base event as defined.

A Base Event			
Text	**Verb**	**Participants**	**Time**
1843 年 10 月，马克思和燕妮一起来到巴黎。 In October 1843, Marx and Yanni came to Paris together.	来到 come to	马克思,燕妮,巴黎 Marx, Yanni, Paris	1843 年 10 月底 October 1843

3 CN-StartEnd Data Model

3.1 Event Definition

We use verb-centric event definitions as [6] does. A verb and its dominated semantic elements including time and participants constitute a base event. Table 2 provides the structure of an event example. The number of participants (called actor in following sections) in an event can be one or more.

3.2 Event Model

SEM defines a Simple Event Model with four core classes: Event, Actor, Place and Time [2]. However, in practice, the locations of the events are often missing and less important, so when we model an event, the location is not a core class. Instead, Evidence becomes one of the core classes. According to our definition, the data model of an event in CN-StartEnd is shown in Fig. 1. We use the 'cnse:' prefix to represent the concept in CN-StartEnd. There are four classes cnse:Event (what happens), cnse: Time (when), cnse:Actor (who or what participated) and cnse:Evidence (data sources referring to this event) working as subclasses of cnse:Core. The solid lines in Fig. 1 represent the relations between instances of different classes while the dotted line points to properties. An instance can hold several properties such as place, gender and reason which are not listed in the figure. Two properties cnse:hasLiteral and cnse:hasData-Source are highlighted in Fig. 1 since they play roles in representation and storage. Each instance of cnse:Event, cnse:Actor and cnse:Time is bound to a literal text. One event in CN-StartEnd may be mentioned in several documents since we extract cases from multiple data sources, therefore we reserve every mention for an event as evidence.

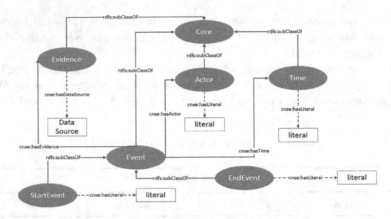

Fig. 1. Data model of event in CN-StartEnd.

As we mentioned earlier, our event cases are mainly extracted from Chinese encyclopedias. Instances of cnse:Event, cnse:Actor and cnse:Time may be same as entities in some knowledge bases which can be represented via relation owl:sameAs.

3.3 Start-End Pair Definition

An event instance will be treated as a cnse:StartEvent if it describes something begin. Similarly, if an event describes an ending, it is a cnse:EndEvent. Or it's simply a cnse: Event without any start or end meaning.

Two events that describe the beginning and end of the same thing constitute a start-end pair. CN-StartEnd is designed to store start-events, end-events and matched pairs. As shown in Fig. 1, an instance of cnse:EndEvent may have a cnse:hasStartEvent relation linked to a matched cnse:StartEvent instance. The event relation cnse:hasEndEvent plays a similar role.

3.4 Representation and Storage

We use triples to represent instances and the relations between them. Each event instance has a unique id and a complete literal description. If two cnse:Events hold the same cnse:Actor, cnse:Time and the event verb, they will be stored as one. That's how we deduplicate the event cases in CN-StartEnd. Finally, complete events will be represented and stored as Fig. 2 shows. Figure 2 provides <event 127> and <event 128> as examples in CN-StartEnd. The literal text of the case <event 127> is

马克思在 1864 年又创立了第一国际。

Marx founded the First International in 1864.

which describes a historical event that Marx founded the First International. The case <event 128> just describes an event opposite to <event 127> that Marx dissolved the First International. According to our definition, these two events constitute a start-end pair. The common participants "马克思/Marx" and "第一国际/the First International" are stored as cnse:Actors for the events. Temporal expressions are regularized to standard form as detailed as possible.

```
......
<event 127>        rdf:type              cnse:StartEvent
<event 127>        cnse:hasLiteral       马克思在1864年又创立了第一国际。
                                         (Marx founded the First International in 1864.)
<event 127>        cnse:hasActor         马克思 (Marx)
<event 127>        cnse:hasActor         第一国际(First International)
<event 127>        cnse:hasTime          1864
<event 127>        cnse:hasEndEvent      <event 128>
<event 127>        cnse:hasEvidnece      https://baike.baidu.com/view/10007
<event 127>        cnse:hasEvidence      https://baike.com/wiki/%E6%94%BF%E5%85%9A
<event 128>        rdf:type              cnse:EndEvent
<event 128>        cnse:hasLiteral       马克思在1876年解散了第一国际。
                                         (Marx dissolved the First International in 1876.)
<event 128>        cnse:hasActor         马克思(Marx)
<event 128>        cnse:hasActor         第一国际(First International)
<event 128>        cnse:hasTime          1876
<event 128>        cnse:hasStartEvent    <event 127>
<event 128>        cnse:hasEvidnece      https://baike.baidu.com/view/10007
......
```

Fig. 2. Examples of representation and storage for events in CN-StartEnd.

4   CN-StartEnd Construction Pipeline

The pipeline of constructing CN-StartEnd is show in Fig. 3. First, the dumps of the reference sources are collected. Data sources include pages from Baidu baike, Hudong baike and Wikiedia-zh. In the rough extraction step, we first collect the infobox triples with temporal expressions which can naturally be treated as events. We also collect sentences with temporal expressions as event candidates. After temporal tagging and event extraction, we get a Chinese event base. For temporal tagging, we build a Chinese temporal detector in a distant supervision way as [7] dose. The popular system LTP is used to identify semantic roles as semantic elements of events.

Fig. 3. CN-StartEnd construction pipeline.

text with time range	卡尔·马克思（1818年5月5日－1883年3月14日），马克思主义的创始人之一，第一国际的组织者和领导者。 Karl Marx (May 5, 1818 - March 14, 1883), one of the founders of Marxism, the organizer and leader of the First International.
the time range	1818年5月5日－1883年3月14日 May 5, 1818 - March 14, 1883
event at start of time range	卡尔·马克思1818年5月5日出生于普鲁士王国莱茵省一个律师家庭。 Karl Marx was born on May 5, 1818 in a family of lawyers in the province of Prussia.
start event verb	出生(be born)
event at end of time range	1883年3月14日中午，马克思安详地辞世了。 At noon on March 14, 1883, Marx died peacefully.
end event verb	辞世(pass away)
start-end template	出生 (be born)-逝世 (pass away)

Fig. 4. How time ranges provide start-end templates.

Finding cases from the Chinese event base to form start-end pairs requires an understanding of the start-end pairing pattern. A large number of time ranges in the encyclopedic corpus we use give us ready-made templates. The example in Fig. 4 shows how a time range provides a template. Suppose there are two events with the same actors, one at the start of the time range and the other at the end of the time range, then the verbs of the two events form a start-end template like the example "出生 (be born)-逝世 (pass away)" shown in Fig. 4. We collect start-end templates and use them for start-end matching to generate more start-end pairs.

5 Statistics and Evaluation

We collect as many event cases with temporal expressions and actors as possible from existing Chinese encyclopedias. Both infoboxes and natural texts are used as sources for event extraction as Fig. 3 shows. More than 3 million event-temporal cases are collected. Matching with start-end templates, more than 150, 000 start-end pairs are found. Unsurprisingly, the most common start-end pairs are birth-death pairs. Over 100,000 birth-death pairs are recorded. Counts for most common pairs are listed in the Table 3. In the matching process, those events that are not paired are also recorded as start-events and end-events separately. Statistics of most common events are listed in Table 4. It's easy to find an imbalance between start-events and end-events. The most common starting events contribute little to start-end pairs. For example, a book often has a publishing event that represents its beginning with no corresponding end-event.

Since there is no similar work that focus on start-event and end-event for comparison, we simply compare it to existing event-centric works. Comparisons with other event bases are shown in the Table 5. It can be seen that although CN_StartEnd is a single language event library, the total number of recorded events is more than EventKG. Further, we have filtered and divided the events into two categories: start and end. The event lists of Wikipedia-zh, Baidu baike and Hudong baike are mainly recorded in pages of their year entities and date entities. Because in our definition, timestamps are indispensable elements of events, all recorded events have their known time.

Table 3. Counts for most frequent start-end pairs.

Start-End Pair	Count
出生-逝世 / Birth-Death	107355
开园-闭园 / Open-Close	3734
开工-竣工 / Start Building-Complete	811
开始-结束 / Start-Over	522
服役-退役 / Serve-Retire	453
建国-灭亡 / Nation Start-Nation Demise	298

Table 4. Statistics for top events.

Event	Count	Start or End
出版 / publish	1534666	Start
成立 / Established	493660	Start
出生 / Birth	387682	Start
毕业 / Graduate	354787	End
去世 / Death	151130	End
发行 / Issue or Release	108537	Start
授予 / Grant	107959	Start
创作 / Literal Create	77745	Start
发生 / Happen	76411	Start
改名 / Rename	74728	End

Table 5. Comparisons with existing event bases.

Event base	Count	Language	Known time
CN-StartEnd	≥ 3,000,000	Chinese	100%
EventKG	≥ 320,000	Multilingual	50.82%
Wikipedia-zh Event List	≥ 18,000	Chinese	100%
Baidu baike Event List	≥ 68,000	Chinese	100%
Hudong baike Event List	≥ 51,000	Chinese	100%

There are two kinds of events in CN-StartEnd, those from infoboxes and those extracted from sentences. For events from infoboxes, we simply believe that they are of high quality, except for a few editorial errors. We are mainly concerned with the quality of events extracted from sentences. We randomly sampled 600 cases from start-events and end-events for evaluation. We calculate the accuracy of rdf:type, cnse:hasTime, cnse:hasAct and cnse:hasActor for these cases based on their literal evidences.

Table 6. Accuracy of event element extraction

	Accuracy (%)		
	Start-event	End-event	Overall
cnse:Time	99.33	99.67	99.5
cnse:Act	94	96.33	95.17
cnse:Actor	93	89.67	91.33
rdf:type	98	97	97.5

The values in Table 6 show the accuracy of the core elements and type of events in CN-StartEnd. The overall scores are over 90% while the performance of cnse:Actor extraction is relatively poor. To improve the recognition of cnse:Actors needs better NER methods. Very few cases have incorrect event categories which contributes a good accuracy of rdf:type.

For paired start-end pairs, we can't estimate their true recall, still we sample random cases and calculate accuracy. Overall, the accuracy of event pairs is around 0.87. We find that there are two main causes of wrong event pairs. One is due to errors in the events themselves that constitute the pairs, for example an event which is not belong to cnse:startEvent or cnse:endEvent is put in a pair. Another is that there is no semantic pairing between the two events in a pair.

6   Conclusion

Focusing on two types of events in Chinese with special meanings: start and end, we build an event base CN-StartEnd which aims to record start and end for everything in Chinese. In this paper, we present an event-centric approach to record the beginning and end. We collected a large number of event-temporal cases from multiple sources and pick out those with our target meanings: start and end. After template matching, we built a largest set of start-end pairs which directly provide the time range in which some entity, relation and states exist.

References

1. Gottschalk, S., Demidova, E.: EventKG: a multilingual event-centric temporal knowledge graph. In: Gangemi, A., et al. (eds.) ESWC 2018. LNCS, vol. 10843, pp. 272–287. Springer, Cham (2018). https://doi.org/10.1007/978-3-319-93417-4_18
2. Van Hage, W.R., Malaisé, V., Segers, R.H., Hollink, L., Schreiber, G.: Design and use of the simple event model (sem). Soc. Sci. Electron. Publ. 9(2), 128–136 (2011)
3. Hienert, D., Wegener, D., Paulheim, H.: Automatic classification and relationship extraction for multi-lingual and multi-granular events from wikipedia. In: Detection, Representation, and Exploitation of Events in the Semantic Web (DeRiVE 2012), vol. 902, pp. 1–10 (2012)
4. Yubo, C., Shulin, L., Xiang, Z., Kang, L., Jun, Z.: Automatically Labeled Data Generation for Large Scale Event Extraction (2017)
5. Xu, B., et al.: CN-DBpedia: a never-ending Chinese knowledge extraction system. In: Benferhat, S., Tabia, K., Ali, M. (eds.) IEA/AIE 2017. LNCS (LNAI), vol. 10351, pp. 428–438. Springer, Cham (2017). https://doi.org/10.1007/978-3-319-60045-1_44
6. Wei, X., Ke, Z., Yatao, L.: An event model adapted for analysis of verb sense in natural language. In: International Conference on Artificial Intelligence & Computational Intelligence. IEEE Computer Society (2009)
7. Zhang, H., Liu, L., Cheng, S., Shi, W.: Distant supervision for Chinese temporal tagging. In: Zhao, J., Harmelen, F., Tang, J., Han, X., Wang, Q., Li, X. (eds.) CCKS 2018. CCIS, vol. 957, pp. 14–27. Springer, Singapore (2019). https://doi.org/10.1007/978-981-13-3146-6_2

Overview of CCKS 2018 Task 1: Named Entity Recognition in Chinese Electronic Medical Records

Jiangtao Zhang[1,2(✉)], Juanzi Li[2], Zengtao Jiao[3], and Jun Yan[3]

[1] The 305 Hospital of PLA, Beijing 100017, China
[2] Tsinghua University, Beijing 100084, China
zhang-jt13@tsinghua.org.cn, lijuanzi@tsinghua.edu.cn
[3] Yidu Cloud Beijing Technology Co., Ltd., Beijing 100191, China
{zengtao.jiao,jun.yan}@yiducloud.cn

Abstract. The CCKS 2018 presented a named entity recognition (NER) task focusing on *Chinese* electronic medical records (EMR). The Knowledge Engineering Group of Tsinghua University and Yidu Cloud Beijing Technology Co., Ltd. provided an annotated dataset for this task, which is the only publicly available dataset in the field of *Chinese* EMR. Using this dataset, 69 systems were developed for the task. The performance of the systems showed that the traditional CRF and Bi-LSTM model were the most popular models for the task. The system achieved the highest performance by combining CRF or Bi-LSTM model with complex feature engineering, indicating that feature engineering is still indispensable. These results also showed that the performance of the task could be augmented with rule-based systems to determine clinical named entities.

1 Introduction

With the development of hospital information technology, a large amount of electronic medical records (EMR) data has been accumulated. Especially, unstructured data in the form of free text is the most important part of EMR, such as discharge summary, progress nots, which contain substantial detailed and valuable medical knowledge and health information. Identifying medical-related entity names from these massive EMR texts and classifying them into predefined categories (e.g., diseases, treatments, symptoms, drugs) is a key step in EMR data mining and information extraction. This task is often referred to as clinical named entity recognition (CNER) [13]. It is not only an important foundation for NLP related tasks [5] such as information retrieval, information extraction and question answering system [8], but also has greatly promoting effect to many practical clinical applications such as comorbidity analysis, syndrome monitoring, adverse drug event detection and drug interaction analysis [1,2,9]. A traditional NER task usually relies on a supervised model over a high quality training data. However, in the clinical domain, annotated data is not

© Springer Nature Singapore Pte Ltd. 2019
X. Zhu et al. (Eds.): CCKS 2019, CCIS 1134, pp. 158–164, 2019.
https://doi.org/10.1007/978-981-15-1956-7_14

only expensive but also often unavailable due to patient privacy and confidentiality requirements. Although there are some public evaluations and annotated datasets for the CNER task, such as i2b2 [11], ShARe CLEF eHealth [10] and SemEval [6], most of these existing evaluations focused on the *English* EMR. For the better promotion of the development of CNER for *Chinese* EMR, the Knowledge Engineering Group of Tsinghua University and Yiducloud Beijing Technology Co., Ltd. jointly organized a evaluation task in China Conference on Knowledge Graph and Semantic Computing 2018 (CCKS 2018) and provided the only publicly available dataset in the field of Chinese EMR.

2   Task Description

The evaluation is a traditional named entity recognition task for Chinese EMR, that is, given a set of plain texts in EMR documents [3], the goal of the task is to identify and extract entity mentions related to clinical concepts and to classify the extracted entity mentions into predefined categories such as symptoms, drugs, surgery. To the best of our knowledge, this is one of the earliest comprehensive evaluation tasks for *Chinese* CNER based on the annotated *Chinese* clinical datasets.

2.1   Formalized Definition

The input and output of our task are defined as follows.

Input:

1. A natural language text collection of EMR:

$$\mathcal{D} = \{d_1, d_2, \cdots, d_{|\mathcal{D}|}\}, d_i = \langle w_{i1}, w_{i2}, \cdots, w_{i|d_i|}\rangle \tag{1}$$

2. A set of predefined categories:

$$\mathcal{C} = \{c_1, c_2, \cdots, c_{|\mathcal{C}|}\} \tag{2}$$

Output:

1. Collections of mention-category pairs:

$$\mathcal{O} = \{\langle m_1, c_{m_1}\rangle, \langle m_2, c_{m_2}\rangle, \cdots, \langle m_{|\mathcal{O}|}, c_{m_{|\mathcal{O}|}}\rangle\} \tag{3}$$

where $m_i = \langle d_j, b_k, e_k\rangle, 1 \leq j \leq |\mathcal{D}|, 1 \leq k \leq |d_j|$ is the clinical entity mention appeared in the document $d_j \in \mathcal{D}$ and b_k, e_k denote the starting and ending position of m_i in d_j, respectively. $c_{m_i} \in \mathcal{C}$ denotes the predefined category to which it belongs. It is required that there is no overlap between entity mentions, that is $e_k < b_{k+1}$.

2.2 Pre-defined Categories

The entity type of this task focuses on three main categories: symptoms, drugs, and surgery. Since most of the symptoms appeared in Chinese EMR are structured, this task further subdivided the symptoms into three sub categories: the anatomical site (the subject of the symptoms), the symptom description (the description of the symptoms), and the independent symptoms. Finally, the pre-defined categories of this task are limited to the following five categories:

1. **Anatomical Site:** The subject of a symptom which refers to a structural unit composed of a variety of tissues that perform certain function, such as "腹部" (abdomen).
2. **Symptom Description:** The description of a symptom which refers to the patient's own experience and feeling of abnormal physiological function. It needs to be combined with an anatomical part to express a complete symptom, such as "不适" (discomfort), combined with "腹部" to output "腹部不适" (abdominal discomfort).
3. **Independent Symptom:** a complete symptom which can be output independently, such as "眩晕" (dizziness).
4. **Drug:** A chemical substance used to treat, prevent diseases, or promote health.
5. **Surgery:** The treatment of the patient's body with a medical device such as resection, suturing.

3 Dataset

The dataset used in this task was provided by Yidu Cloud Beijing Technology Co., Ltd. A doctor team was organized spending considerable time to process and annotate the data. The annotated data[1] were deidentified and released to evaluation participants with data use agreements.

The statistics of the annotated dataset are shown in the following Table 1.

Table 1. The statistics of annotated dataset

Dataset	Documents	Independent symptoms	Symptom descriptions	Anatomical sites	Drugs	Surgeries	Total
Training set	600	3055	2066	7838	1005	1116	15080
Test set	400	1327	918	6339	813	735	10132

---

[1] The annotated dataset has not been deposited in a public repository but is available to the research community under data use agreements from the corresponding author on request.

4   Evaluation Metrics

We employ the standard NER evaluation metrics, namely, precision, recall and F1 to measure the performance of our task.

The output result of the system is denoted as $\mathcal{S} = \{s_1, s_2, \cdots, s_m\}$, and the set of the manual annotation (Gold Standard) is denoted as $\mathcal{G} = \{g_1, g_2, \cdots, g_n\}$. The element of the collection is an entity mention, which is denoted as a quaternion $\langle d, b, e, c \rangle$, where d is the document, b and e correspond to the starting and ending position of the entity mention appeared in the document d, respectively. c indicates pre-defined category that the entity mention belongs to.

The evaluations were performed on the following two levels.

Strict Metrics. We define $s_i \in \mathcal{S}$ is strictly equivalent to $g_j \in \mathcal{G}$, if and only if:

$$s_i.d = g_j.d, s_i.b = g_j.b, s_i.e = g_j.e, s_i.c = g_j.c \tag{4}$$

Based on the above equivalence relations, we define the strict intersection of the set $\mathcal{S}$ and $\mathcal{G}$ as $\cap_s$. This leads to strict evaluation metrics:

$$P_s = \frac{|\mathcal{S} \cap_s \mathcal{G}|}{|\mathcal{S}|}, R_s = \frac{|\mathcal{S} \cap_s \mathcal{G}|}{|\mathcal{G}|}, F1_s = \frac{2P_s * R_s}{P_s + R_s} \tag{5}$$

Relaxed Metrics. We define $s_i \in \mathcal{S}$ is loosely equivalent to $g_j \in \mathcal{G}$, if and only if:

$$s_i.d = g_j.d, max(s_i.b, g_j.b) \leq min(s_i.e, g_j.e), s_i.c = g_j.c \tag{6}$$

Based on the above equivalence relations, we define the related intersection of the set $\mathcal{S}$ and $\mathcal{G}$ as $\cap_r$. This leads to relaxed evaluation metrics:

$$P_r = \frac{|\mathcal{S} \cap_r \mathcal{G}|}{|\mathcal{S}|}, R_r = \frac{|\mathcal{S} \cap_r \mathcal{G}|}{|\mathcal{G}|}, F1_r = \frac{2P_r * R_r}{P_r + R_r} \tag{7}$$

At last, according to five different predefined categories, each sub-category is evaluated separately. Thus a total of 12 evaluation results (F1 scores) for each competitor are obtained.

5   Results

The evaluation task attracted more than 100 teams from computer academia, industry and medical institutions. 69 teams submitted the valid results among which 12 teams submitted evaluation papers. The evaluation results are listed on Table 2 (sorted according to the strict metrics).

Table 2. The evaluation results

Rank	Team	Anatomical Site	Symptom description	Independent symptoms	Drugs	Surgery	Total
1	Ali Health	0.882	0.904	0.923	0.944	0.85	**0.893**
2	Personal	0.879	0.903	0.916	0.923	0.876	**0.889**
3	Dalian University of Technology	0.876	0.908	0.917	0.915	0.861	**0.886**
4	Zhejiang University	0.874	0.903	0.916	0.891	0.866	0.883
5	NUDT + Xiangya Hospital	0.867	0.891	0.907	0.912	0.856	0.877
6	East China University of Science and Technology	0.858	0.905	0.913	0.905	0.845	0.872
7	Tongji University	0.868	0.900	0.915	0.813	0.846	0.871
8	Shanghai University	0.869	0.895	0.908	0.827	0.831	0.870
9	Unisound	0.863	0.897	0.911	0.842	0.860	0.870
10	Xi'an University of Posts	0.859	0.871	0.890	0.892	0.844	0.866

6 Discussion

Based on comparative analysis of 12 submitted evaluation papers, we have come to the following conclusions:

1. Being a classic sequence labeling problem, CRF and BiLSTM models are still the most commonly used models in CNER. Almost all teams use these two traditional models [4,7,12], in which Ali Health Lab uses only the CRF model combined with complex feature engineering to achieve the first position in this evaluation, which indicates that our evaluation is slightly lack of innovation of models and methods.

2. Although the representation learning method has achieved great success in the general field, feature engineering is still indispensable for the specific tasks in the clinical field. In this evaluation, all teams use a large amount of manually defined features, including part-of-speech tagging, pinyin characteristics, roots, radicals and dictionary features, etc, which shows that the use of embedded representation without feature engineering is not applicable in clinical medical texts when only a small annotated dataset is available.

3. Due to the particularity of the clinical entity names, the construction of the thesaurus is crucial. In all submitted evaluation papers, a large number of external thesaurus resources, such as ICD-10, the DrugBank database, anatomical lexicons are used. Besides, a large number of technical terms are collected from the well-known health websites such as "寻医问药" (http://www.xywy.com) and "好大夫" (https://www.haodf.com) to build multiple types of terminological dictionaries.

4. The hybrid model has become a mainstream method. Most teams combine multiple models in a variety of ways, such as CRF, BiLSTM+CRF and BiL-STM+CNN+CRF, and use manually defined rules to improve their performance.

5. Due to the particularity of the clinical text, all teams have abandoned the Chinese word segmentation. Instead, they directly train the Chinese character embedding vector on the provided clinical data set. The joint method that models the word segmentation and named entity recognition tasks jointly has not yet appeared.

7   Conclusion

This paper presents a detailed introduction and description of CCKS 2018 Task 1 for CNER in Chinese EMR, including task settings, data set description, evaluation metrics and evaluation results. Comparing with English evaluations such as i2b2 and ShARe CLEF eHealth, our task achieves much higher performance due to the difference distribution of clinical entities between different datasets. That is, the recurrence rate of entities appeared in our dataset is far higher than in those English datasets, which leads to lower the degree of difficulty of entity recognition. However, the innovation of method and model is slightly insufficient in our task. We hope that through this evaluation, we could promote research progress and practical use of technology of CNER for Chinese EMR by providing a publicly available annotated dataset.

References

1. de Bruijn, B., Cherry, C., Kiritchenko, S., Martin, J., Zhu, X.: Machine-learned solutions for three stages of clinical information extraction: the state of the art at i2b2 2010. J. Am. Med. Inf. Assoc. **18**(5), 557 (2011)
2. Jiang, M., et al.: A study of machine-learning-based approaches to extract clinical entities and their assertions from discharge summaries. JAMIA **18**, 601–606 (2011)
3. Kundeti, S.R., Vijayananda, J., Mujjiga, S., Kalyan, M.: Clinical named entity recognition: challenges and opportunities. In: IEEE International Conference on Big Data, pp. 1937–1945 (2016)
4. Luo, L., Li, N., Li, S.S., Yang, Z., Lin, H.: Dutir at the ccks-2018 task1: a neural network ensemble approach for chinese clinical named entity recognition. In: CCKS Tasks (2018)
5. Meystre, S.M., Savova, G.K., Kipper-Schuler, K.C., Hurdle, J.F.: Extracting information from textual documents in the electronic health record: a review of recent research. In: Yearbook of Medical Informatics, pp. 128–144, January 2008
6. Pradhan, S., Elhadad, N., Chapman, W.W., Manandhar, S., Savova, G.: Semeval-2014 task 7: analysis of clinical text. In: SemEval@COLING, pp. 54–62 (2014)
7. Qiu, W., Chen, M., Ding, R., Xie, P.: Heiheihahei at ccks clinical entity recognition task: a neural-based ensemble approach. In: CCKS Tasks (2018)
8. Ratinov, L., Roth, D.: Design challenges and misconceptions in named entity recognition. In: CoNLL, June 2009

9. Settles, B.: Biomedical named entity recognition using conditional random fields and rich feature sets. In: JNLPBA, pp. 104–107 (2004)
10. Suominen, H., et al.: Overview of the ShARe/CLEF eHealth evaluation lab 2013. In: Forner, P., Müller, H., Paredes, R., Rosso, P., Stein, B. (eds.) CLEF 2013. LNCS, vol. 8138, pp. 212–231. Springer, Heidelberg (2013). https://doi.org/10.1007/978-3-642-40802-1_24
11. Uzuner, O., South, B.R., Shen, S., DuVall, S.L.: 2010 i2b2/va challenge on concepts, assertions, and relations in clinical text. J. Am. Med. Inf. Assoc. **18**(5), 552 (2011)
12. Yang, X., Huang, W.: A conditional random fields approach to clinical name entity recognition. In: CCKS Tasks (2018)
13. Zhang, J., et al.: Category multi-representation: a unified solution for named entity recognition in clinical texts. In: PAKDD, pp. 275–287 (2018)

A Conditional VAE-Based Conversation Model

Junfan Chen[1], Richong Zhang[1]($\boxtimes$), Yongyi Mao[2], Binfeng Wang[3],
and Jianhang Qiao[3]

[1] Beihang University, Beijing, China
{chenjf,zhangrc}@act.buaa.edu.cn
[2] University of Ottawa, Ottawa, Canada
ymao@uottawa.ca
[3] Big Data Center, Qihoo 360, Beijing, China
wangbinfeng@360.cn, qiaojianhang@360.cn

Abstract. The recent sequence-to-sequence with attention (S2SA) model achieves high generation quality in modeling open-domain conversations. However, it often generates generic and uninformative responses. By incorporating abstract features drawn from a latent variable into the attention block, we propose a Conditional Variational Auto-encoder based neural conversation model that directly models a conversation as a one-to-many problem. We apply the proposed model on two datasets and compare with recent neural conversation models on automatic evaluation metrics. Experimental results demonstrate that the proposed model can generate more diverse, informative and interesting responses.

Keywords: Conversation · Conditional VAE · Reponse generation

1 Introduction

Conversation modeling is a challenging task in Artificial Intelligence. With large datasets available, end-to-end neural network based methods have become the state-of-the-art. Recently, sequence-to-sequence with attention model was proposed to model conversation and made significant improvement in response generation task [11,13]. Originally, it was used to solve machine translation problem [1,3]. However, these models tend to generate dull and uninformative responses like "me too" or "I don't know", due to high frequency of such patterns in the data [8] and limited variability injection [10].

Different methods have been proposed to tackle this issue. The Maximum Mutual Information (MMI) objective proposed by the work of [8] was used, instead of Maximum Likelihood Estimation (MLE), to generate more varied and interesting outputs. The Latent Variable Hierarchical Recurrent Encoder-Decoder model (VHRED) [10] introduced a latent variable into a hierarchical sequence-to-sequence model to explicitly model generative processes with

© Springer Nature Singapore Pte Ltd. 2019
X. Zhu et al. (Eds.): CCKS 2019, CCIS 1134, pp. 165–174, 2019.
https://doi.org/10.1007/978-981-15-1956-7_15

multiple levels of variability. And the Topic Aware Sequence-to-Sequence (TA-Seq2Seq) model [14] improved response quality by adding additional topic attention into the model and leverage topic information as prior knowledge.

Unlike the above methods, and motivated by recent works on image modeling and generation using Conditional VAE [12,15] to map a single input to many possible outputs, we propose a Conditional VAE-based neural conversation model (CVAE) which directly models a conversation using the Conditional VAE framework. This allows the model to draw abstract properties of sentences such as style, topic, and high-level syntactic features [2]. Unlike the VHRED model, generating responses from a latent variable z, we incorporate z into attention block to let the latent variable influence the decoding process significantly. The latent variable conditions on both the source and target sentences, allowing it to capture more mutual relation between the source and target. Although VAE-Based models have been successfully applied to image modeling, they suffer optimization difficulties when modeling language using VAEs since Recurrent Neural Networks (RNNs) as decoder depend heavily on context information resulting in the latent representation being ignored. We train our proposed model with KL cost annealing [2,16] to alleviate the problem. The contributions of this paper are:

- We propose a Conditional VAE-Based neural conversation model that introduces a latent variable, thereby incorporating the attention model to capture abstract language features and generate diverse responses.
- We compare our proposed model with S2SA model and VHRED model using entropy-based methods and distinct-based metrics in the Sina Weibo and OpenSubtitles datasets.
- We propose item-level distinct to evaluate the ability of a model in continually generating diverse responses given a message and analyze its generation quality through examples.

2   Background

2.1   Seq2seq-Attention Model

The S2SA model is a generative model that uses the encoder-decoder framework. Given a source sequence $X = (x_1, x_2, \cdots, x_{N_x})$ and a target sequence $Y = (y_1, y_2, \cdots, y_{N_y})$. The encoder converts the source sequence X into a set of high-dimensional hidden representations $H = (h_1, h_2, \cdots, h_{N_x})$ by

$$h_t = f(x_t, h_{t-1}), \tag{1}$$

where h_t is the hidden state at time step t and f is often a Long-Short Term Memory unit (LSTM) [6] or a Gated Recurrent Unit (GRU) [4]. The decoder generates sequence Y word by word conditioned on a context vector c and previously generated words. The objective is to maximize the generation probability of Y conditioned on X

$$p\left(Y \mid X\right) = p\left(y_1 \mid c\right) \prod_{t=2}^{N_y} p\left(y_t \mid c, y_1, \cdots, y_{t-1}\right), \tag{2}$$

where y_1 is an initialized vector representing the start token of a sentence and c is often the last hidden representation

$$c = h_{N_x}, \tag{3}$$

We use GRU in both encoder and decoder that is parameterized as

$$\begin{aligned} g &= \sigma\left(W^g x_t + U^g h_{t-1}\right) \\ r &= \sigma\left(W^r x_t + U^r h_{t-1}\right) \\ s &= \tanh\left(W^s x_t + U^s\left(h_{t-1} \circ r\right)\right) \\ h_t &= (1 - g) \circ s + g \circ h_{t-1}, \end{aligned} \tag{4}$$

where σ is a sigmoid function and $\circ$ is the element-wise product. The decoder predicts next word by a probability distribution p_t, which is computed by

$$s_t = f\left(y_{t-1}, s_{t-1}, c\right) \tag{5}$$

An attention mechanism can be introduced to the Seq2Seq model to improve the decoding process. With the attention mechanism, each y_i corresponds to a context vector c_i, which is a weighted average of all hidden states $\{h_t\}_{t=1}^{N_x}$. Namely, c_i is calculated as

$$c_i = \sum_{j=1}^{N_x} \alpha_{ij} h_j, \tag{6}$$

where

$$\begin{aligned} \alpha_{ij} &= \frac{exp\left(e_{ij}\right)}{\sum_{k=1}^{N_x} exp\left(e_{ik}\right)} \\ e_{ij} &= \eta\left(s_{i-1}, h_j\right). \end{aligned} \tag{7}$$

η is a multi-layer perceptron (MLP) with tanh activation function.

2.2 VHRED Model

The VHRED model augments the HRED model with a latent variable at the decoder, which is trained by maximizing a variational lower-bound on the log-likelihood. The VHRED model consists of three parts as the same in the HRED model. The encoder RNN encodes a single sub-sequence into a vector. The context RNN takes the output of the encoder RNN as input, and encodes all previous sub-sequences into a context vector. The decoder RNN is used to generate target sequences. Instead of directly decoding from the context vector, VHRED model first samples the latent variable, and then generates target sequences from it. The detailed architecture is described in [10].

3 Model

We propose a Conditional VAE-Based neural conversation model. Instead of modeling the conditional probability $p(Y \mid X)$ directly as in Eq. (2), we first generate a continuous latent vector representation z from a Gaussian prior $p(z \mid X)$ with CVAE-encoder, and then generate sequence Y from a conditional distribution $p(Y \mid X, z)$ with CVAE-decoder. To estimate the model's parameters, we need to maximize the marginal probability

$$p(Y \mid X) = \int p(Y \mid X, z) \, p(z \mid X) \, dz \tag{8}$$

The marginal probability is intractable, but we can use the following variational lower bound as an objective

$$\begin{aligned} \log p_\theta(Y \mid X) \geq & -\mathbf{KL}\left(q_\phi(z \mid X, Y) \,\|\, p_\theta(z \mid X)\right) \\ & + E_{q_\phi(z \mid X, Y)}\left[\log p_\theta(Y \mid X, z)\right], \end{aligned} \tag{9}$$

We rewrite the objective as

$$\begin{aligned} \mathcal{L}(\theta, \phi; X, Y) = & -\mathbf{KL}\left(q_\phi(z \mid X, Y) \,\|\, p_\theta(z \mid X)\right) \\ & + \frac{1}{L} \sum_{l=1}^{L} \log p_\theta\left(Y \mid X, z^{(l)}\right), \end{aligned} \tag{10}$$

where $z^{(l)} = G_\phi\left(X, Y, \epsilon^{(l)}\right)$, and $\epsilon^{(l)} \sim N(\mathbf{0}, \mathbf{I})$, G is a deterministic, differentiable function. ϵ is a noise variable, and L is the sample times. This reparameterization trick [5,7] overcomes the non-differentiable sample function problem, so that the model can be trained with stochastic gradient descent.

The architecture of the proposed model in training is shown in Fig. 1. CVAE-encoder consists of three parts: Encoder-X, Encoder-Y and Encoder-Q. Encoder-X and Encoder-Y are both implemented with Bidirectional Gated Reccurent Neural Networks (bi-GRU) [9], which summarize the sequence of source words and target words into high-demensional representations $H_x = (h_{x1}, h_{x2}, \cdots, h_{xN_x})$ and $H_y = (h_{y1}, h_{y2}, \cdots, h_{yN_y})$, respectively. Encoder-Q computes the mean μ and variance Σ of distribution $p(z \mid X, Y)$ by MLP

$$\begin{aligned} H_{xy} &= \tanh\left(h_{xN_x} W_x + h_{yN_y} W_y\right) \\ \mu &= W_\mu H_{xy} + b_\mu \\ \log \Sigma^2 &= W_\Sigma H_{xy} + b_\Sigma. \end{aligned} \tag{11}$$

The sampling block takes μ, Σ and a random ϵ sampled from $N(\mathbf{0}, \mathbf{I})$ as input, and: (1) draw z from distribution $N(\boldsymbol{\mu}, \boldsymbol{\Sigma})$. (2) compute the KL-divergence in objective function (10) by

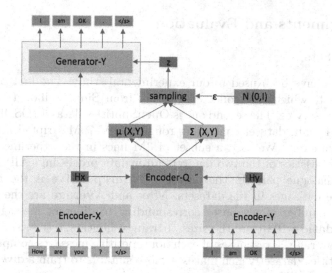

Fig. 1. Conditional VAE-Based Neural Conversation Model architecture in training

$$KL\left(N\left(\boldsymbol{\mu}, \boldsymbol{\Sigma}\right) \parallel N\left(\mathbf{0}, \boldsymbol{I}\right)\right) = -\frac{1}{2}\sum_{i=1}^{I}\sum_{j=1}^{J}\left(1 + \log\left(\left(\Sigma_{i,j}\right)^2\right)\right)$$

$$+\frac{1}{2}\sum_{i=1}^{I}\sum_{j=1}^{J}\left(\left(\mu_{i,j}\right)^2 + \left(\Sigma_{i,j}\right)^2\right), \qquad (12)$$

where i denotes the i-th datapoint and j denotes the j-th element. We assume the latent variable z is statistically independent of the source input X (similar to [7,12]) and z is drawn from distribution $N\left(\mathbf{0}, \boldsymbol{I}\right)$.

CVAE-decoder consists of Generator-Y. It takes H_x and z as input and generates responses from distribution $p\left(Y \mid X, z\right)$ word by word. Generator-Y is the same as the decoder of the S2SA model except for an additional input z. We incorporate z into the attention block to capture abstract features and introduce variation in the decoding process. z is concatenated with every summarized representation in H_x, and the context vector c in equation (3) is modified as

$$c_i = \sum_{j=1}^{N_x} \alpha_{ij}\left[h_j, z\right]. \qquad (13)$$

We use the reconstruction cross-entropy error as the second term loss. While testing, we just use Generator-Y with representation H_x and sample z drawn from $N\left(\mathbf{0}, \boldsymbol{I}\right)$ as input to generate target sequences.

4   Experiments and Evaluation

4.1   Data Sets

Two datasets have been used in our experimental study. The first one is Sina Weibo dataset, which was collected by [11] from Sina Weibo, a twitter-like microblogging service. The second one is OpenSubtitles dataset (OSDb), a large, noisy, open-domain dataset containing roughly 60M-70M scripted lines spoken by movie characters. We used a subset of 3M lines in the experiment. Table 1 shows some statistics of the two datasets after data processing. **All** is the total number of dialogue pairs in the datasets. **Nonrepetitive** is the number of nonrepetitive messages in the datasets. **Max** and **Average** are the maximum and average number of responses corresponding to different message. Finally, **Train/Validation/Test** are the sizes of train/validation/test sets. Sina Weibo dataset has average 20 responses of each nonrepetitive messages compared to 1.7 in OpenSubtitles dataset which makes it more suitable to train a diverse output (one-to-many) model.

Table 1. Statistics of the two datasets.

Datasets	Sina Weibo	Datasets	OSDb
All	4382160	All	2698819
Nonrepetitive	219294	Nonrepetitive	1562787
Max	2127	Max	9067
Average	20	Average	1.7
Train	4300000	Train	2645580
Validation	80000	Validation	26490
Test	1000	Test	1000

4.2   Training

We implement the S2SA model and the CVAE model using open source deep learning framework Blocks[1], and the VHRED model is implemented by using the open source code[2] provided by [10].

For Sina Weibo dataset, we construct two separate vocabularies for messages and responses by using most frequent 40,000 words on each side, covering 97.8% usage of words for post and 96.2% for response, respectively. We set the dimensions of the hidden states of the encoder and the decoder as 1000, the dimensions of word embeddings as 620 and the dimensions of latent variables as 500 in the CVAE model. We set the batch size as 256, dropout ratio as 0.3 and Gradient clipping threshold as 1.0. We train the models with AdaDelta algorithm. In the VHRED model, we set the dimensions of the hidden states of the encoder and the decoder as 1000, the dimensions of word embeddings as 512, batch size 128

---

[1]   https://github.com/mila-udem/blocks.
[2]   https://github.com/julianser/hed-dlg-truncated.

and learning rate 0.0002. We optimize the VHRED model with Adam algorithm. We apply KL cost annealing in the CVAE model and the VHRED model at first 60000 iterations. For the OpenSubtitles dataset, we follow the above setting and decrease the dimensions of hidden states, word embeddings, latent variables to 800, 500, 400, respectively. We use multimodal sampling to generate words at every time step in the S2SA model to output diverse responses.

4.3   Evaluation

Basic Evaluation: Following [10], we report the average entropy per word and per response to measure the infomation contained by generated responses. A unigram model is trained on the training set to compute the entropy. We also evaluate the response diversity by distinct-1 and distinct-2 that were introduced by [8], the number of distinct unigrams and bigrams divided by total number of generated words. Basic evaluation results are shown in Tables 2 and 3. **w-entropy** and **r-entropy** are the reported average entropy per word and per response, respectively.

Table 2. Evaluation results of Sina Weibo datasets.

Model	w-entropy	r-entropy	distinct-1	disinct-2
S2SA	10.0208	156.2649	0.2451	0.0011
VHRED	**10.6575**	**244.4940**	0.2077	0.0007
CVAE	10.1884	89.2604	**0.2980**	**0.0020**

Table 3. Evaluation results of OpenSubtitles datasets.

Model	w-entropy	r-entropy	distinct-1	distinct-2
S2SA	9.5635	88.5485	0.1981	**0.0009**
VHRED	8.8895	**120.6392**	0.1560	0.0006
CVAE	**9.7766**	95.6739	**0.2142**	**0.0009**

Item-level Distinct: Instead of using beam search to generate the best responses, we implement the decoder of the three models with multinomial sampling in every word generation step. This methods can to generate random responses and efficiently measure the ability a model generating many diverse responses. We sample diverse responses and compute distinct value for each test message on their corresponding generated responses. We report the average distinct value across the test set as Item-level distinct. A model with higher Item-level distinct can generate more diverse responses. We randomly choose 100 messages from the test data and calculate their Item-level distinct in 100 sample times. We compared the result of the S2SA model and the CVAE model in the Sina Weibo datasets in Fig. 2.

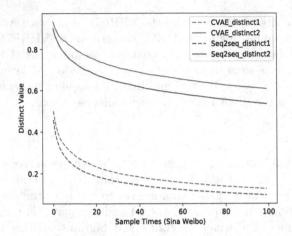

Fig. 2. Item-level distinct1 and distinct2 of Sina Weibo.

4.4 Evaluation Results

In both the Sina Weibo and OpenSubtitles dataset, the VHRED model get much higher per response entropy compared to the other models because the VHRED model is designed for incorporating long contexts and tend to generate longer sentences with more semantic content as [10] analysed. Results suggest that the CVAE model generates more informative responses than S2SA model due to its higher per word entropy. The CVAE model get the highest distinct-1 and distinct-2 score in both the Sina Weibo and OSDb dataset indicates the latent variable injection into attention block significantly increases generation diversity. It's clear in Fig. 2, as sample times increases, the diversity of each message responses in the CVAE model would be much higher than the S2SA model. In Table 4, we select the best 5 responses from 20 generated examples

Table 4. Generated examples

Message	Want me to put peanut butter cups in your eggs ?
S2SA	no one that mixed sugar ?
	no one searched or allergic to cyanide.'
	i burned everything like this.
	no today.
	no.
CVAE	no, thank you very much, mrs UNK.
	nothin' and juicy milk, please ?
	all right with jelly tea on leisure UNK ?
	aw, sure, but a good one here ?
	just something else, lots of things.

for each model. We can see that the CVAE model generates logical and topic related responses because the latent variable captures global topic and syntactic features.

5 Conclusion

We proposed a Conditional VAE-Based neural conversation model to tackle the issue of response diversity in dialogue systems. We experimented on the Sina Weibo dataset and the OpenSubtitles dataset and compared the proposed model with the Seq2seq-attention model and the VHRED model. We evaluated the generated responses with entropy-based methods and distinct-based metrics. Experimental results show the CVAE model improves generation diversity of dialogue responses. In future work, we will enhance the model by incorporating more context infomation and introduce human annotation in evaluation.

Acknowledgements. This work is supported partly by the National Natural Science Foundation of China (No. 61772059, 61421003), by the Beijing Advanced Innovation Center for Big Data and Brain Computing (BDBC), by State Key Laboratory of Software Development Environment (No. SKLSDE-2018ZX-17) and by the Fundamental Research Funds for the Central Universities and the Beijing S&T Committee.

References

1. Bahdanau, D., Cho, K., Bengio, Y.: Neural machine translation by jointly learning to align and translate. CoRR (2014)
2. Bowman, S.R., Vilnis, L., Vinyals, O., Dai, A.M., Józefowicz, R., Bengio, S.: Generating sentences from a continuous space. In: Proceedings of the 20th SIGNLL Conference on Computational Natural Language Learning, CoNLL 2016, Berlin, Germany, 11–12 August 2016, pp. 10–21 (2016)
3. Cho, K., van Merrienboer, B., Bahdanau, D., Bengio, Y.: On the properties of neural machine translation: encoder-decoder approaches. In: Proceedings of SSST@EMNLP 2014, Eighth Workshop on Syntax, Semantics and Structure in Statistical Translation, Doha, Qatar, 25 October 2014, pp. 103–111 (2014)
4. Cho, K., van Merrienboer, B., Gülçehre, Ç., Bougares, F., Schwenk, H., Bengio, Y.: Learning phrase representations using RNN encoder-decoder for statistical machine translation. CoRR (2014)
5. Doersch, C.: Tutorial on variational autoencoders. CoRR (2016)
6. Hochreiter, S., Schmidhuber, J.: Long short-term memory. Neural Comput. **9**(8), 1735–1780 (1997)
7. Kingma, D.P., Welling, M.: Auto-encoding variational bayes. CoRR (2013)
8. Li, J., Galley, M., Brockett, C., Gao, J., Dolan, B.: A diversity-promoting objective function for neural conversation models. In: NAACL HLT 2016, The 2016 Conference of the North American Chapter of the Association for Computational Linguistics: Human Language Technologies, San Diego California, USA, 12–17 June 2016, pp. 110–119 (2016)
9. Schuster, M., Paliwal, K.K.: Bidirectional recurrent neural networks. IEEE Trans. Signal Process. **45**(11), 2673–2681 (1997)

10. Serban, I.V., et al.: A hierarchical latent variable encoder-decoder model for generating dialogues. In: Proceedings of the Thirty-First AAAI Conference on Artificial Intelligence, San Francisco, California, USA, 4–9 February 2017, pp. 3295–3301 (2017)
11. Shang, L., Lu, Z., Li, H.: Neural responding machine for short-text conversation. In: Proceedings of the 53rd Annual Meeting of the Association for Computational Linguistics and the 7th International Joint Conference on Natural Language Processing of the Asian Federation of Natural Language Processing, ACL 2015, Beijing, China, 26–31 July 2015, vol. 1: Long Papers, pp. 1577–1586 (2015)
12. Sohn, K., Lee, H., Yan, X.: Learning structured output representation using deep conditional generative models. In: Advances in Neural Information Processing Systems 28: Annual Conference on Neural Information Processing Systems 2015, Montreal, Quebec, Canada, 7–12 December 2015, pp. 3483–3491 (2015)
13. Vinyals, O., Le, Q.V.: A neural conversational model. CoRR (2015)
14. Xing, C., et al.: Topic aware neural response generation. In: Proceedings of the Thirty-First AAAI Conference on Artificial Intelligence, San Francisco, California, USA, 4–9 February 2017, pp. 3351–3357 (2017)
15. Yan, X., Yang, J., Sohn, K., Lee, H.: Attribute2Image: conditional image generation from visual attributes. In: Leibe, B., Matas, J., Sebe, N., Welling, M. (eds.) ECCV 2016. LNCS, vol. 9908, pp. 776–791. Springer, Cham (2016). https://doi.org/10.1007/978-3-319-46493-0_47
16. Yang, Z., Hu, Z., Salakhutdinov, R., Berg-Kirkpatrick, T.: Improved variational autoencoders for text modeling using dilated convolutions. CoRR (2017)

Emerging Entity Discovery
Using Web Sources

Lei Zhang[1(✉)], Tianxing Wu[2], Liang Xu[3], Meng Wang[3], Guilin Qi[3],
and Harald Sack[1]

[1] FIZ Karlsruhe – Leibniz Institute for Information Infrastructure,
Eggenstein-Leopoldshafen, Germany
{lei.zhang,harald.sack}@fiz-karlsruhe.de
[2] Nanyang Technological University, Singapore, Singapore
wutianxing@ntu.edu.sg
[3] Southeast University, Nanjing, China
{lxu,mwang,gqi}seu.edu.cn

Abstract. The rapidly increasing amount of entities in knowledge bases
(KBs) can be beneficial for many applications, where the key issue is to
link entity mentions in text with entities in the KB, also called *entity
linking* (EL). Many methods have been proposed to tackle this problem.
However, the KB can never be complete, such that *emerging entity discovery* (EED) is essential for detecting emerging entities (EEs) that are
mentioned in text but not yet contained in the KB. In this paper, we propose a new topic-driven approach to EED by representing EEs using the
context harvested from online Web sources. Experimental results show
that our solution outperforms the state-of-the-art methods in terms of
F1 measure for the EED task as well as Micro Accuracy and Macro
Accuracy in the full EL setting.

1 Introduction

As large knowledge bases (KBs) of individual entities became available, it
enabled the linking of words or phrases in text to entities in the KB. The challenges of entity linking (EL) lie in entity recognition and disambiguation. The
first stage, i.e., entity recognition (ER), is to identify the word sequences in
text that refer to an entity, also called *mentions*, for which no KB is required.
The second stage, i.e., entity disambiguation (ED), aims at mapping ambiguous
mentions onto entities like persons, organizations or movies in the KB.

In spite of the rapidly increasing quantities of entities in the KB, the knowledge can never be complete due to (1) the ever-changing world, e.g., *new entities*
appear under the same names as existing ones in the KB, and (2) a *long-tail of
entities* that are not captured by the KB because they lack the importance.
In [1], a survey to thoroughly investigate various types of challenges that arise
from out-of-KB entities in the context of EL has been provided. We refer to
such out-of-KB entities as *emerging entities* (EEs) and EL methods must cope
with this issue, i.e., mentions that have no corresponding entities in the KB. In

© Springer Nature Singapore Pte Ltd. 2019
X. Zhu et al. (Eds.): CCKS 2019, CCIS 1134, pp. 175–184, 2019.
https://doi.org/10.1007/978-981-15-1956-7_16

this work, the key problem is to determine when a mention refers to an EE by discriminating it against the existing candidate entities in the KB. The task is also called *emerging entity discovery* (EED). The examples of two kinds of EEs, i.e., new entities and long-tail entities, are given in the following.

Example (New Entities). Suppose an EL method is fed with the input text "*Alphabet*, Google's new parent company, is boldly restructuring the search engine giant and its subsidiaries." from one of the early news articles on this topic, before the entity Alphabet_Inc. being added into the KB due to its lagging behind news [2]. The EL method needs to determine that the mention "*Alphabet*" does not refer to Alphabet_(poetry_collection), a 1981 book by Danish poet Inger Christensen that exists in the KB, e.g., Wikipedia, for quite a long time, and instead should be mapped to an EE.

Example (Long-tail Entities). Consider the news about *Michael Jordan*, a professor of English at the University of St. Thomas, who does not exist in the KB. An EL method needs to decide that the mention "*Michael Jordan*" in such a news should refer to an EE, instead of a candidate entity in the KB, such as Michael_Jordan, an American retired professional basketball player, or Michael_I._Jordan, a professor in machine learning, statistics, and artificial intelligence at the University of California, Berkeley.

However, most existing EL methods cannot robustly deal with mentions that have no correct entity candidate in the KB. As soon as there is a candidate entity for a mention in the input text, these algorithms are destined to choose one. In order to identify mentions that have no good match in the KB, a simple solution is to employ a confidence threshold to disregard the candidate entities in the KB yielded by an algorithm, such that a mention with a low confidence score for all KB entities is determined to refer to an EE.

In contrast, Hoffart et al. [3] has introduced a new approach, which models an EE as a set of weighted keyphrases collected from news articles by looking back some days before the publishing date of the input text and introduces an additional EE candidate for each mention. Once the candidate space is expanded with EEs, the EL problem is fed back to a prior EL method (i.e., AIDA [4]), which is based on the same keyphrase features, such that it can treat EEs in the same way as it treats KB entities. This is the state-of-the-art method for EED and also the most related work to ours.

The main drawback of the method in [3] is that adding an EE candidate for each mention would potentially introduce noise, which, as showed in our experiments, resulted in degraded EL decisions for the mentions referring to an existing entity in the KB. In order to address this problem, we propose a new solution to EED. Different from [3], our approach employs a prior EL method as a black box and takes its results (i.e., the mappings between each mention and its most likely referent entity in the KB) as the input for further EE detection. In addition, it does not affect existing EL decisions for KB entities yielded by the prior EL method.

Towards a robust solution to EED in the context of EL, we provide in this work the following contributions:

- In order to capture both new entities and long-tail entities, we accurately harvest the context of such emerging entities from online Web sources using a Web search engine.
- We enrich KB entities and EE candidates with an appropriate representation as topic distributions of their contexts, based on that develop a principled method of topic-driven EED.
- The experiments conducted on a benchmark dataset for EED show the superior quality of our solution compared to the state-of-the-art methods in terms of F1 measure of EE results as well as Micro Accuracy and Macro Accuracy of EL results.

2   Approach

Firstly, we formally formulate the task of EL by taking into account EEs. Then, we present our solution to EED in the context of EL.

Definition 1 (Entity Linking). *Let $M = \{m_1, \ldots, m_k\}$ denote the set of all words and phrases in a document D. Given a knowledge base KB containing a set of entities $E = \{e_1, \ldots, e_n\}$, the objective of* entity linking (ER) *is to determine the referent entities for the mentions in M, where two functions are to be found: (1) an* entity recognition (ER) *function $f : D \rightarrow 2^M$ that aims to identify the set of entity mentions $\mu \subseteq M$ from D, and (2) an* entity disambiguation (ED) *function $g : \mu \rightarrow E \cup \{EE\}$ that maps the set of mentions μ yielded by the recognition function to entities in KB or to* emerging entities *that are not yet contained in KB, denoted by the label EE.*

We assume that the KB used in this work is Wikipedia, or any others where each entity has a corresponding Wikipedia page, such as DBpedia [5] and YAGO [6]. Now we recap the computational model of EL. Firstly, the text document is processed by a method for ER, e.g., the Stanford NER Tagger [7], which detects the boundaries of entity mentions. These detected mentions serve as the input of ED in the next step, where the goal is to infer the actual referent entities in the KB or the label EE in case that the corresponding entities do not exist in the KB. In many existing EL methods (e.g., [8–10]), the output also includes a confidence score for each mapping between a mention and its most likely referent entity in the KB.

In our approach, we firstly employ a probabilistic EL method [10], which models the interdependence between different EL decisions as a graph to capture both local mention-entity compatibility and global entity-entity coherence, where evidences for EL can be collectively reinforced into high-confidence decisions based on a random walk process. In principle, many EL methods can be applied here as long as they provide a confidence score for the individual outputs (i.e., mention-entity mappings). Instead of thresholding on the confidence score to directly determine EE, we only use a threshold to filter out the mentions that have a high-confidence mapping to an existing entity in the KB. Then, the remaining mentions are considered as EE candidates and fed into an additional model of EED, which involves *entity context harvesting* (Sect. 2.1), *context representation learning* (Sect. 2.2) and *EE detection* (Sect. 2.3).

2.1   Entity Context Harvesting

For each mention m as an EE candidate, we firstly collect its entity context from Wikipedia, where each page describes a corresponding KB entity. Also, a Wikipedia page often contains hyperlinks pointing to the pages of other entities and the anchor text of a hyperlink provides the mention of the linked entity. Based on that, we define the context of a mention m w.r.t. KB entities, denoted by $\mathbf{C_{KB}} = \{p_i\}_{i=1}^{|\mathbf{C_{KB}}|}$, as a set of Wikipedia pages p_i linked from the anchor text m, where each page corresponds to a KB entity referred to by m.

Although EEs do not have textual information in Wikipedia, there might exist some associated Web pages. Therefore, we decide to acquire the entity context for a mention m as an EE candidate by querying the Web with a search engine[1]. To accurately get such context, we firstly perform coreference resolution [11] to find all expressions that refer to the same entity as m in the input document and based on POS tagging [12] to extract the noun phrases that co-occur with all coreferences of m in the same sentences. Then, the mention m and the extracted noun phrases are jointly submitted to the search engine to retrieve a set of relevant Web pages p_j as the *actual* entity context of m, denoted by $\mathbf{C_{Actual}} = \{p_j\}_{j=1}^{|\mathbf{C_{Actual}}|}$.

Given a mention m, its actual entity context $\mathbf{C_{Actual}}$ could correspond to either a KB entity or an EE, while $\mathbf{C_{KB}}$ captures the context of all existing entities in the KB that can be referred to by m. In order to perform EED on m as an EE candidate, our basic idea is to check if the actual entity context $\mathbf{C_{Actual}}$ is dissimilar enough to the KB entity context $\mathbf{C_{KB}}$. If so, we assume that there should be an EE that has quite different context from all the referent KB entities of m. To compare the textual contexts $\mathbf{C_{KB}}$ and $\mathbf{C_{Actual}}$, the bag-of-words (BOW) model is the most common method to represent text as vectors, and based on that we can apply standard functions (e.g., Euclidian distance, dot product and cosine) to calculate the vector similarity. However, the textual contexts are extracted from different sources, i.e., Wikipedia and various websites, that vary a lot in wording styles, such that the same words in $\mathbf{C_{KB}}$ and $\mathbf{C_{Actual}}$ could be of low frequency even though they share common information. Therefore, the BOW model may not work well in this scenario.

2.2   Context Representation Learning

To address the problem of the BOW model, we try to discover the topics of $\mathbf{C_{KB}}$ and $\mathbf{C_{Actual}}$ with a topic model, i.e., Latent Dirichlet allocation (LDA) [13], such

---

[1] We choose Microsoft Bing as the Web search engine in this work.

Algorithm 1. Generative Process of $\mathbf{C_{KB}}$ and $\mathbf{C_{Actual}}$

---

1 **initialize:** (1) *set the number of topics K;*
2   (2) *set the values of Dirichlet priors α and β;*
3 **foreach** *topic $k \in [1, K]$* **do**
4 | **sample:** $\phi_k \sim Dir(\beta)$;

5 **sample:** $\theta \sim Dir(\alpha)$;
6 **foreach** *Wikipedia page $p_i \in \mathbf{C_{KB}}$* **do**
7 | **foreach** *of N_i word $w_{in} \in p_i$* **do**
8 | | **sample:** $z_{in} \sim Multinonimal(\theta_i)$;
9 | | **sample:** $w_{in} \sim Multinonimal(\phi_{z_{in}})$;

10 **foreach** *Web page $p_j \in \mathbf{C_{Actual}}$* **do**
11 | **foreach** *of N_j word $w_{jn} \in p_j$* **do**
12 | | **sample:** $z_{jn} \sim Multinonimal(\theta_j)$;
13 | | **sample:** $w_{jn} \sim Multinonimal(\phi_{z_{jn}})$;

---

that we can compare these two kinds of contexts based on their representations as topic distributions.

Suppose the corpus $\mathbf{C} = \mathbf{C_{KB}} \cup \mathbf{C_{Actual}} = \{p_j\}_{j=1}^{|\mathbf{C_{KB}}|} \cup \{p_i\}_{i=1}^{|\mathbf{C_{Actual}}|}$ contains $|\mathbf{C_{KB}}| + |\mathbf{C_{Actual}}|$ documents, W distinct words and K topics expressed over the individual words in these documents. The topic indicator variable is denoted by $z_{in} \in [1, K]$ and $z_{jn} \in [1, K]$ for the n-th word in the Wikipedia page $p_i \in \mathbf{C_{KB}}$ and in the Web page $p_j \in \mathbf{C_{Actual}}$, respectively. For each topic k, the corresponding word distribution is represented by a W-dimensional multinomial distribution ϕ_k with entry $\phi_k^w = P(w|z = k)$. In addition, we employ a K-dimensional multinomial distribution $\theta_i = \{\theta_i^k\}_{k=1}^K$ and $\theta_j = \{\theta_j^k\}_{k=1}^K$ with $\theta_i^k = \theta_j^k = P(z = k)$ to describe the topic distributions of each $p_i \in \mathbf{C_{KB}}$ and each $p_j \in \mathbf{C_{Actual}}$. Following the convention of LDA, the hyperparameters α and β are set as the Dirichlet priors. Based on that, the generative process of $\mathbf{C_{KB}}$ and $\mathbf{C_{Actual}}$ is described in Algorithm 1. Accordingly, the probability of generating both $\mathbf{C_{KB}}$ and $\mathbf{C_{Actual}}$ can be expressed as follows:

$$
\begin{aligned}
&P(\mathbf{C_{KB}}, \mathbf{C_{Actual}}|\alpha, \beta) \\
&= \prod_{k=1}^{K} P(\phi_k|\beta) \prod_{i=1}^{|\mathbf{C_{KB}}|} \left[P(\theta_i|\alpha) \big[\prod_{n=1}^{N_i} \sum_{z_{in}} P(z_{in}|\theta_i) P(w_{in}|z_{in}, \phi) \big] \right] \\
&\times \prod_{j=1}^{|\mathbf{C_{Actual}}|} \left[P(\theta_j|\alpha) \big[(\prod_{n=1}^{N_j} \sum_{z_{jn}} P(z_{jn}|\theta_j) P(w_{jn}|z_{jn}, \phi) \big] \right]
\end{aligned} \tag{1}
$$

It is usually intractable to perform exact inference in such a probabilistic model, therefore we adopt Gibbs sampling [14] to conduct approximate inference. More specifically, we estimate the posterior distribution on z_{in} (z_{jn}) and then sample the topic for each word w_{in} (w_{jn}). Based on the sampling results after a sufficient number of iterations, we can estimate the parameters θ_i and θ_j that represent the topic distributions of each Wikipedia page $p_i \in \mathbf{C_{KB}}$ and each Web page $p_j \in \mathbf{C_{Actual}}$. In our experiments, we set the number of topics K as 25. For the hyperparameters α and β, we take the fixed values, i.e., $\alpha = 50/K$, $\beta = 0.01$.

2.3   Emerging Entity Detection

Given the topics derived from $\mathbf{C_{KB}}$ and $\mathbf{C_{Actual}}$, we represent the topic distributions of the KB entity context, denoted by θ^{KB} and the actual entity context, denoted by θ^{Actual}, as follows:

$$\theta^{KB} = \frac{1}{|\mathbf{C_{KB}}|} \sum_{i=1}^{|\mathbf{C_{KB}}|} \theta_i \tag{2}$$

$$\theta^{Actual} = \frac{1}{|\mathbf{C_{Actual}}|} \sum_{j=1}^{|\mathbf{C_{Actual}}|} \theta_j \tag{3}$$

Then, we measure the difference between $\mathbf{C_{KB}}$ and $\mathbf{C_{Actual}}$ using the Kullback Leibler (KL) divergence between the topic distributions θ^{KB} and θ^{Actual} as follows:

$$D_{KL}(\theta^{KB}||\theta^{Actual}) = \sum_{t=1}^{K} \theta_t^{KB} \cdot \log_2 \frac{\theta_t^{KB}}{\theta_t^{Actual}} \tag{4}$$

Equation 4 measures how one probability distribution, i.e., θ^{KB}, diverges from another distribution, i.e., θ^{Actual}, which is equal to zero when $\theta_t^{KB} = \theta_t^{Actual}$ for all topics t. As the KL divergence is asymmetric, we apply a symmetric measure to calculate the final divergence between $\mathbf{C_{KB}}$ and $\mathbf{C_{Actual}}$ as follows:

$$D(\mathbf{C_{KB}}, \mathbf{C_{Actual}}) = \frac{1}{2}[D_{KL}(\theta^{KB}||\theta^{Actual}) + D_{KL}(\theta^{Actual}||\theta^{KB})] \tag{5}$$

Based on Eq. 5, we learn a threshold τ for $D(\mathbf{C_{KB}}, \mathbf{C_{Actual}})$ to determine whether a mention m refers to a KB entity or an EE. The assumption behind it is that if the actual entity is an EE that is not yet contained in the KB, its context $\mathbf{C_{Actual}}$ should be generated by a topic distribution that is to some extent divergent from the topic distribution of the context $\mathbf{C_{KB}}$ for the candidate KB entities.

3   Experiments and Achieved Results

We now discuss the experiments we have conducted to assess the performance of our approach to EED.

3.1 Experimental Settings

We firstly describe the experimental settings with respect to *Data* and *Evaluation Measures*.

Data. In the experiments, we employ the AIDA-EE dataset, also used by [3], which consists of 150 news articles published on October 1st and 150 published on November 1st, 2010, taken from the GigaWord 5 corpus [15], where each mention was manually annotated with EE if the referent entity is not present in Wikipedia as of 2010-08-17, otherwise the correct entity. The statistics of the dataset is given in Table 1. Accordingly, the knowledge base used in the experiments is based on the Wikipedia snapshot from 2010-08-17.

Table 1. AIDA-EE GigaWord dataset statistics.

Total number of documents	300
Total number of mentions	9,976
Total number of mentions with EE	561
Average number of words per article	538
Average number of mentions per article	33
Average number of entities per mention	104

Evaluation Measures. We evaluate the quality of the overall EL (for both KB entities and EEs) with *Micro Accuracy* and *Macro Accuracy*. Additional measures to evaluate the quality of EED include *EE Precision*, *EE Recall* and *EE F1*. Let D be the collection of documents, G_d be all mentions in document $d \in D$ annotated by a human annotator with a gold standard entity, G_d^{EE} be the subset of G_d annotated with an emerging entity EE, A_d be all mentions in $d \in D$ automatically annotated by a method and A_d^{EE} be the subset of A_d annotated with EE. Based on that, the measures of *Micro Accuracy* and *Macro Accuracy* are defined as follows:

$$\text{Micro Accuracy} = \frac{|\bigcup_{d \in D} G_d \cap \bigcup_{d \in D} A_d|}{|\bigcup_{d \in D} G_d|} \tag{6}$$

$$\text{Macro Accuracy} = \frac{\sum_{d \in D} \frac{|G_d \cap A_d|}{|G_d|}}{|D|} \tag{7}$$

Regarding the *EE Precision* and *EE Recall*, we firstly calculate these two measures for each document $d \in D$ as follows:

$$\text{EE Precision}_d = \frac{|G_d^{EE} \cap A_d^{EE}|}{|A_d^{EE}|} \tag{8}$$

$$\text{EE Recall}_d = \frac{|G_d^{EE} \cap A_d^{EE}|}{|G_d^{EE}|} \tag{9}$$

Based on Eqs. 8 and 9, the final *EE Precision* and *EE Recall* are averaged over all documents in D. The *EE F1* is the harmonic mean of *EE Precision* and *EE Recall*, calculated per document then averaged.

3.2   Evaluation Results

We evaluate our EED approach on top of a EL system, denoted by **RW-EE$_{our}$**, where we adopt a probabilistic EL model based on random walks [10], denoted by **RW**, which generates mention-entity mappings with their probabilities as a direct confidence measure. We compare our solution with two state-of-the-art EED approaches [3], denoted by **AIDA-EE$_{sim}$** and **AIDA-EE$_{coh}$**, which are accordingly based on two variants of the AIDA EL system [4], denoted by **AIDA$_{sim}$** and **AIDA$_{coh}$** respectively, where the difference lies in using keyphrase-based similarity or graph link-coherence for disambiguation. As additional baselines, we also consider the traditional EL methods, i.e., **RW**, **AIDA$_{sim}$** and **AIDA$_{coh}$**, which all detect EE based on a threshold of the output confidence score.

Table 2. Evaluation results (with the best results in bold font).

Measure	EL Methods			EED Methods		
	AIDA$_{sim}$	AIDA$_{coh}$	RW	AIDA-EE$_{sim}$	AIDA-EE$_{coh}$	RW-EE$_{our}$
Mic. Acc.	0.7602	0.7581	0.7616	0.7611	0.7133	**0.7900**
Mac. Acc.	0.7340	0.7258	0.7522	0.7290	0.7040	**0.7709**
EE Prec.	0.7284	0.5349	0.4328	**0.9797**	0.9392	0.8847
EE Rec.	0.8909	**0.9092**	0.7111	0.7069	0.7172	0.7478
EE F1	0.6661	0.4980	0.4023	0.6892	0.6792	**0.6954**

Similar to [3], we estimate the parameters for all methods using the set of 150 documents from 2010-10-01 and based on that, the experiments are run on the 150 documents from 2010-11-01. All the methods use the same Stanford NER Tagger [7] for entity recognition, such that our comparison can focus on the ability of different methods to distinguish between existing and emerging entities, not the ability to recognize mentions in the input text.

The evaluation results in Table 2 clearly show that our approach **RW-EE$_{our}$** achieves the best result in terms of EE F1. It is observed that the traditional EL methods (i.e., **AIDA$_{sim}$**, **AIDA$_{coh}$** and **RW**) yield relatively high EE recall but low EE precision. This is because they determine EE only based on the absence of indication for KB entities such that a mention will be simply considered as an EE if there are no enough evidences for existing entities that can be extracted from the KB. Instead, the EED approaches (i.e., **AIDA-EE$_{sim}$**, **AIDA-EE$_{coh}$** and **RW-EE$_{our}$**) detect EE by leveraging its direct positive indication harvested from external sources, where **RW-EE$_{our}$** achieves an optimal trade off between EE precision and recall, which results in a better EE F1.

Furthermore, the results in Table 2 also show that $\mathbf{RW\text{-}EE}_{our}$ outperforms all the competitors in terms of Micro Accuracy and Macro Accuracy in the full EL setting (w.r.t. both KB entities and EEs). While $\mathbf{RW\text{-}EE}_{our}$ improves the performance of $\mathbf{RW}$ for the general EL, $\mathbf{AIDA\text{-}EE}_{sim}$ and $\mathbf{AIDA\text{-}EE}_{coh}$ yield degraded EL performance compared with $\mathbf{AIDA}_{sim}$ and $\mathbf{AIDA}_{coh}$ in some cases, such as Micro Accuracy for $\mathbf{AIDA\text{-}EE}_{coh}$ and Macro Accuracy for both $\mathbf{AIDA\text{-}EE}_{sim}$ and $\mathbf{AIDA\text{-}EE}_{coh}$. This is due to the fact that for each mention $\mathbf{AIDA\text{-}EE}_{sim}$ and $\mathbf{AIDA\text{-}EE}_{coh}$ add an additional EE candidate for disambiguation and feed the expanded set of candidate entities back to the prior EL methods, i.e., $\mathbf{AIDA}_{sim}$ and $\mathbf{AIDA}_{coh}$, which would potentially introduce noise and result in degraded EL decisions for KB entities. In contrast, $\mathbf{RW\text{-}EE}_{our}$ uses a prior EL method (i.e., $\mathbf{RW}$) as a black box to generate the EE candidates for further EE detection, such that it does not affect existing EL decisions for KB entities yielded by the prior EL method.

4   Conclusions

In this paper, we aimed to address the challenge of discovering EEs in text by discriminating them against existing entities in the KB. In order to resolve the problems of existing methods, we devised a new EE detector for each mention as an EE candidate by comparing its KB entity context collected from Wikipedia and its actual entity context harvested from online Web sources based on the context representation learned as topic distributions. Our experiments show the superior quality of our solution in terms of higher F1 measure in detecting EEs compared with the state-of-the-art methods. More importantly, our approach considerably outperforms the existing methods in the full EL setting, where the measures of Micro Accuracy and Macro Accuracy w.r.t. both KB entities and EEs are considered. As future work, we would like to develop methods and tools to add the detected EEs with a canonicalized representation into the KB to improve its up-to-dateness and completeness.

References

1. Färber, M., Rettinger, A., Asmar, B.E.: On emerging entity detection. In: EKAW, pp. 223–238 (2016)
2. Fetahu, B., Anand, A., Anand, A.: How much is Wikipedia lagging behind news? In: WebSci, pp. 28:1–28:9 (2015)
3. Hoffart, J., Altun, Y., Weikum, G.: Discovering emerging entities with ambiguous names. In: WWW, pp. 385–396 (2014)
4. Hoffart, J., et al.: Robust disambiguation of named entities in text. In: EMNLP, pp. 782–792 (2011)
5. Auer, S., Bizer, C., Kobilarov, G., Lehmann, J., Cyganiak, R., Ives, Z.G.: Dbpedia: a nucleus for a web of open data. In: ISWC, pp. 722–735 (2007)
6. Suchanek, F.M., Kasneci, G., Weikum, G.: Yago: a core of semantic knowledge. In: WWW, pp. 697–706 (2007)

7. Finkel, J.R., Grenager, T., Manning, C.D.: Incorporating non-local information into information extraction systems by gibbs sampling. In: ACL, pp. 363–370 (2005)

8. Kulkarni, S., Singh, A., Ramakrishnan, G., Chakrabarti, S.: Collective annotation of wikipedia entities in web text. In: KDD, pp. 363–370 (2009)

9. Ratinov, L., Roth, D., Downey, D., Anderson, M.: Local and global algorithms for disambiguation to Wikipedia. In: ACL, pp. 1375–1384 (2011)

10. Han, X., Sun, L., Zhao, J.: Collective entity linking in web text: a graph-based method. In: SIGIR, pp. 765–774 (2011)

11. Raghunathan, K., et al.: A multi-pass sieve for coreference resolution. In: EMNLP, pp. 492–501 (2010)

12. Toutanova, K., Klein, D., Manning, C.D., Singer, Y.: Feature-rich part-of-speech tagging with a cyclic dependency network. In: HLT-NAACL (2003)

13. Blei, D.M., Ng, A.Y., Jordan, M.I.: Latent dirichlet allocation. J. Mach. Learn. Res. **3**, 993–1022 (2003)

14. Griffiths, T.L., Steyvers, M.: Finding scientific topics. In: PNAS, vol. 101, suppl. 1, pp. 5228–5235 (2004)

15. Parker, R.: English gigaword fifth edition. Technical report (2011)

Named Entity Recognition
for Open Domain Data Based
on Distant Supervision

Junshuang Wu[1,2], Richong Zhang[1,2(✉)], Ting Deng[1,2], and Jinpeng Huai[1,2]

[1] SKLSDE, School of Computer Science and Engineering, Beihang University,
Beijing, China
{wujs,zhangrc,dengting,huaijp}@act.buaa.edu.cn
[2] Beijing Advanced Institution on Big Data and Brain Computing,
Beihang University, Beijing, China

Abstract. Named Entity Recognition (NER) for open domain data is
a critical task for the natural language process applications and attracts
many research attention. However, the complexity of semantic dependencies and the sparsity of the context information make it difficult for
identifying correct entities from the corpus. In addition, the lack of annotated training data makes impossible the prediction of fine-grained entity
types for detected entities. To solve the above-mentioned problems in
NER, we propose an extractor which takes both the near arguments and
long dependencies of relations into consideration for the entities and relations mention discovery. We then employ distant-supervision methods to
automatically label mention types of training data sets and a neural network model is proposed for learning the type classifier. Empirical studies
on two real-world raw text corpus, NYT and YELP, demonstrate that
our proposed NER approach outperforms the existing models.

Keywords: Named entity recognition · Information extraction ·
Knowledge graph · Distant supervision

1 Introduction

With the increasing number of digital contents, there are a considerable number
of research areas [3,14,21] which focusing on better understanding these data.
Among these efforts, Named Entity Recognition (NER) is one of the most important tasks because of their ability to facilitate more efficient access to the public
available information. In general, a typical named entity recognition (NER) system includes two sub-modules: *entity mention extraction* and *entity mention
typing*. Previous researchers [6,18,34] have studies the NER problem from different views. However, the need for more fine-grained entity types [22] and a
large number of nominal mentions (such as *36th avenue, the living room*) [32] in
open domain NER provide a great challenge for sequence-labeling based models. FIGER [22] and ClusType [26] are introduced to solve those two sub-tasks
separately. In this paper, we follow the second research line.

© Springer Nature Singapore Pte Ltd. 2019
X. Zhu et al. (Eds.): CCKS 2019, CCIS 1134, pp. 185–197, 2019.
https://doi.org/10.1007/978-981-15-1956-7_17

To solve the *entity mention extraction*, researchers proposed various methods, such as Conditional random field (CRF) [17], boot strapping [13], and jointly entity and relation extraction models [9,16,20]. Among these existing studies, *Reverb* [9] is one of the most popular models for jointly extracting entities and relations from text. However, the limitation of *Reverb* merely considers the near arguments of the semantic dependency. It does not take the long distance *semantic dependencies* into account. In this study, we propose an entity mention extractor *Reverb-DP* which incorporates both of these two considerations to improve the performance.

Existing *entity mention typing* task is modeled as classification problem [7, 10]. [12,31,32] use different combination and variants of LSTM, GRU and CNN to learn the distributed representations of the entity mention features for entity typing problem. Inspired by their works, we build a DNN based entity type classifier by jointly embedding local *content feature* and global *dependencies relation features* for entity mentions.

Another critical issue for utilizing machine learning techniques for *open-domain* entity mention typing is limited by the *availability* of the training data, only a specified set of types (*Location, Person, Organization*) are identified. The knowledge sharing platforms, such as Wikipedia, provide us opportunities to build a knowledge graphs (KGs) which stores the relations between entities. Freebase [4], YAGO [30] and DBpedia [2] are all based on the information from this platform. In these KGs, the type of entities and relation labels are well defined. So it is possible to link the un-annotated data with a knowledge graph and generate a training set for NER systems to discover entities and their corresponding types [22,26]. With the rich type information in the open domain knowledge bases (KB), researchers start to study the *fine-grained* entity typing problem which can automatically tag an entity mention with the most relevant fine-grained type from a large entity type set [22,26]. In this paper, we utilize *distant-supervision* to automatically generate training data set with Freebase type schema for entity mentions extracted by our extractor Reverb-DP. To sum up, our contributions in this paper are mainly three-fold:

- We propose a novel information extractor Reverb-DP to jointly consider near argument and long dependencies.
- To solve the unavailability of training data for entity mention generated by Reverb-DP, we utilize the distant-supervision to generate training data set by linking the entity mention into KG.
- We employ a novel DNN type classifier model to jointly embed the local content and global relation features for entity mentions.

2   Problem Definition and System Framework

The general pipeline of NER within a specific domain is to detect the named entity mentions and then to generate annotated training data with distant-supervision and finally to train a type classifier which can be used to automatically distribute type for entity mentions. As shown in Fig. 1, our entity

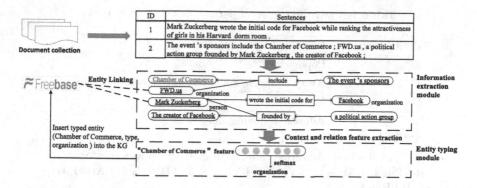

Fig. 1. The framework of our named entity recognition and classification system

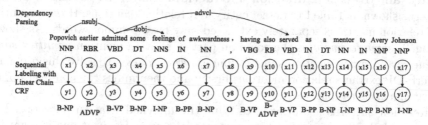

Fig. 2. An example of Dependency Parser and CRF sequential labeling

recognition system consists of three parts, namely information extraction module, simply entity linking and entity typing module.

To generate training data set for entity typing, we utilize the distant supervision method to automatically generate training data. Given a sentence with detected entity mentions, distant supervision merely utilize string matching to link entity mention into entity in KG *without* consider local context information. Entity mentions which have mapped KG entities are regarded as seed entity mentions M_s. And we utilize the type information of KG entities to automatically label those seed entity mentions.

3 NER Pipeline

3.1 Information Extraction

Given corpus $\mathcal{D}$, a KB Δ with type schema $\mathcal{T}_\Delta$, the goal of information extraction is to extract entity mentions M, relation mentions R from $\mathcal{D}$ and generate triples F.

Entity mention is a noun phrase and relation mention is a verb phrase. A triple consists of two entity mentions (called arguments) and one relation mention. In this paper, we propose an information extractor **Reverb-DP** which extracts entity mentions and relation mentions simultaneously by utilizing POS tag pattern and then generates triples F by jointly considering near arguments and semantic dependency parser (DP) results.

Table 1. Entity and relation pattern based on POS tags

Entity pattern	Example
17*	Popovich
17*2+7*	Avery Johnson, some feelings of awkwardness
Relation pattern	Example
37*	Admitted, having, served as
37*[456]+7*	Having also
37*[12456]+7	Admitted some feeling of, served as a mentor to

B-NP is 1, I-NP is 2, B-VP is 3, I-VP is 4, B-ADVP is 5, I-ADVP is 6, B-PP is 7

Entity and Relation Mention Extraction. Reverb-DP utilizes POS tag patterns shown in Table 1 to detect entity and relation mentions. However, entity and relation mentions separately extracted may have common words. As shown in Fig. 2, *some feeling of* is the common part of relation mention *admitted some feeling of* and entity mention *some feeling of awkwardness*. To solve this problem, Reverb-DP extracts relation mentions firstly and then mines the non-overlapped entity mentions as follows.

Relation patterns are utilized to mine the matched relation mentions. If a verb is included in several relation patterns, the most frequent one is regarded as relation. Adjacent relations are merged together to create a long relation.

After obtaining the relation mention, entity patterns are used to extract entity mentions which have no common words with relation mentions. If a noun word appears in several patterns, the most frequent mention is regarded as the entity mention. Similar to relation mentions generation, adjacent entity mention are also merged together to from a new entity mention with composition name.

Triple Generation. Reverb-DP combines Reverb nearest argument strategy [9] and semantic dependency rules to generate $\langle m_l, r, m_r \rangle$ triples. In this paper, five semantic dependency rules, *nsubj, dobj, verb conj, advcl, noun conj*, [1], are utilized to extract long range relation between entity mentions. These five rules can model different semantic relationships between entity and relation mentions in a natural language sentence. However, those rules are still ignored in the previous triple extraction researches. More specifically, we heuristically generate long dependency relation by utilizing those five SDs as follows:

- If an entity mention and a relation mention have *nsubj* (*dobj*), the entity mention should be the left (right) argument for relation mention.
- If two relation mentions have *advcl* (or *verb conj*) dependency, they should share the same left argument.
- If two entity mentions have *noun or conj*, they should share the same relation.

The detail triple generation algorithm for Reverb-DP is shown in Algorithm 1.

---

[1] These five labels are introduced in Stanford Dependency notations. http://nlp.stanford.edu/software/dependencies_manual.pdf.

Algorithm 1. Reverb-DP Triple Generation Method

Require: sentence s; its entity mentions $M(s)$; relation mentions $R(s)$ and dependency parsing results $DP(s)$
Ensure: sentence triples $F(s)$

```
1:  for r_i ∈ R(s) do
2:      Find its nearest left and right entity mention pair (m_l, m_r), where m_r, m_l ∈ M(s)      ▷ Near Argument
3:      if r_i has dependency item (m_dpi, rel, r_i) in DP(s) and m_dpi in M(s) then
4:          if rel is nsubj and m_dpi is not m_l then                                                ▷ nsubj
5:              m_l = m_dpi
6:          if rel is dobj and m_dpi is not m_r then                                                 ▷ dobj
7:              m_r = m_dpi
8:      else if (r_t,conj or advcl,r_i) in DP(s) and r_t in R(s) then                                ▷ verb conj, advcl
9:          if r_t has triples ml_{r_t}, r_t, mr_{r_t} in F(s) and ml_{r_t} is not m_l then
10:             m_l = ml_{r_t}
11:     insert (m_l, r_i, m_r) into F(s)
12:     if (m_r,conj,m_i) in DP(s) and (m_l, r_i, m_i) not in F(s) for each m_i ∈ m(e) then          ▷ noun conj
13:         insert (m_l, r_i, m_i) into F(s)
14: for m_i ∈ M(s) do
15:     if m_i does not appear in the triples F(s) then
16:         find m_i nearest relation r_i and (m_l, r_i, m_r) in the triples F(s)                    ▷ Near Argument
17:         if m_i in the left of r_i then
18:             insert (m_i, r_i, m_r) into F(s)
19:         else
20:             insert (m_l, r_i, m_i) into F(s)
```

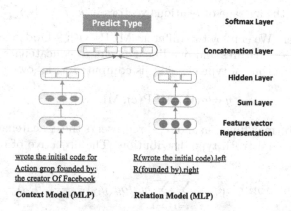

Fig. 3. Entity mention typing model based on Deep Neural Network

3.2 Entity Mention Typing Model

Let $\mathcal{T}$ denote the given type set of data set for entity mention typing within an open-domain. In a sentence of interest, the triples (m_l, r, m_r) have been extracted by Reverb-DP, namely we can get entity mentions and its related relations $(m, \kappa := (r_1, \cdots, r_{|\kappa|}))$. The objective of a (*sentence-level*) entity mention typing is to find the appropriate types in $\mathcal{T}$. Let $\mathcal{D}$ denote the training data, which takes the following form: $\mathcal{D} := \{(s_i, m_i, \kappa_i, y_i), i = 1, 2, \cdots, M\}$, where in each triple, $y_i \in \{0, 1\}^{|\mathcal{T}|}$ is a binary type vector, namely types associated with the entity $e(m_i)$ corresponding to m_i. Figure 3 shows us the whole framework for entity mention typing model.

Content Feature: To reduce the impact of popular entity mention names, we only extract the words $\{l_1, l_2, \cdots, l_c\}$ around m_i as content information.

Table 2. Statistic of triples generated by Reverb-DP.

Dataset	Dependency rules (%)					Near argument (%)
	nsubj	dobj	noun conj	verb conj	advcl	
YELP	0.34	0.17	0.08	0.12	0.03	0.33
NYT	0.28	0.19	0.07	0.07	0.03	0.42

Let $A(l_i)$ denote the embedding of word l_i, the representation of content feature is simply computed by averaging the words vector of context words: $\hat{c} = \frac{1}{c} \sum_{i=1}^{c} A(l_i)$.

Relation Feature: We regard one entity relation mention r_i as two relations $\hat{r}_{2i}$ and $\hat{r}_{2i+1}$. If m is the left argument of r_i, $\hat{r}_{2i+1}$ should be inserted into relation set κ and vice versa. Let $B(r_i)$ denote the embedding of relation r_i, the relation feature for m is the average of relations vectors in κ: $\hat{r} = \frac{1}{|\kappa|} \sum_{i=1}^{|\kappa|} B(\hat{r}_i)$.

Type Classifier: We employ two different MLPs with 2-hidden layers to encode the entity mention features and one linear layers to concatenate those two features. The final output of type classifier is computed as follows:

$$\tilde{y} = \sigma(W_f[\mathrm{MLP}(\hat{c}), \mathrm{MLP}(\hat{r})]) \tag{1}$$

where σ is the softmax function and $[*, *]$ represents the concatenation operation. Let y denote ground truth type distribution. The objective of our model is as follow:

$$minimize \quad -\sum_{i=1}^{|M|} \sum_{j=1}^{|T|} y_{ij} log(\tilde{y}_{ij}) + \frac{\lambda_\theta}{2}(\|\theta\|_2^2) \tag{2}$$

where θ represents all the training parameters in our model and λ_θ is the regularization hyper-parameter.

4   Experiment

4.1   Datasets

In our experiment, we evaluate our NER pipeline on three different data sets, one structure data set FB15K [5] and two raw text corpus YELP, NYT [26] As the entity in FB15k data set only has relation information, we extract its description in KG as its content information.

4.2   Information Extraction Analysis

The statistic of triples generated by our proposed Reverb-DP is shown on Table 2. From the table, we can find that dependency rules generate a large mount of new triples that can not be extracted by near argument strategy. What is more,

Table 3. Data statistic of YELP, NYT and FB15K. M_s denotes the seed entity mention. M_{ns} denotes the non-seed entity mention having relation with seed entity. M_{nsf} denotes other entity mentions.

Dataset	#M_s	#M_{ns}	#M_{nsf}	#Type	#Entity	# Relation	#Triple	Noisy
YELP	57198	166539	35384	3	7023	31103	241110	20%
NYT	94705	175088	423829	3	21122	36940	235622	18%
FB15K	-	-	-	50	13445	1333	483142	-

one same triple can be generated simultaneously by dependency rules and near argument strategy.

The statistic of YELP, NYT and FB15K are shown at Table 3. The top three frequent types for YELP are LOC (Location), FOOD (food), and ORG (Organization). The top three frequent types of NYT are LOC (Location), PER (Person), and ORG (Organization). We filter the most popular 50 types as the target types for FB15K. So that FB15K has a fine-grained entity type schema. We ignore the entity mentions which appear less than three times. Those detected entity mentions can be split into three groups: seed entity mentions with mapped KG entities E_s, non-seed entity mention which have relation with seed entities and other mentions. Finally, we need pay attention to the fact that our training data generated by distant supervision have *noisy type label*. The entity mention with noisy label may have more than one entity types in YELP and NYT. What is more, one entity mention may have more than one types in FB15K which has a fine-grained entity type schema.

4.3   Experiment Settings

For NYT and YELP, we extract 10% of the data as testing set and others as training set. For FB15K, we utilize training and testing data provided by [31]. The hidden dimension for MLPs is 128. The dimension of the word vector and relation vector are 300 and 150. Word vectors are initialized by pre-trained word embedding provided by [19]. The learning rate is 0.001. We utilize batch normalization [15] to regularize the hidden output. Dropout [29] are utilized to prevent the neural network over-fitting.

4.4   Evaluation Results

In this part, we first evaluate our entity typing with several baseline models on structure data set FB15K. Then we evaluate the whole system performance on YELP and NYT datasets.

Comparision with Fine-Grained Entity Mention Typing: We compare our entity mention typing model with Distributed Bag of Words and SDType [25] on the FB15k data set. Mean Average Precision (MAP) is utilized to measure

Table 4. MAP for entity type classification in KG

Method	Feature	MAP
BOW	Context	0.86
SDType	Relation	0.85
NType_ctx	Context	0.87
NType	Context + relation	**0.93**

Table 5. NER performance of NType, FIGER and ClusType

System	NYT		YELP	
	Micro-F1	Macro-F1	Micro-F1	Macro-F1
ClusType	59.7	50.7	64.5	36.0
FIGER	72.6	66.9	68.8	36.5
NType_ctx	76.9	71.6	73.1	53.2
NType	**78.4**	**72.9**	**75.4**	**57.4**

type classification performance. **DBOW**: Distributed Bag of Words model simply averages word vectors of the entity mention description context as feature and LR logistic regression classifier is trained on the DBOW features. **SDType**: SDtype utilizes relation feature to infer entity missing type in KG. **NType_ctx**: Our proposed entity typing model utilizes the contextual feature. **NType**: Entity typing model make use of both contextual feature and relation feature. As shown in Table 4, our model **NType_ctx** outperforms two baseline models on FB15K. Adding relation feature can improve our model performance.

Comparison with NER Pipeline Systems: We compare our whole entity recognition system with state-of-art systems FIGER [22] and ClusType [26]. Micro-F1 and macro-F1 are utilized as the measurement to evaluate ER system performance. The comparison of performance are shown on Table 5. From Table 5, we can observe that:

1. Our proposed model NType_ctx achieves better performance than FIGER and ClusType on all data sets. The result verifies that our neural entity typing model has the ability to encode the semantic information.
2. Adding relation feature can improve performance of NType_ctx on all data sets demonstrating that relation feature is helpful for entity typing task.
3. Relation feature contributes more to YELP than to NYT. This result conforms to our intuition. Owing to dense and coherent sentences, content feature in NYT provides a rich information for the model to infer entity mention types. Since YELP sentences are more concise, the model has to rely on relationship among entity mentions to infer their types.

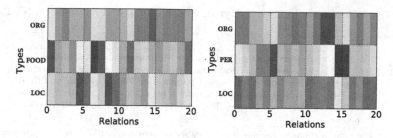

Fig. 4. Entity type distributions for YELP (left) and NYT (right) relation clusters. The darker shade represents that the probability of this type entities appearing in this relation is higher.

4.5   Embedded Relation Analysis

We assume that relation embedding vectors can reflect the type distribution. In other words, similar relation vectors tend to have similar entity type distribution. To verify this assumption, we do clustering analysis on the relation vectors trained on YELP and NYT. As shown in Fig. 4, we obtain ten relation clusters and statistic the type distribution of their left and right arguments. We can find that type *FOOD* appears frequently in the 4-th relation cluster and never appears in left of 3-th and 5-th relation cluster one in YELP data. We can also discover that type *PER* appears frequently in the left of 4-th cluster and never appears in left and right of relation 3-th and 5-th relation clusters. On the Table 6, we give some concrete relation mentions of the 8-th clusters of YELP and the 4-th cluster of NYT.

Table 6. Example relation mention clusters and their frequency in YELP and NYT corpus

Dataset	Relation mention
YELP	Left: ate (28k), become (634), melted (301)
	Right: cooked (2.2k), toasted (330), drop off (63)
NYT	Left: said (4.3k), threw (316), declined to comment (471)
	Right: be dominated by (113), identified as (68), founded by (59)

4.6   Case Study

Table 7 shows entity recognition results of NType, FIGER and ClusType. Following, we give a detail explanation for those results.

- *FWD.us* and *the Chamber of Commerce* have dependency relationship (*nconj*). REVERB-DP extracts two triple, (*The event 's sponsors, include, FWD.us*) and (*The event 's sponsors, include, the Chamber of Commerce*). As *FWD.us* and *the Chamber of Commerce* have the similar relation feature, they tend to have similar type.

Table 7. Results of our local entity typing and its compared methods on NYT data

Dataset	NYT
NType	The event's sponsors include [the Chamber of Commerce]:organization; [FWD.us]:organization, a political action group founded by [Mark Zuckerberg]:people, the creator of Facebook; [the National Immigration Forum]:people; and the Partnership for a New American Economy, which is led by [Mayor Michael R. Bloomberg of New York]:people, [Rupert Murdoch]:people and [Bill Marriott Jr]:people
ClusType	The event's sponsors include [the Chamber of Commerce; FWD.us]:organization, a [political action]:organization group founded by [Mark Zuckerberg]:people, the creator of [Facebook; the National Immigration Forum]:location; and the [Partnership for a New American Economy]:location, which is led by [Mayor Michael R. Bloomberg of New York]:location, [Rupert Murdoch]:people and [Bill Marriott Jr]:people
FIGER	The event's sponsors include the [Chamber of Commerce]:organization; FWD.us, a political action group founded by [Mark Zuckerberg]:people, the creator of [Facebook]:organization; the National Immigration Forum; and the Partnership for a [New American Economy]:organization, which is led by Mayor [Michael R. Bloomberg]:people of [New York]:location, [Rupert Murdoch]:people and [Bill Marriott Jr]:people

- *New American Economy* appears only twice in corpus. It is filtered out from the candidate entity mentions. So that both NType and ClusType do not predict type for it.
- *Mayor Michael R. Bloomberg of New York* appears more than five times in NYT corpus, so that both NType and ClusType treat it as a whole entity mention. What is more, NType gives the right type prediction and ClusType makes the wrong prediction. While FIGER splits it into two entity mentions *Michael R. Bloomberg* and *New York*.

5   Related Work

Type Completion in KG: As KGs are built from manually created data source such as Wikipedia, the completeness of KG would be difficult to guarantee [2,4, 30]. Missing entity type inference is helpful for knowledge base refinement. Aldo Gangemi et al. [11] proposes Tipalo model for automatic typing DBpedia entities based on their NL definition provided by their corresponding Wikipedia pages. Christian Bizer [25] proposes SDType to infer the right type for wikipedia's entities based on relation information. And they also prove that the SDType model can produce a more reasonable result than traditional RDFS reasoner. Recently, embedding based methods are utilized to learn entity type embeddings to complete the knowledge graph [23,24].

Fine-Grained Entity Recognition: The goal of fine-grained entity recognition is to extract entity mentions and predict type distributions for them by KG type schema [22]. Xiao Ling [22] creates a large set of entity types derived from Freebase and proposes a fine-grained entity recognize (FIGER) model. Greg Durrett [8] employs a structured CRF model to jointly tackle three tasks in the entity anlysis, namely coreference resolution, named entity recognition and entity linking. Recently, researchers [1, 27, 28, 33] focus on improving performance on fine-grained entity typing by de-noising the lables in the training data set.

6   Conclusion

In this paper, we propose a novel named entity recognition for domain specific corpus based on deep neural network including information extraction module and entity typing module. In information extraction module, we combine semantic dependency parser structure and REVERB near arguments to solve the long range dependency relationships between entity mentions. Entity typing module utilizes both context and relation feature to predict type distribution for entity mentions. Empirical studies on two real-word raw text corpus, NYT and YELP, demonstrate that our proposed NER system performs better than the state-of-art systems.

Acknowledgments. This work is supported partly by the National Natural Science Foundation of China (No. 61772059, 61602023 and 61421003), by the Beijing Advanced Innovation Center for Big Data and Brain Computing (BDBC), by State Key Laboratory of Software Development Environment (No. SKLSDE-2018ZX-17), and by the Fundamental Research Funds for the Central Universities and the Beijing S&T Committee.

References

1. Anand, A., Awekar, A.: Fine-grained entity type classification by jointly learning representations and label embeddings. In: Proceedings of EACL, pp. 797–807 (2017)
2. Auer, S., Bizer, C., Kobilarov, G., Lehmann, J., Cyganiak, R., Ives, Z.: DBpedia: a nucleus for a web of open data. In: Aberer, K., et al. (eds.) ASWC/ISWC -2007. LNCS, vol. 4825, pp. 722–735. Springer, Heidelberg (2007). https://doi.org/10.1007/978-3-540-76298-0_52
3. Bhattacharya, I., Getoor, L.: Collective entity resolution in relational data. Trans. Knowl. Discov. Data **1**(1), 1–36 (2007)
4. Bollacker, K.D., Evans, C., Paritosh, P., Sturge, T., Taylor, J.: Freebase: a collaboratively created graph database for structuring human knowledge. In: Proceedings of SIGMOD, pp. 1247–1250 (2008)
5. Bordes, A., Usunier, N., García-Durán, A., Weston, J., Yakhnenko, O.: Translating embeddings for modeling multi-relational data. In: Proceedings of NIPS, pp. 2787–2795 (2013)
6. Chieu, H.L., Ng, H.T.: Named entity recognition: a maximum entropy approach using global information. In: Proceedings of COLING (2002)
7. Collobert, R., Weston, J., Bottou, L., Karlen, M., Kavukcuoglu, K., Kuksa, P.P.: Natural language processing (almost) from scratch. JMLR **12**, 2493–2537 (2011)
8. Durrett, G., Klein, D.: A joint model for entity analysis: coreference, typing, and linking. Trans. Assoc. Comput. Linguist. **2**, 477–490 (2014)

9. Fader, A., Soderland, S., Etzioni, O.: Identifying relations for open information extraction. In: Proceedings of EMNLP, pp. 1535–1545 (2011)
10. Finkel, J.R., Grenager, T., Manning, C.D.: Incorporating non-local information into information extraction systems by Gibbs sampling. In: Proceedings of ACL (2005)
11. Gangemi, A., Nuzzolese, A.G., Presutti, V., Draicchio, F., Musetti, A., Ciancarini, P.: Automatic typing of DBpedia entities. In: Cudré-Mauroux, P., et al. (eds.) ISWC 2012. LNCS, vol. 7649, pp. 65–81. Springer, Heidelberg (2012). https://doi.org/10.1007/978-3-642-35176-1_5
12. Gregoric, A.Z., Bachrach, Y., Coope, S.: Named entity recognition with parallel recurrent neural networks. In: Proceedings of ACL, pp. 69–74 (2018)
13. Gupta, S., Manning, C.D.: Improved pattern learning for bootstrapped entity extraction. In: Proceedings of CoNLL, pp. 98–108 (2014)
14. Han, X., Sun, L., Zhao, J.: Collective entity linking in web text: a graph-based method. In: Proceedings of SIGIR, pp. 765–774 (2011)
15. Ioffe, S., Szegedy, C.: Batch normalization: accelerating deep network training by reducing internal covariate shift. In: Proceedings of ICML, pp. 448–456 (2015)
16. Kate, R.J., Mooney, R.J.: Joint entity and relation extraction using card-pyramid parsing. In: Proceedings of CoNLL, pp. 203–212 (2010)
17. Lafferty, J.D., McCallum, A., Pereira, F.C.N.: Conditional random fields: probabilistic models for segmenting and labeling sequence data. In: Proceedings of ICML, pp. 282–289 (2001)
18. Lample, G., Ballesteros, M., Subramanian, S., Kawakami, K., Dyer, C.: Neural architectures for named entity recognition. In: Proceedings of NAACL, pp. 260–270 (2016)
19. Le, Q.V., Mikolov, T.: Distributed representations of sentences and documents. In: Proceedings of ICML, pp. 1188–1196 (2014)
20. Li, Q., Ji, H.: Incremental joint extraction of entity mentions and relations. In: Proceedings of ACL, pp. 402–412 (2014)
21. Lin, T., Mausam, Etzioni, O.: No noun phrase left behind: detecting and typing unlinkable entities. In: Proceedings of EMNLP-CoNLL, pp. 893–903 (2012)
22. Ling, X., Weld, D.S.: Fine-grained entity recognition. In: Proceedings of AAAI, pp. 94–100 (2012)
23. Moon, C., Jones, P., Samatova, N.F.: Learning entity type embeddings for knowledge graph completion. In: Proceedings of CIKM, pp. 2215–2218 (2017)
24. Neelakantan, A., Chang, M.: Inferring missing entity type instances for knowledge base completion: new dataset and methods. In: Proceedings of NAACL-HLT, pp. 515–525 (2015)
25. Paulheim, H., Bizer, C.: Type inference on noisy RDF data. In: Proceedings of ISWC, pp. 510–525 (2013)
26. Ren, X., El-Kishky, A., Wang, C., Tao, F., Voss, C.R., Han, J.: Clustype: effective entity recognition and typing by relation phrase-based clustering. In: Proceedings of SIGKDD, pp. 995–1004 (2015)
27. Ren, X., He, W., Huang, M.Q.L., Ji, H., Han, J.: AFET: automatic fine-grained entity typing by hierarchical partial-label embedding. In: Proceedings of EMNLP, pp. 1369–1378 (2016)
28. Shimaoka, S., Stenetorp, P., Inui, K., Riedel, S.: Neural architectures for fine-grained entity type classification. In: Proceedings of EACL, pp. 1271–1280 (2017)
29. Srivastava, N., Hinton, G.E., Krizhevsky, A., Sutskever, I., Salakhutdinov, R.: Dropout: a simple way to prevent neural networks from overfitting. J. Mach. Learn. Res. **15**(1), 1929–1958 (2014)

30. Suchanek, F.M., Kasneci, G., Weikum, G.: Yago: a core of semantic knowledge. In: Proceedings of WWW, pp. 697–706 (2007)
31. Xie, R., Liu, Z., Jia, J., Luan, H., Sun, M.: Representation learning of knowledge graphs with entity descriptions. In: Proceedings of AAAI, pp. 2659–2665 (2016)
32. Xu, M., Jiang, H., Watcharawittayakul, S.: A local detection approach for named entity recognition and mention detection. In: Proceedings of ACL, pp. 1237–1247 (2017)
33. Xu, P., Barbosa, D.: Neural fine-grained entity type classification with hierarchy-aware loss. In: Proceedings of NAACL, ACL, June 2018
34. Zhou, G., Su, J.: Named entity recognition using an hmm-based chunk tagger. In: Proceedings of ACL, pp. 473–480 (2002)

Geography-Enhanced Link Prediction Framework for Knowledge Graph Completion

Yashen Wang[1(✉)], Huanhuan Zhang[1], and Haiyong Xie[1,2]

[1] National Engineering Laboratory for Public Safety Risk Perception
and Control by Big Data (PSRPC),
China Academy of Electronics and Information Technology of CETC, Beijing, China
`yashen_wang@126.com`, `huanhuanz_bit@139.com`, `haiyong.xie@ieee.org`
[2] University of Science and Technology of China, Hefei, Anhui, China

Abstract. Knowledge graphs contain knowledge about the world and provide a structured representation of this knowledge. Current knowledge graphs contain only a small subset of what is true in the world. Link prediction approaches aim at predicting new links for a knowledge graph given the existing links among the entities. Recent years have witnessed great advance of representation learning (RL) based link prediction models, which represent entities and relations as elements of a continuous vector space. However, the current representation learning models ignore the abundant geographic information implicit in the entities and relations, and therefore there is still room for improvement. To overcome this problem, this paper proposes a novel link prediction framework for knowledge graph completion. By leveraging geographic information to generate geographic units and rules, we construct geographic constraints for optimizing and boosting the representation learning results. Extensive experiments show that the proposed framework improves the performance of the current representation learning models for link prediction task.

Keywords: Link prediction · Geographic constraint · Knowledge Graph Completion · Representation learning

1 Introduction

Knowledge Graphs (KGs) have become a crucial resource for many tasks in machine learning, data mining, and artificial intelligence applications [9,22,25]. In our view, KGs are an example of a heterogeneous information network containing entity-nodes and relationship-edges corresponding to RDF-style triples (h, r, t) where h represents a head entity, and r is a relationship that connects h to a tail entity t. KGs are widely used for many practical tasks, however, their completeness are not guaranteed. Although large-scale KGs contain billions of triples [1], the extracted knowledge is still a small part of the real-world

X. Zhu et al. (Eds.): CCKS 2019, CCIS 1134, pp. 198–210, 2019.
https://doi.org/10.1007/978-981-15-1956-7_18

knowledge and probably contains errors and contradictions. For example, 71% of people in Freebase have no known place of birth, and 75% have no known nationality. Therefore, it is necessary to develop Knowledge Graph Completion (KGC) methods to find missing or errant relationships with the goal of improving the general quality of KGs.

Link prediction over a knowledge graph aims to predict the missing relations r for a triple (h, r, t), which, in turn, can be used to improve or create interesting downstream applications. Recent years have witnessed great advance of representation learning (RL) based link prediction models, which represent entities and relations as elements of a continuous vector space. Although these RL-based models have significantly improved the knowledge graph embedding representations and increased the link prediction accuracy, there is still room for improvement. A major element of this potential could be concluded as, the beneficial constraints based on common knowledge rules are ignored in these RL-based models, i.e., geographic constraints.

There exists abundant geographic information implicit in the entities and relations of the real-world, and could be employed to promote the performance of link prediction. Unfortunately, these previous RL models didn't make use of the implicit *geography* units of entities and relations themselves. In fact, the existing knowledge graph contains a large number of geography-dependent entities and relations. For example, in the triple *(Beyonc Giselle Knowles, WasBornIn, Houston)*, the entity *"Houston"* has the definite geographic characteristics and attributes (e.g., longitude, latitude, area, etc.), which could be used to generate its geographic units and then predict the geographic units implied in another entity *"Beyonc Giselle Knowles"*. With efforts above, we could construct the *geographic rules* and *geographic constraints* by utilizing the implicit geographic unit. This paper proposes a novel link prediction framework for geography-dependent relations. As discussed in [10,18], inclusion, adjacency and intersection are common relationships between geological objects such as faults, geological units, fractures, mineralized zones and reservoirs. Therefore, in our view, the geography-dependent relations is classified into three categories: (i) *geography-inclusion* relation, indicating that the geographical coordinate ranges of two given entities include with each other (as shown in Fig. 1(a)); (ii) *geography-adjacency* relation, indicating that the geographic coordinate ranges of two given entities are separated from each other, but within a certain distance (as shown in Fig. 1(b)); and (iii) *geography-intersection* relation, indicating that the geographical coordinate ranges of two given entities themselves are intersecting (as shown in Fig. 1(c)). In the proposed framework: Firstly, for different types of entities, different implicit geographic units are extracted, consisting of its geographic attributes (e.g., longitude, latitude, etc.,) and its radiation range (details in Sect. 3.3). Secondly, for different types of relations, different geographic rules are generated (details in Sect. 3.3). Finally, these geographic rules are utilized for constraining the current representation learning models and improving the link prediction results (details in Sect. 3.4), as shown in Fig. 2. Note that, arbitrary representation learning models could be adopted here, because of generality of the proposed framework.

Our contributions are summarized as follows: (i) We propose a novel link prediction framework for knowledge graph, which inherits the advantages of the representation learning models and introduces the implicit geographic information. (ii) By leveraging geographic information to generate geographic units and rules, we construct geographic constraints for boosting the current representation learning models for knowledge graph completion. Moreover, this is a general framework, in which arbitrary representation learning models and constraint rules could be flexibly adopted and changed. (iii) Extensive experiments show that our framework improves the performance of the current representation learning models significantly for link prediction of knowledge graph.

2 Related Work

During the past two decades, several knowledge graphs (KGs) containing (perhaps probabilistic) facts about the world have been constructed. These KGs have applications in several fields including search, question answering, natural language processing, recommendation systems, etc. Due to the enormous number of facts that could be asserted about our world and the difficulty in accessing and storing all these facts, KGs are incomplete. However, it is possible to predict new links in a KG based on the existing ones. Link prediction and several other related problems aiming at reasoning with entities and relationships are studied under the umbrella of statistical relational learning.

To complete or predict the missing relation element of triples, such as $(h, ?, t)$, Representation Learning (RL) is widely deployed. RL embeds entities and relations into a vector space, and has produced many successful translation models including TransE [2], TransH [21], TransR [8], TransG [23], etc. These models aim to generate precise vectors of entities and relations following the principle $\mathbf{h} + \mathbf{r} \approx \mathbf{t}$, which means t is translated from h by r. Besides, these methods usually learn continuous, low-dimensional vector representations (i.e., embeddings) for entities and relationships by minimizing a margin-based pairwise ranking loss. The most widely used embedding model in this category is TransE [2], which views relationships as translations from a head entity to a tail entity on the same low-dimensional plane.

Based on the initial idea of treating two entities as a translation of one another (via their relationship) in the same embedding plane, several models have been introduced to improve the initial TransE model. The newest contributions in this line of work focus primarily on the changes in how the embedding planes are computed and/or how the embeddings are combined. E.g., the entity translations in TransH [21] are computed on a hyperplane that is perpendicular to the relationship embedding. In TransR [8] the entities and relationships are embedded on separate planes and then the entity-vectors are translated to the relationships plane. Structured Embedding (SE) [3] creates two translation matrices for each relationship and applies them to head and tail entities separately. Knowledge Vault [6] and HolE [13], on the other hand, focus on learning a new combination operator instead of simply adding two entity embeddings element-wise. RESCAL [15] is a restricted form of Tucker decomposition for discovering previously unknown triples in a knowledge graph. [19] demonstrated that simple changes in the architecture of the underlying model could outperform the aforementioned models without the need for complex unit engineering.

Unfortunately, the beneficial constraints based on common knowledge rules are ignored in these models. [5] examined non-negativity constraints on entity representations and approximate entailment constraints on relation representations. The former help to learn compact and interpretable representations for entities. The latter further encode regularities of logical entailment between relations into their distributed representations. [16] proposed a co-regularized multiview nonnegative matrix factorization method with correlation constraint for nonnegative representation learning, which jointly exploits consistent and complementary information across different views. [7] proposed a hybrid method to learn the representation of MWEs from their external context and component words with a compositionality constraint, which could make use of both the external context and component words. This paper investigates how to introduce geographic rules and constraints based on the available geographic information, and how to constrain and optimize the representation learning results based on these geographic constraints.

3   Methodology

The proposed framework consists of: (i) geographic unit and rule generation (described in Sect. 3.3). Firstly, we extract the geographic units of entities in triples with the help of external knowledge graph (such as GeoName[1], Lniked-GeoData[2], and so on), then automatically recognize or classify the relations of triples based on these geographic units. (ii) link prediction based on geographic constraints (described in Sect. 3.4). Firstly, the triple is trained by representation learning models, and then the results are constrained and optimized by geographic rules. The sketch of the proposed framework is shown in Fig. 2.

3.1   Notation and Definition

This paper represents vectors with lowercase letters and matrices with uppercase letters. Let $\mathbf{v} \in R^d$ be vectors of length d. Let E and R represent the set of entities and relations respectively. A triple is represented as (h, r, t), where $h \in E$ is the head entity, $r \in R$ is the relation (geography-dependent relation is emphasized here, and in this paper geography-dependent relation refer to the situation that a triple contains at least one entity which could generate geographical attributes or meanings from geographical knowledge graph, e.g., GeoName and LnikedGeoData.), and $t \in E$ is the tail entity of the triple. A knowledge graph (KG) is denoted as G. An embedding is a function from an

---

[1] http://www.geonames.org/.
[2] http://linkedgeodata.org.

entity or a relation to one vector. Given entity e, notation lng_e denotes the longitude, lat_e denotes the latitude, and rad_e of given entity e denotes the radius value of the administrative region which e represents. A representation learning model generally defines the embedding functions for entities and relations and the values of the embeddings are learned using the triples in a KG G.

Given entity $e \in E$, we define its geographic unit as $\Phi_{geo}(e) = [lng_e, lat_e, rad_e, add_e]$, which could be derived from the current knowledge graph or some external knowledge graph, such as Yago, GeoName, LnikedGeoData, and so on. As shown in Fig. 1, for entity $h \in E$, lng_h denotes the longitude of entity h, similarly lat_h denotes its latitude, rad_h denotes its radius, and add_h denotes the address description of entity h. Obviously, the blue circle in Fig. 1 represents the radius range of entity h, and notation (lng_e, lat_e) represents the its geographic coordinate.

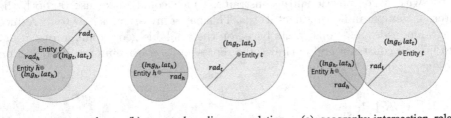

(a)   geography-inclusion relation   (b) geography-adjacency relation   (c) geography-intersection relation

Fig. 1. Different geography-dependent relations between the geographic units of entity h and entity t. (Color figure online)

As discussed in [10,18], generally speaking, *inclusion*, *adjacency* and *intersection* are common relationships between geological objects such as faults, geological units, fractures, mineralized zones and reservoirs. Hence, this paper provides the following definitions for a triple (h, r, t) with geography-dependent relation[3]:

(i) if $\sqrt{|(lng_h - lng_t)^2 + (lat_h - lat_t)^2|} < |rad_h - rad_t|$, there exists geography-inclusion relation between the geographic units of h and t, denoted as $\mathtt{Inclusion}(h, t) \sim true$ (Fig. 1(a));

(ii) if $|rad_h + rad_t| \leq \sqrt{|(lng_h - lng_t)^2 + (lat_h - lat_t)^2|} < \eta|rad_h + rad_t|$, there exists geography-adjacency relation between the geographic units of h and t, denoted as $\mathtt{Adjacency}(h, t) \sim true$ (Fig. 1(b)), wherein $\gamma > 1$ is the range parameter which is needed to be adjusted according to different tasks or datasets (details in Sect. 4);

and (iii) if $|rad_h - rad_t| \leq \sqrt{|(lng_h - lng_t)^2 + (lat_h - lat_t)^2|} < |rad_h + rad_t|$, there exists geography-intersection relation between the geographic units of h and t, denoted as $\mathtt{Intersection}(h, t) \sim true$ (Fig. 1(c)).

---

[3] This paper denotes this kind of triple as "geography-dependent triple".

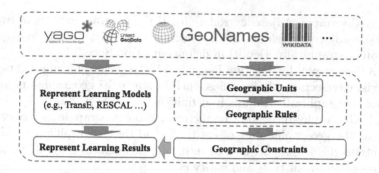

Fig. 2. The sketch of the proposed link prediction framework by leveraging the geographic constraints.

3.2 Geographic Unit Generation

Given a geography-dependent triple (h, r, t), Firstly, we extract the geographic units of entities in the triple. For example, in the triple *(Beyonc Giselle Knowles, WasBornIn, Houston)*, by matching the entities *"Beyonc Giselle Knowles"* and *"Houston"* with current knowledge graph and external knowledge graphs (such as Yago, GeoName, LinkedGeoData, etc.), we can conclude that the entity *"Houston"* is a city name, i.e., geography name. Furthermore, we could obtain the geographic information (e.g., longitude, latitude, radius, address, etc.) of this entity. Finally, the geographic unit $\Phi_{geo}(Houston)$ of entity *"Houston"* could be generated.

Then we need to classify relation *"WasBornIn"* into geography-inclusion relation, geography-adjacency relation, or geography-intersection relation. Intuitively, for such classification task: (i) For the relation wherein both head entity and tail entity have geographic units, such as *"LocatedIn"* relation or *"Nearby"* relation, we could utilize the entity's geographic units to classify the relation (as discussed at the end of Sect. 3.1). (ii) For other relations, manual annotation is effective due to the limited number of geography-dependent relations. Therefore, in the preceding example, we finally recognize that the relation *"WasBornIn"* belongs to geography-inclusion relation. Interestingly, for the situation that none of the two entities could directly obtain explicit geographic information, the proposed framework can still achieve an appreciable improvement (discussed in details in the following experimental section).

3.3 Geographic Rule Definition

Overall, this paper mainly focuses on the following geographic rules:

- Rule_1 (Geography-Inclusion Relation): If the geographic units of two entities exist inclusion relation, these entities may exist geography-inclusion relation geographically. Details in definition (i) in Sect. 3.1.

- Rule_2 (Geography-Adjacency Relation): If the geographic units of two entities exist adjacency relation, these entities may exist geography-adjacency relation geographically. Details in definition (ii) in Sect. 3.1.
- Rule_3 (Geography-Intersection Relation): If the geographic units of two entities exist intersection relation, these entities may exist geography-intersection relation geographically. Details in definition (iii) in Sect. 3.1.
- Rule_4 (Geography-Inclusion Conduction): If the geographic unit of entity e_3 contains the geographic unit of entity e_2 and the geographic unit of entity e_2 contains the geographic unit of entity e_1, there exists geography-inclusion relation between entity e_3 and entity e_1.
- Rule_5 (Geography-Adjacency Reflexivity): If the geographic unit of entity e_1 exists adjacency relation with entity e_2, there exists directed geography-adjacency relation from entity e_1 and entity e_2 and there also exists directed geography-adjacency relation from entity e_2 and entity e_1.
- Rule_6 (Geography-Intersection Reflexivity): If the geographic unit of entity e_1 exists intersection relation with entity e_2, there exists directed geography-intersection relation from entity e_1 and entity e_2 and there also exists directed geography-intersection relation from entity e_2 and entity e_1.
- Rule_7 (Entity Type Filtering): Specific relations have specific types of entities.

3.4 Link Prediction Based on Geographic Constraints

Given a knowledge graph G, it contains $|E|$ entities and $|R|$ types of relations. The set of triples $T = \{(h, r, t)\}$ could be obtained by the representation learning models, and a variety of low-dimensional representation learning models have been developed to work on the KGC task. These models usually learn continuous, low-dimensional vector representations (i.e., embeddings) for entities and relations by minimizing a margin-based pairwise ranking loss. Arbitrary representation learning models could be adopted in the proposed framework, because of generality of the proposed framework. Here we only investigate two mature representation learning models: (i) TransE, and (ii) RESCAL.

Motivated by the linear translation phenomenon observed in well trained word embeddings [11], TransE [2] represents the head entity h, the relation r and the tail entity t with vectors $\mathbf{h}, \mathbf{r}, \mathbf{t} \in R^d$ respectively, which were trained so that $\mathbf{h} + \mathbf{r} \approx \mathbf{t}$. They define the energy function as

$$f_r(h, t) = \| \mathbf{h} + \mathbf{r} - \mathbf{t} \|_l \tag{1}$$

where $l = 1$ or $l = 2$, which means either the l_1 or the l_2 norm of the vector $\mathbf{h} + \mathbf{r} - \mathbf{t}$ will be used depending on the performance on the validation set.

We follow previous work to minimize the following hinge loss function:

$$\ell = - \sum_{(h,r,t) \sim \Delta, (h',r,t') \sim \Delta'} [\gamma + f_r(h, t) - f_r(h', t')]_+ \tag{2}$$

Wherein Δ is the training set consisting of correct triples (i.e., fact), Δ' is the distribution of corrupted triples (i.e., negative samples), and $[\cdot]_+ = max(\cdot, 0)$.

RESCAL [15] maps each relation r into a matrix $\mathbf{M}_r \in R^{d \times d}$, and utilize the following energy function:

$$f_r(h, t) = \mathbf{h}^\top \mathbf{M}_r \mathbf{t} \tag{3}$$

The loss function is defined as follows:

$$\ell = -\sum_{r \in R} \sum_{h \in E} \sum_{t \in E} [\chi(h, r, t) - f_r(h, t)]^2 \tag{4}$$

Wherein, $\chi(h, r, t) = 1$ if (h, r, t) is a "fact".

Based on the loss function above, we could define the problem of geography rule constraints of representation learning results, as the following form:

$$\ell = -\sum_{r \in R} \sum_{h \in E} \sum_{t \in E} [\chi(h, r, t) - f_r(h, t)]^2$$

s.t.   Rule_1. $\displaystyle\sum_{r \in R_{inclusion}} \chi(h, r, t) \geq 1, \quad \forall h \in E, t \in E, \texttt{Inclusion}(h, t)$

Rule_2. $\displaystyle\sum_{r \in R_{adjacency}} \chi(h, r, t) \geq 1, \quad \forall h \in E, t \in E, \texttt{Adjacency}(h, t)$

Rule_3. $\displaystyle\sum_{r \in R_{intersection}} \chi(h, r, t) \geq 1, \quad \forall h \in E, t \in E, \texttt{Intersection}(h, t)$

Rule_4. $\displaystyle\sum_{r \in R_{inclusion}} \chi(h, r, t) \geq 1,$

$\forall h, e', t \in E, \texttt{Inclusion}(h, e'), \texttt{Inclusion}(e', t)$

Rule_5. $\chi(t, r, h) = 1, \quad \forall r \in R_{adjacency}, h, t \in E, \texttt{Adjacency}(h, t), \chi(h, r, t) = 1$

Rule_6. $\chi(t, r, h) = 1, \quad \forall r \in R_{intersection}, h, t \in E, \texttt{Intersection}(h, t), \chi(h, r, t) = 1$

Rule_7. $\chi(h, r, t) = 0, \quad \forall r, \forall h \notin E_h^r, \forall t \notin E_t^r$

$$\tag{5}$$

In Eq. (5) of the proposed framework, we denote the set of geography-inclusion relations as $R_{inclusion}$, denote the set of geography-adjacency relations as $R_{adjacency}$, and denote the set of geography-intersection relations as $R_{intersection}$. Given each relation $r \in R$, E_h^r represents the set of the head entities corresponding to relation r, and similarly E_t^r represents the set of the tail entities corresponding to relation r.

4   Experiments

We evaluate our framework on standard Link Prediction task with benchmark statistic datasets.

4.1 Datasets and Baselines

Three datasets are utilized in our experiments: (i) WIKI-500K, derived from WikiData [20]; (ii) WN-100K derived from WordNet [12]; and (iii) FB-500K derived from FreeBase [1]. For these datasets, the triples which with geographic information, i.e., geography-dependent triples, are distilled from the whole triples. Besides, some external knowledge bases, such as Yago, GeoNames, and LinkedGeoData, are leveraged for providing geographic information for each entity in the filtered dataset, to generate its geographic unit $\Phi_{geo}(\cdot)$.

Arbitrary representation learning models could be adopted in the proposed framework, because of generality of the proposed framework. The experimental section mainly focuses on whether the geographic constraint (i.e., geographic units and geographic rules) could improve the performance of the current representation learning models. Therefore, we select several competitive representation learning models here, including: (i) **TransE** [2], uses a margin-based pairwise ranking loss function, which measures the score of each possible result as the L_n distance between $\mathbf{h} + \mathbf{r}$ and $\mathbf{t}$. (ii) **RESCAL** [15], is a restricted form of tucker decomposition for discovering previously unknown triples in a knowledge graph. (iii) **TRESCAL** [4], leverages relational domain knowledge about entity type information based on **RESCAL**. (iv) **HolE** [14], learns more expressive combination operators, instead of simply adding $\mathbf{h} + \mathbf{r}$. (v) **DKRL** [24], uses word embeddings of entity content in addition to multi-hop paths, but relies on the machinery of a Convolution Neural Network (CNN) to learn entity and relation embeddings. (vi) **ProjE** [19], presents a shared variable neural network model that fills-in missing information in a knowledge graph by learning joint embeddings of the knowledge graph's entities and relations, and through subtle changes to the standard loss function.

Furthermore, we denote their extended version as **geo+TransE**, **geo+RESCAL**, **geo+TRESCAL**, **geo+DKRL**, **geo+HolE**, **geo+ProjE**, which are constrained with geographic rules in the proposed framework.

4.2 Experiment Settings

For each dataset, we divide the geography-dependent triples into training-set, validation-set and testing-set according to the ratio of 6:3:1. HITS@N, which is widely-used, is considered as evaluation metrics in our experiments, indicating the proportion of original triples whose rank is not larger than N. Specially, HITS@10 is used here, and higher HITS@10 mean better performance. Following the methodology described in Sect. 3.3, in the proposed framework: (i) given entity, we should generate its explicit geographic unit $\Phi_{geo}(\cdot)$, by matching each entity with exact geographic information provided by the external knowledge bases (such as Yago, GeoName, LinkedGeoData, etc.). (ii) Then, we classify the relations in the dataset. (iii) Finally, we could generate the implicit geographic unit $\Phi_{geo}(\cdot)$ for the entity with no explicit geographic information. Besides, We have attempted several settings on the validation-set to get the best configuration. We set the margin γ to 5 and dimension of embedding d to 50 for dataset

WIKI-500K and dataset WN-100K, and $\gamma = 1$, $d = 100$ for dataset FB-500K. The learning rate is 0.01 on for dataset WIKI-500K and dataset WN-100K, and 0.1 on FB-500K. For the geographic constraints (Eq. (5)), parameters η is set as 1.3, which release the best performance in all most situations. The toolkit [17] is used to solve the problem of Eq. (5), And all the models are implemented with Theano.

4.3   Experimental Results and Analysis

Link prediction aims at predicting the missing relation when given two entities, i.e., we predict r given $(h, ?, t)$. We adopt the same protocol used in previous studies. For each triple (h, r, t) in the testing-set, we replace the tail t (or the head h) with every entity in the dataset. We calculate the energies of all replacement triples and rank these energies in descending order. We follow [2] to report the *filter* results, i.e., removing all other correct candidates r' in ranking.

Table 1. Evaluation results of link prediction for different types of geography-dependent relations (HITS@10).

Model	geo-inclusion	geo-adjacency	geo-intersection	geo-#1	geo-#2	geo-#0
RESCAL	71.89	45.89	53.56	74.36	72.54	62.92
TransE	71.76	44.85	51.77	78.26	63.05	67.11
TRESCAL	72.93	46.15	52.26	72.28	65.26	64.48
DKRL	74.39	47.07	53.31	73.73	**69.25**	65.77
HolE	75.13	**48.97**	53.84	74.46	67.23	66.43
ProjE	**77.39**	47.54	**55.45**	**76.70**	66.57	**68.42**
geo+RESCAL	78.13	49.27	54.86	62.66	68.26	65.26
geo+TransE	73.84	46.02	52.65	91.00	65.39	64.09
geo+TRESCAL	74.36	49.14	50.96	**91.39**	63.96	64.87
geo+DKRL	80.34	50.84	57.57	79.62	74.19	71.03
geo+HolE	**83.40**†‡	**54.36**†‡	58.23†	82.65†‡	**74.63**†‡	**73.73**†‡
geo+ProjE	81.26†	49.92†	**59.76**†	80.53†	69.89†	71.84†

The superscript $\dagger$ and $\ddagger$ respectively denote statistically significant improvements over **ProjE** and **geo+ProjE** ($p < 0.05$).

We compare the results of different geography-dependent relation types (defined in Sect. 3.1), as shown in Table 1, wherein we report the average results of 30 repeats here. In Table 1, "geo-inclusion", "geo-adjacency" and "geo-intersection" represent geography-inclusion relation, geography-adjacency relation and geography-intersection relation, respectively. Given a triple (h, r, t), if we could obtain the explicit geographic information of both h and t, we denote this situation as "geo-#2". For the relation wherein both head entity and tail entity have geographic units, such as "LocatedIn" relation or "Nearby" relation, we utilize the entity's geographic units to classify the relation (as discussed at the end of Sect. 3.1). If only h or t has explicit geographic information, we denote this situation as "geo-#1". While "geo-#0" means no explicit geographic information could be obtained from h and t of the given triple. For the situations of "geo-#1" and "geo-#0", manual annotation is effective due to the limited number of geography-dependent relations. Moreover, the notation "ave." in Table 1 indicates the results averaged across the aforementioned three datasets. The statistical t-test is employed here: To decide whether the improvement by algorithm A over algorithm B is significant, the t-test calculates a value p based on the performance of A and B. The smaller p is, the more significant the improvement is. If the p is small enough ($p < 0.05$), we conclude that the improvement is statistically significant. From the result, We observe that, the use of geographic units and rules has significantly improved the link prediction performance of specific relations. This is most pronounce in **RESCAL**, **DKRL**, **HolE**. Especially for **HolE**, its geographic variant **geo+HolE** even outperforms **geo+ProjE**, while performance of original **HolE** is not as good as that of original **ProjE**. This demonstrates that our framework successfully utilizes the geographic information, and geographic constraints could capture the different semantics of every entity more accurately. Moreover, from the experimental results, we could also conclude that, the promotion impact of the proposed framework for the geography-inclusion relation (i.e., row "geo-inclusion" in Table 1) is significantly higher. Take **geo+ProjE** and **geo+HolE** as example, **geo+ProjE** improve **ProjE** by 5.00% for the geography-inclusion relation, and **geo+ProjE** improve **ProjE** by 11.01%. As far as entities are concerned, if both entities can directly generate the geographic units (i.e., "geo-#2"), prediction results is advanced obviously, and this result is as expected.

5   Conclusions

In summary, we propose a novel link prediction framework for knowledge graph. By leveraging geographic information to generate geographic units and rules, we construct geographic constraints for boosting the current representation learning models for knowledge graph completion. The key discovery is that, this framework could make full use of implicit geographic information, and accurately captures semantic units of entities (and relations). Empirically, we show the proposed framework can improve the performance of the current representation learning models on three benchmark datasets.

Acknowledgement. This work was supported in part by National Key Research and Development Project (Grant No. 2017YFC0820503), the China Postdoctoral Science Foundation (No. 2018M641436), the Joint Advanced Research Foundation of China Electronics Technology Group Corporation (CETC) (No. 6141B08010102), 2018 Culture and tourism think tank project (No. 18ZK01), and the New Generation of Artificial Intelligence Special Action Project (18116001).

References

1. Bollacker, K., Evans, C., Paritosh, P., Sturge, T., Taylor, J.: Freebase: a collaboratively created graph database for structuring human knowledge. In: SIGMOD Conference, pp. 1247–1250 (2008)
2. Bordes, A., Usunier, N., Garcia-Duran, A., Weston, J., Yakhnenko, O.: Translating embeddings for modeling multi-relational data. In: Advances in Neural Information Processing Systems, pp. 2787–2795 (2013)
3. Bordes, A., Weston, J., Collobert, R., Bengio, Y.: Learning structured embeddings of knowledge bases. In: AAAI Conference on Artificial Intelligence, AAAI 2011, San Francisco, California, USA, August 2011
4. Chang, K.W., Yih, W., Yang, B., Meek, C.: Typed tensor decomposition of knowledge bases for relation extraction. In: EMNLP (2014)
5. Ding, B., Quan, W., Wang, B., Li, G.: Improving knowledge graph embedding using simple constraints (2018)
6. Dong, X., et al.: Knowledge vault: a web-scale approach to probabilistic knowledge fusion. In: ACM SIGKDD International Conference on Knowledge Discovery and Data Mining, pp. 601–610 (2014)
7. Li, M., Lu, Q., Long, Y.: Representation learning of multiword expressions with compositionality constraint. In: Li, G., Ge, Y., Zhang, Z., Jin, Z., Blumenstein, M. (eds.) KSEM 2017. LNCS (LNAI), vol. 10412, pp. 507–519. Springer, Cham (2017). https://doi.org/10.1007/978-3-319-63558-3_43
8. Lin, Y., Liu, Z., Sun, M., Liu, Y., Zhu, X.: Learning entity and relation embeddings for knowledge graph completion. In: Twenty-Ninth AAAI Conference on Artificial Intelligence, pp. 2181–2187 (2015)
9. Ma, S., Ding, J., Jia, W., Wang, K., Guo, M.: TransT: type-based multiple embedding representations for knowledge graph completion. In: Ceci, M., Hollmén, J., Todorovski, L., Vens, C., Džeroski, S. (eds.) ECML PKDD 2017. LNCS (LNAI), vol. 10534, pp. 717–733. Springer, Cham (2017). https://doi.org/10.1007/978-3-319-71249-9_43
10. Mainguenaud, M.: Manipulations of graphs with a visual query language: application to a geographical information system. In: Ifip Wg26 Working Conference on Visual Database Systems (1997)
11. Mikolov, T., Sutskever, I., Chen, K., Corrado, G., Dean, J.: Distributed representations of words and phrases and their compositionality. Adv. Neural Inf. Process. Syst. **26**, 3111–3119 (2013)
12. Miller, G.A.: Wordnet: a lexical database for English. Commun. ACM **38**(11), 39–41 (1995)
13. Nickel, M., Rosasco, L., Poggio, T.: Holographic embeddings of knowledge graphs. In: Thirtieth AAAI Conference on Artificial Intelligence, pp. 1955–1961 (2016)
14. Nickel, M., Rosasco, L., Poggio, T.A.: Holographic embeddings of knowledge graphs. In: AAAI (2016)
15. Nickel, M., Tresp, V., Kriegel, H.P.: A three-way model for collective learning on multi-relational data. In: International Conference on International Conference on Machine Learning (2011)
16. Ou, W., Fei, L., Yi, T., Yu, S., Wang, P.: Co-regularized multiview nonnegative matrix factorization with correlation constraint for representation learning. Multimedia Tools Appl. **77**(10), 12955–12978 (2018)
17. Perazzolo, R.: Programmazione lineare open-source come alternativa a cplex: indagine sul programma lpsolve (2010)

18. Pouliot, J., Bdard, K., Kirkwood, D., Lachance, B.: Reasoning about geological space: coupling 3D geomodels and topological queries as an aid to spatial data selection. Comput. Geosci. **34**(5), 529–541 (2008)
19. Shi, B., Weninger, T.: ProjE: embedding projection for knowledge graph completion. In: AAAI (2016)
20. Vrandei, D., Krtzsch, M.: Wikidata: a free collaborative knowledgebase. Commun. ACM **57**(10), 78–85 (2014)
21. Wang, Z., Zhang, J., Feng, J., Chen, Z.: Knowledge graph embedding by translating on hyperplanes. In: Twenty-Eighth AAAI Conference on Artificial Intelligence, pp. 1112–1119 (2014)
22. Xiao, H., Huang, M., Meng, L., Zhu, X.: SSP: semantic space projection for knowledge graph embedding with text descriptions. In: AAAI (2017)
23. Xiao, H., Huang, M., Zhu, X.: Transg: a generative model for knowledge graph embedding. In: Meeting of the Association for Computational Linguistics, pp. 2316–2325 (2016)
24. Xie, R., Liu, Z., Jia, J.J., Luan, H., Sun, M.: Representation learning of knowledge graphs with entity descriptions. In: AAAI (2016)
25. Yi, T., Luu, A.T., Hui, S.C.: Non-parametric estimation of multiple embeddings for link prediction on dynamic knowledge graphs. In: Thirty First Conference on Artificial Intelligence (2017)

Author Index

Printed in the United States
by Book...

Printed in the United States
By Bookmasters